W9-BOB-949

The Girls in Blue. Pan American 1964-1967; Real Stories of a Bygone Era.

ISBN 0-13-978-0615925646

For

Dan

Lauren and Joanna

Hannah and Patrick

and

Pan Am Class 12 of 1964

On December 4, 1991, Pan Am ceased operations.
Newsweek ran an article about the airline's history, beginning with
this statement:

"This is not a story about planes.
It's about romance…
air travel was an adventure;
airlines once had a soul.
Pan Am certainly did."

PAN AMERICAN WORLD AIRWAYS

In the 1960s Pan American was the world leader in air transportation and the premier international airline with an air network that spanned the world.

Pan American's fleet of aircraft derived from the clipper sailing ships originating in the 1830s, the fastest ocean-going vessels of their time. Hence, the 707 jet planes were referred to as Jet Clippers.

The 707 was named by Boeing executives who felt the number 707 was catchier than 700 for marketing purposes for the company's first commercial jet. Since the 707, all Boeing's commercial jets have been named in succession: 727,737,747,757,767,777,787. The 717 was given to a military version.

The title Purser stemmed from the senior steward on a ship. At Pan Am more stewardesses were being promoted to the purser position and they, along with the male pursers, were responsible for the flight service crew and because of their experience were looked to for leadership and advice. They made the decisions regarding all aspects of the in-flight service, especially the timing of meal services and any necessary revisions.

The stewardesses were members of the flight service crew and were responsible to the purser and for looking after the many needs of the passengers.

The stewardesses of Pan Am Training Class 12, 1964 experienced hundreds of flights that ran smoothly, left and arrived on time, enjoyed perfect food services and happy passengers. And, being so well-run and organized, the flights have dimmed in our memories.

The following stories are real. They are the vivid memories of unforeseen mishaps, the turmoil of unexpected turbulence, the hazards of the Vietnam War and political uprisings in Asia…and all the fun times, the romances, and group dynamics we experienced along the way.

PAN AM TRAINING CLASS 12
March 24, 1964

NEW YORK

Barbara, England
Edith, Germany
Karin, Sweden
Louise, Sweden
Kate, England
Tina, Sweden
Gunnel, Sweden
Lesley, England
Mona, Norway
Roberta, USA
Lilibi, Sweden
Sigi, Germany
Jenny, USA
Mary, England
Bonnie, USA
Reidun, Sweden

PROLOGUE

A sleek Pan American World Airways 707 jet sat on the searing hot runway at Tan Son Nhut Air Base, Saigon, South Vietnam. The Jet Clipper heralded the Jet Age of flying with its glossy white body and Pan Am blue stripe running along the full length of the fuselage, its tail adorned with the pride of all – the round blue Pan Am logo sitting high and centered – sometimes irreverently referred to as the blue meatball!

In the mid-1960s the Vietnam War was in full force; a Cold War-era military conflict with United States involvement escalating in hopes of preventing a communist takeover of South Vietnam. Pan Am had a government contract to fly military personnel and refugees into and out of this war-torn country. The airplane and its crew were on the runway to uphold this duty.

Heart-breaking lines of Vietnamese refugees struggled across the steaming tarmac; the mirage effect from the shimmering heat produced a scene of human ghosts walking through water. They hurriedly climbed up the two stairway ramps leading to the fore and aft doorways of the aircraft.

Short and slight in build, some of the women were wearing the ao dai, a long tunic with slits up the sides over silk pantaloons, while others were clad in Western style summer dresses. The men were trying to keep cool in loose pants and short-sleeved sun-faded shirts with thong-like rubber or leather sandals on their calloused feet. Many wore the ubiquitous 'leaf' conical hat held in place by a cloth chin strap, the perfect protection from the burning sun.

The aircraft cabin lacked a bulkhead divider making one configuration with all the seats in threes each side of a center aisle. The young and old, men, women, and children were filling the cabin to capacity, fleeing from their war-torn homeland to the safety and uncertainty of refugee camps in Thailand. From there most would face the monotony of waiting, sometimes for years, for sponsorship to the great United States of America.

We welcomed these sad souls with happy smiles, though their expressions belied a deep anguish. Boarding the plane was a long, arduous process and was further hindered by the unwelcome oppressive heat and high humidity pouring into the cabin through the gaping cabin doors.

I was assigned to work in the forward half of the cabin amidst this emotional sea of passengers. I was a twenty-one year old English stewardess on my first flight to Vietnam. The cabin crew consisted of six girls - one purser and two stewardesses working forward, and a junior purser and two stewardesses working aft.

The refugees had little understanding of what the seat numbers meant, and as we guided them to their rows we stowed their overflowing bags under seats and in the overhead shelves. With trembling hands they hung onto their small cloth and straw bags filled with personal and sentimental belongings, afraid they might never see them again – so little to last them the rest of their lives.

We helped fasten their seat belts, a tedious task as few passengers knew how to use them, and when they didn't understand our English we resorted to communication in French.

The cabin became a cocoon of frayed nerves, haggard faces, weary bodies, and forlorn souls. They had bravely left their lives behind them – walking away from their homes, families, friends and country – never to return, now staring into the face of the unknown. And we, very young naïve girls from European and Scandinavian countries, came face to face with the reality of war and the terrible consequences for these innocent families caught up in the middle of the bombing and destruction of their homes, villages, and towns.

When all the passengers and crew were aboard and counted, the pursers closed the doors with an ominous thud. We tried to allay the refugees' fears of being enclosed in an airplane as most had never seen or been aboard one in their lives before now. We were caught up in our own heart-rending emotions, but we fought hard to show a front of calm and control.

As the plane started up and taxied down the short runway, the deafening roar of the four jet engines sent a new tremble of fear through the cabin. One painfully thin young girl, no older than thirteen and prettily clad in a flowery cotton dress, collapsed across two seats and shook uncontrollably from head to toe. Her long black hair was wet with anxiety and plastered to her tiny round pale face. I tried to console her by gently stroking her back, but she continued shivering and quietly sobbing. I covered her with a Pan Am blanket and reluctantly left her in order to work my way through the cabin to reach the forward crew seats.

The purser gave the welcome and emergency announcements in French and English – France had conquered Vietnam as far back as 1859 and for years Saigon was known as the Paris of the Far East. She introduced the captain and crew, while the stewardesses demonstrated the use of life vests and oxygen masks. The plane rumbled like an impending storm, finally lifting off the runway into the freedom of the skies.

Astrid, our attractive blonde German purser, helped me lower the seat tables and set up the drinks cart. I was working with a Norwegian stewardess, Bryn, who was preparing the food in the galley. Astrid and I steered the cart down the aisle, offering everyone a much-needed drink. Water, which we quickly learned was 'nuoc' in Vietnamese, was the most requested beverage and was poured carefully from a metal Pan Am-etched pitcher – convenient plastic bottled water was a thing of the future.

Bryn was busy plating the food in the galley. Lunch was a delicious mound of fresh, plump, rosy-pink shrimp with a thick cocktail sauce, alongside a mixed greens salad, and warmed sourdough bread rolls. Astrid and I placed a prepared lunch plate on each serving tray and walked the aisle to place them on the passengers' tables. The service was proceeding quietly and efficiently. Until…

The plane suddenly and violently shuddered and shook. We instinctively stopped in our tracks and clung onto the nearest seat back as the sensation felt as if a bomb had struck us!

"What's happening?" I desperately asked Astrid, as we slowly continued handing out the last of the food trays. The plane was now vibrating noisily and we felt ourselves being jerked up and down as we tried to walk the aisle.

"The plane must have hit a bad pocket of turbulence," Astrid explained, as the captain's voice boomed over the speakers, "Everyone sit down and fasten your seat belts!"

We struggled to reach our crew seats, gripping onto the seat backs to keep upright as the jolting worsened. We were walking on air one minute and being weighted down and pulled to the floor the next – a strange and disconcerting feeling.

Throughout this turmoil we were trying hard to smile to allay the passengers' fears. We knew we had to present the feeling of security even though we didn't feel it ourselves. Thankfully, we reached our crew seats without injuries and, remembering our training instructions, fastened our seatbelts as tightly as possible just as we heard another loud BOOM and the cabin lurched up and crashed down violently.

And then there was chaos.

Meal trays, plates, cups and cutlery flew everywhere, tossed throughout the cabin in a cacophony of clanging and breakage. The passengers gasped in unified terror and as we craned our necks from our jump seats to look around the cabin, we were horrified by what we saw. The color drained from my face and I could feel my heart beating rapidly as I wondered if a bomb really had hit the plane.

The cabin was a bloodbath.

Still restrained in our seats, we could see red ooze dripping from the passengers and splattered throughout the entire cabin creating a war-like scene.

As we slowly recovered from our initial shock and scanned the aisles again, we realized with enormous relief that no bodies or body parts were strewn down the aisle. In fact, the passengers seemed wholly intact. We quickly realized the imagined 'blood' was globs of sticky red cocktail sauce! Unfinished shrimp, leafy green salads, and crimson goo had splattered onto everyone and everything.

We giggled nervously while realizing our foolish mistake, but the passengers were gripped with fear from not understanding what was happening. Some moaned quietly, but most kept a hushed silence. They had come from the atrocities of war and were in panic that it had caught up with them in the skies above. Their quiet sounds were truly unnerving, but we pulled ourselves together and again acted with a serenity we didn't feel.

'Keep your cool, and keep calm, under *all* circumstances,' was a slogan pounded into us during training until ingrained in our Pan Am souls.

Action resumed as Astrid yelled at us, "Grab as many of the towels as you can and hand them out to the passengers to help them clean the food spills off themselves." These were tight rolls of damp white 'hot towels' stowed in the galley as part of the food service to offer as an after-meal freshen-up.

The one thing worse than our fears of bomb-induced carnage was the stark reality that we had to clean up the worst of the mess, wiping down and clearing up all the sticky red sauce that had sprayed all over the seats, the floor, the windows, and even stuck on the ceiling. We had to pick up the worst of the food debris, the meal trays, the cutlery, broken glassware, chipped plates, and coffee cups that were littered throughout the cabin like the devastation from a hurricane.

For us this clean-up was an unpleasant but necessary chore, and was the dark side of our so-called 'glamorous' job. The cabin had to be cleared to see us through to our destination in Thailand. When the plane landed and the shaken passengers had disembarked, an official maintenance crew came aboard to give the cabin a thorough cleaning. We were happy to get off the plane and leave them to the task.

These incidents had to have detailed written reports entered into the plane's flight log book and we hoped Pan Am would consider omitting cocktail sauce from its menu on future flights out of the war zone.

Our training had been intense and covered all the basics, but unpredictable situations like this one were left to our instincts and ingenuity to handle with grace and calm.

1

BACKGROUND

My home was a small farming village, three miles from the Roman city of Chichester in Sussex, on the south coast of England.

Our idyllic garden was landscaped with rock gardens, apple trees, gooseberry bushes and an old wooden swing overgrown with pink rose vines. I remember many summer days lazing on the lawn staring up at the English blue sky and watching puffy white clouds slowly drifting far above. I imagined them being foreign lands far, far away and wished someday to travel and explore all the countries of the world.

After attending the all-girls Chichester High School and then secretarial college on the outskirts of London, I moved to the bustling city center.

My college girlfriend, Linda, and I lived in an antiquated, basement flat on the Old Brompton Road in Earls Court. To us it was refuge and independence. We walked to the 'tube' (rail underground), shops, prolific Indian restaurants and a popular local coffee bar called The Troubador, where we spent many relaxing hours drinking coffee, listening to music and visiting with friends.

Reminiscent of the television series "Downton Abbey" we dwelt in the 'downstairs' basement part of what was once a small upper-class city home. We had two rooms. One was a bedroom/living room, with one bed folding up into the wall, and the other bed doubling as a sofa. Across the narrow hall was the large, dark kitchen in which stood a huge antique dresser, a small wooden table and two chairs, an old stove and a large stone kitchen sink which doubled as our wash basin.

Iron bars covered the windows giving us a feeling of security. We shared an old-fashioned separate loo, the long pull-chain flusher style, with the elderly maid, Nellie. She took care of the 'upstairs' landlady, Mrs. Buckmaster, who was very much a 'lady.'

Our grand landlady allowed us only two baths a week and we had to venture cautiously 'upstairs' to use her personal bathroom. There were strict rules to clean and dry the tub after use and not waste the water. Other days we had to wash in the kitchen sink where looking up one could see the legs of pedestrians on the sidewalk outside. In the winter any water left in the sink froze overnight. The panic of having no hot water sent us scrounging in our purses for a shilling to put in the meter – no shilling, no hot water.

One cold November evening in 1963, I was listening to our portable radio (television was a luxury in those days) and heard the horrifying news that American President John F. Kennedy had been fatally shot in Texas. News of this nature was unheard of, and stunned me so far away in London.

Every morning in all weathers, I walked around the corner to the Earls Court underground tube station and descended the many escalators through the dank stale air into the bowels of the earth and the platforms below. I commuted by the tube train to Green Park and then walked to Berkeley Square and to the London office of the American advertising agency J. Walter Thompson.

I was enjoying my work as the personal secretary to Senior Vice President, Mr. Douglas Caton. My very first experience at the agency as a brand new, fresh from college secretary, was filling in for a personal secretary on the exalted Board of Directors floor working for Sir John Rogers, a member of the House of Lords. I was hailed into his plush office, pen and notebook in hand, and was asked to call the *Treasury*! I looked at the three official-looking telephones sitting in a row along the side of his polished oak desk and with my heart beating fast, tried to guess which one was the direct line to the Government Office. His Lordship then explained, sensing my trepidation, that all I had to do was pick up the red phone and ask the switchboard operator to put me through. I learned the hard way there were no direct telephone lines and most calls went through the company switchboard.

The Beatles were about to take over the music world with their Beatlemania. Another group to hit the charts and follow the Beatles was Mick Jagger and his Rolling Stones. Everyone was rocking to their hit song 'Ain't Got No Satisfaction.'

On the fashion front, Twiggy became a world supermodel. Her very thin build, huge round eyes and short hair became the face of London's 'mod' scene.

Cigarette smoking was widespread though I hadn't succumbed to the temptation, and the drug scene was slowly emerging.

In America, Lyndon Johnson became President and the country was becoming embroiled in the Vietnam War.

It was during these tumultuous times that I left England for the United States of America.

2.

THE TURNING POINT

In the year 1963, on a chill December afternoon, I was comfortably seated in my boss's warm oak-paneled office at J. Walter Thompson Advertising Agency. Mr. Caton was dictating an especially long and important business letter to a prestigious client. I was frantically scribbling down every word in Pitman shorthand knowing I had to translate it back with all the advertising jargon. I was also thinking of the arduous task ahead of typing it onto letterhead with the dreaded carbon paper inserted between each of five sheets. A single typing error would result in the stigma of imperfection, the tell-tale smudge of whiteout or an erasure on each copy.

Dictation over, Mr. Caton looked at me across his heavy, but neatly kept, leather-topped desk and asked, "Lesley, what would you really like to do with your life?"

I was completely taken aback by the suddenness of the question. Maybe he sensed an aura of disquiet in my demeanor, but sitting stiffly in the rigid-backed chair, I replied with little hesitation, "I would love to travel and see the world. My dream would be to fly as an air hostess with BOAC (British Overseas Airways Corporation, now British Airways)." I didn't tell him that I was concerned about the rigorous testing. In the early Sixties being an air hostess was considered one of the most glamorous jobs in the world – offering the wonder of worldwide travel and romance – and it was not easy to pass the stringent requirements and intense interview process.

A few days after our exchange, Mr. Caton walked briskly into the office – it was New Years Day 1964. He passed my desk, smiled and casually announced, "I remembered what you told me about wishing to be an air hostess. Traveling home last evening, I was reading the Evening Standard newspaper and noticed a small advertisement from Pan American World Airways. I thought you might be interested that Pan Am is interviewing for stewardesses to train in New York." He continued walking into his office and I was left thinking about what he'd said – all day long!

Mr. Caton was a charming gentleman in his early fifties. He was slightly built, had a thinning hairline and was always immaculately dressed. I enjoyed working for him as he was considerate and kind. He had confided to me one day that he and his wife were unable to have children, and I felt he looked upon me as a daughter. Now he had handed me a golden opportunity to pursue the dream of a lifetime.

At age twenty-one, and in the 1960s, the prospect of going to New York was not commonplace and therefore enormously exciting. At the same time, the thought of leaving behind my family and friends and all things familiar was daunting. I could hardly concentrate the rest of the day. The United States of America – New York! Was it possible?

After work that evening, I walked briskly to keep warm in the bitterly cold air, my curiosity to see the Pan Am advertisement at bursting point. I stopped at a corner newsstand and looked for the Evening Standard newspaper. I grabbed a copy from the rack, paid for it and off I went.

Jostling around on the stuffy underground train, jammed in body touching body, I had to exercise patience. I was unbelievably lucky to land into a vacated seat when a passenger jumped up at the next station. I took the chance to open my paper and with little room to open it widely, I scanned through every page, frantically searching for the announcement. Just as I was about to give up, I found it on the back page in one small paragraph:

Pan American World Airways.
Stewardesses needed.
Training in New York, USA.

This was an American, all-international airline and they were interviewing interested girls at the Westbury Hotel in London.

Stumbling along with the flood of travelers pouring off the train, I rode up the almost perpendicular escalator and was ejected into the welcome fresh air at Earl's Court station. I walked as fast as possible darting around the crush of commuters past the familiar Indian restaurants and their beckoning aromas, the small coffee bars and bustling shops, and turned the corner into the Old Brompton Road and home.

I ran down the worn stone steps to our basement flat and let myself in the back door, formerly the tradesmen's entrance. I hurried down the dark hall, unlocked our door and found the flat silent and devoid of life. My roommate, Linda, was still at work.

The old bed creaked as I slumped onto it, opened the newspaper and scanned the Pan Am advertisement again. I stared at it for a long, long time. Thoughts were spinning through my head. This would turn my cozy, comfortable world completely upside down. Could I handle the upheaval? How would my parents react to their older daughter leaving for another country?

That little voice deep down inside was telling me 'You have to do it.'

Dashing into the kitchen, I filled the kettle, and lit the stove to boil water for a fortifying cup of tea. I rummaged through a bureau drawer and found a plain writing pad, a fountain pen and a matching envelope. With my cup of tea I sat down at our small kitchen table and stared at the stark white paper. Slowly I began to write a rough draft. When satisfied with my work, I carefully hand wrote and signed my formal application letter. I neatly folded and placed the precious page into the envelope, wrote the address, licked the stamp and sealed the back flap.

Linda arrived home an hour later and I breathlessly told her what I'd done. She was somewhat surprised but didn't over-react.

Linda was a good friend and she had just worked a long ten-hour day for a London solicitor and had a lot on her mind.

The next morning on my way to work, I clutched the application letter and with shaking gloved fingers dropped it into the depths of the big Royal red letterbox on the street corner. The deed was done and I was committed.

I had to be patient and remain calm while waiting for a reply, knowing I'd be devastated if it was a turndown for the initial interview.

What an exciting way to start the New Year 1964.

Caught up in the anticipation of this adventure I wanted to make sure I was prepared for every aspect of an interview process, even before I heard back from the airline. At that time the major international airlines gave preference to girls who were nurses or who had some medical or first aid training. With this in mind, I looked for and found an evening First Aid course within walking distance of our flat and decided to give it a try.

A bitter cold wind was blowing and I walked five streets to find the building where the class was held. The evening was dark and damp and the street was hard to find but finally I saw the house number. I climbed the steps to the big black front door which was slightly ajar. I stepped inside feeling a rather foreboding atmosphere, but I was there to learn and bolster my confidence.

The instructor looked like a character out of a Charles Dickens novel. He was eccentric-looking, tall and gangly, with long wisps of graying hair covering a bulging forehead ('a sign of brains' my mother always said). He wore a threadbare knitted cardigan over a white shirt and a loose-knotted tie. He introduced himself as 'Mr. Johnson.' There were only six of us present, four women and two young men. Along with them I plunged with gusto into all the sling making, bandage wrapping and rules of first aid.

My friends must have dreaded my return to the flat, as I instantly started practicing on them. They were good sports as I made slings for pretend broken arms and bandaged them for various injuries. They took my enthusiasm in good stride, although telling me at the same time that I was taking this whole first-aid thing a bit far.

Proficiency and fluency in a foreign language was also a requirement which had stifled me from applying in the past. I dug around in my cardboard box of books and found my high school French and German volumes. I refreshed many years of education by immersing myself in both.

At college I had taken a Business Spanish course but as that entailed little conversation it hardly counted.

Every evening after long days at work, I checked the old cane-back chair placed just inside the basement entrance door. All the mail was delivered 'upstairs' and every day Nellie would bring ours 'downstairs' to the letter chair. I eagerly looked for an envelope with a Pan Am logo on the upper left corner.

A whole week passed by, seven harrowing days filled with anguish and hope. Then, on the eighth day, a jolt of adrenaline shot through me – there it was, the long-awaited letter.

I picked it up with my heart racing, afraid to open it as I didn't want to face bad news. The envelope felt rather thin, but that could mean anything. I took a deep breath to calm myself, ran down the narrow hall to our flat and straight into the kitchen. I put down my handbag, grabbed a sharp knife from the kitchen drawer and slit open the envelope. I slowly pulled out the enclosed letter, unfolded it and started reading. I gasped and jumped with joy for there was the hoped-for news – *I was invited to an interview*. I had made it over the first hurdle.

Enclosed with the short acceptance letter was a typewritten list of needed qualifications and a request for a full-length photograph. The intimidating list of qualifications for Flight Service employment read as follows:

- Age: 21 to and including 27 at time of employment
- Height: 5'3" to 5'8"
- Weight: 110 to 135 lbs., well proportioned
- Marital Status: Single

- Education: Two years' college preferred
- Must be fluent in English plus one of the following languages: French, Italian, German, Portuguese, Dutch, Swedish, Danish, Norwegian, Finnish, Turkish, Arabic, Hindustani or Greek
- Must be a citizen of the United States or be able to obtain an Immigration Visa to the U.S.
- Must be able to obtain and maintain passport, visas and resident status, and be able to travel freely and perform duties as assigned while in all countries to which the Company flies
- Must be in excellent health and able to pass flight physical (medical) examination
- Vision must be 20/50 in each eye correctable to 20/20
- Eyeglasses or contact lenses not permitted
- Must have good posture and appearance
- Must be of good moral character
- Must have pleasant speaking voice and habitually use good English
- Must have pleasing personality, tact and diplomacy, and possess a genuine liking for people
- Must be willing, adaptable, and prepared for hard work
- Must be able to swim
- Although domicile normally is New York, applicant must be willing to accept an overseas assignment up to three years' duration, should the need arise
- Stewardesses cannot be married nor have children
- Mandatory retirement age – 32

All applicants are required to pass a check of qualifications (height, weight, languages etc.) *before* being interviewed.

With the anti-discrimination laws of today, most of the above wouldn't be tolerated.

The following weekend I took the express train from Victoria Station to Chichester to spend time with my parents who were stoically supporting my excitement. I made an appointment with a local photographer to have the requested full-length photo taken. My hair was cut and set, I put on my best black and red knit suit, and headed out to the photo studio. The photographer took many pictures and said he'd send me the proofs in a few days.

Back in London, I was fortunate to meet most of the stated requirements so I was taking everything in stride. I didn't feel too nervous about the upcoming interview day.

I should have known better!

When the actual day arrived my nerves took over. I realized how desperately I wanted this opportunity to go to New York, to travel and explore the world.

3.

THE INTERVIEW

Wednesday morning, January 22nd, my boss willingly allowed me leave from the office for the all-important interview. He shook my hand firmly and wished me good luck.

The Westbury Hotel was on Bond Street in Mayfair. The weather had remained damp and cold, so I donned my heavy winter-wool coat and strode off through Berkeley Square. I was feeling very alone and full of apprehension. Was I doing the right thing? I kept repeating the saying 'Nothing ventured, nothing gained' as I walked toward the hotel, my pace increasing to keep warm. The interview was scheduled for ten o'clock, and my nerves acted up with a vengeance. My heart was thumping and my whole body felt tingly.

The Westbury loomed before me, a tall grey-stone building in a slight U-shape with the huge entrance in the center. I walked slowly toward the imposing entry doors and a smartly dressed doorman in a black suit with gold trim opened the center door and ushered me inside.

Full of anxiety as I entered the plush spacious lobby, I immediately saw a printed sign sitting on a large easel with directions to the Pan Am Interview Suite. I looked for the lift, climbed in, and with fingers numb and white with cold, pushed the button for the third floor.

I walked down the long gold-carpeted corridor in a daze and was relieved to see the suite number and a *Pan Am Interview Waiting Room* sign outside. The door was wide open and I cautiously peered inside. The small room was full of gorgeous young girls seated against cream-colored walls.

I warily stepped through the doorway and looked for a vacant chair, but the only one I could see was at the far end of the room. This meant I had to walk in front of all those girls with their critical gazes upon me. I fixed my eyes on the chair, and advanced determinedly, wishing I was invisible.

The room was warm so I carefully took off my coat and draped it over the back of the chair; I felt much better being dressed in my black wool knit suit. I sat down and discreetly looked around. I was unprepared to see so many strikingly attractive, model-like glamour girls, sporting the most stylish clothes and looking like they'd stepped out of a Vogue magazine. Some were clad in expensive fur coats, and others were bedecked in the latest fashionable long-sleeve wool dresses or tailored suits. Even more demoralizing was hearing the multiple languages as they talked – fluent German, French, Italian, and others I didn't recognize. The noise level was on the rise from all their chatter. Was I the only English girl in the room?

Witnessing this scene of perfection around me, I perched on the edge of the chair quietly wondering what on earth I was doing there, stricken with panic and feeling a sinking loss of all my confidence. The devastating thought went through my mind that maybe I should LEAVE – immediately – as I hadn't a chance whatsoever against this bevy of beautiful foreign young women.

But I reasoned with myself that I had come this far and wasn't about to quit now. I leaned back in the chair, tried to relax, and watched and listened. What I heard actually filled me with rays of hope. Some of these elegant girls were returning from the initial interview obviously upset. They had been asked to cut off their shiny long tresses to just one inch above their collars. Many vehemently refused to comply, some seemed insulted by the request, and I realized then that such an attitude would eliminate some of the competition. Their hair was more important to them than being a Pan Am stewardess. They were probably NOT asked back for the second interview.

In the midst of these thoughts, I was jolted alert by hearing my name, "Lesley Peters," announced loudly at the door by a severe-looking, dark-haired woman with clipboard in hand. With wobbly legs I managed to rise from the chair and nonchalantly walk across the room. I took a long, deep breath and followed the woman, who was wearing a smart grey dress and black heels, down the long hallway where I was ushered into a small windowless interview room.

One man was seated behind a large wooden desk. I was initially relieved because a one-on-one interview seemed so much easier than fielding questions from a multitude of interviewers. The middle-aged gentleman rose from his chair, shook my hand and introduced himself in an unmistakable American accent as "Mr. Rigby." He was wearing a casual camel-brown sport coat, crisp white shirt, and blue-striped tie. He told me he was from the San Francisco base and smiled warmly which made me feel very much at ease.

I was able to answer all the standard, expected questions: "Why Pan Am; Why did I want to be a stewardess; Had I ever flown before?" When suddenly he switched to "Do you always wear your hair short?" I didn't have long-flowing hair. I blushed profusely at the question and Mr. Rigby noticed and actually apologized for upsetting me (though he hadn't at all). I explained that my hair was naturally wavy and was much easier to keep manageable by wearing it short. He seemed to like that answer.

After chit chat and questions about my schooling and work in London, he rose from his chair and said "Thank you, Miss Peters." I was stricken silent as I waited for the all-important request. Then out of the fog I heard him add, "I would like you to come back this afternoon for the SECOND interview at five-fifteen." I was so elated on hearing those words, I thanked him and left grinning with relief.

Another hurdle cleared.

I grabbed my overcoat, flew down the corridor, missed the lift, rushed down the staircase and out the main doors. Now I had the rest of the day to concentrate on work at the office before returning for the second interview.

Mr. Caton seemed as excited as I was at the good news and graciously let me leave work early for the second interview that afternoon. It was dark by four-thirty, and even colder as I walked back to the hotel. The streets were crowded with people at this hour and my breath was leaving white puffs as I hurried along with a purpose in my stride.

I was thrilled to get this far but knew the next session was critical to being hired. I still had a big challenge ahead to reach my goal. Again, I faced the interminable wait in a room full of other optimistic girls.

This time they were all quiet, all wore short hair and all seemed serious. We sat rigidly in our chairs sick with apprehension and anticipation. The same lady with the clipboard stopped by the door, poked her head in and announced they were running an hour behind schedule. She apologized for the extra long wait but what could we do. I had to sit there in that state of nervous tension for another sixty minutes.

I finally heard my name called. I jumped up, tried to calm down and accompanied the 'clipboard lady' down the same long, plush-carpeted hallway to the second interview room. The double doors were open wide showing a much larger room. As I entered I surveyed the scene and could see a huge, long table with a panel of four gentlemen and one woman seated behind it. I was directed to a lone chair facing them in the center of the room.

I felt I was facing the jury at a trial.

All eyes were on me as I sat down. Should I cross my legs, or not cross them? I decided to cross them. I was trying to assess each one of the panel members before me. One by one they questioned me, and each time I was waiting for the dreaded questions in French or German. I did notice one fellow on the panel, a Mr. Bamberger, who didn't say a word the whole time. He just watched and listened, which was unnerving. After answering a barrage of questions, I was, quite unexpectedly, asked to stand up and please walk back and forth in front of them.

I felt rather self-conscious parading up and down in front of all those watchful eyes. I was wondering what they were checking – my legs, my walk, my posture or probably all three? I was told to sit down. And then, abruptly, it was all over. No questions in the foreign languages.

They thanked me for coming and said I would be notified by mail of the interview result. I received zero indication to sense what they were thinking. I left the hotel feeling numb, with a glamorous future in the balance, having no idea what their decision would be.

4.

LETTER OF ACCEPTANCE

Every day after work I returned to the flat full of apprehension in the hopes of finding another Pan Am letter waiting for me on the little antique chair. Then one evening amongst our stack of mail I saw *the* envelope with the impressive gold embossed Pan Am logo. With my heart a-flutter I picked up the pile of letters and carried them along to our flat. Once inside, I quickly closed the door and cautiously pulled out the important letter. As before, with shaking fingers, I found a knife in the cutlery drawer, and while leaning against the sink for support I slit the envelope across the top. I carefully pulled out the enclosed letter and started reading.

I sat down fast. I couldn't believe my eyes. There, in black and white, were the words I had dreamed of seeing. I had been accepted to join the Pan American Stewardess Training School in New York for flight service employment with the most prestigious airline in the world.

My dream had come true!

In a state of high exhilaration, I grabbed the phone to call my parents with the wonderful news. The phone rang and rang for what seemed forever. No-one answered. What a let-down. In those days you couldn't leave a message as there were no answering machines and no voicemail.

There I was all alone in the empty, silent flat bursting with life-changing news. I had to tell someone, anyone, and the nearest person I could think of was the old matriarch landlady 'upstairs.' With no thought I flew up the narrow, curved, back staircase into the hallowed rooms above and found Mrs. Buckmaster in her private sitting room. She was relaxing in a very ornate Queen Anne style chair reading a book. She looked alarmed at my flustered, unannounced entrance but I didn't wait and blurted out breathlessly, "Please excuse me, Mrs. Buckmaster, but I have to tell someone my incredible news, I am flying to New York in America to train to become an air stewardess!"

She lowered the book to her lap and looked at me through her wire-framed eyeglasses and replied, "Why on earth would you want to do that?"

"Because I want to travel and see the world beyond London," I replied.

"Well, in that case, I wish you the very best of luck young lady!"

My very upstanding landlady was the first person to hear the news about my leaving London for New York. She was probably thinking about having to find new renters for the flat.

When I again phoned and finally reached my parents, I couldn't understand why they weren't as excited as I was. Being rather young and naïve I didn't stop to consider how devastated they must have been at the prospect of their daughter going so far away. With typical British 'stiff upper lip' they were quietly encouraging. They never uttered a negative word about my leaving home, not wanting to shatter their daughter's fondest dream.

My mother told me years later that she knew once I landed in America I would never return home for good. In those days the United States was years ahead of Europe in technology and modern living. How heartbreaking it must have been for my parents, but they supported me all the way.

Interviewed in January
Accepted in February
Flight to New York in March

No time for a change of heart and backing out. And so little time to get everything done.

I took the bus to Swan and Edgars, a department store in Piccadilly Circus, to have photographs taken for my visa and files.

The American Embassy sent me a letter requesting my appearance for an appointment prior to being issued the all-important Green Card. This was the United States Permanent Resident Card which allowed the holder the right to live and work in the US.

Three days later, on the stated date and time, I arrived at the impressive American Embassy in Grosvenor Square, Westminster. The building had a large gleaming gilded bald eagle on the roof with a wingspan over thirty-five feet, which made it easy to find. Once inside the wall of glass doors, I approached the official-looking young man behind the reception desk and was asked to produce my letter with the appointment time.

I was directed up the wide staircase to the next level. There I found the appropriate office and in the waiting room I was given many forms to read through and fill out with all the visa and alien registration information required before being issued the Green Card, my key to the future.

My confidence was at an all-time high. I was ushered into a huge, light and airy room with views over the rooftops of London. A young man shook my hand and asked me to sit in a comfortable black leather chair in front of his very modern, glass-topped desk. He was unmistakably American, speaking in a relaxed American drawl. He appeared to be fortyish with short hair and light brown eyes. After being asked a checklist of many general questions, I was horrified and embarrassed at being asked if I had been a prostitute, had committed any crimes, or been in jail!

The Green Card had to be carried with me at ALL times and I was not to forget the renewal in January of each year to update my whereabouts.

The next major step was to give in my notice at JWT, where I was required to sign resignation forms in the Employment Office. There was no going back now.

Mr. Caton was positive and encouraging about my future career and insisted on taking me out for a celebration lunch. I was so surprised when he produced a small gift wrapped in gold paper. As I opened the box, I saw a beautiful red soft-leather passport cover with the Pan Am logo stamped in gold on the front corner. Mr. Caton explained that he hoped the color red would help me to always 'find' my all-important passport. He was so thoughtful and such a gentleman and I knew I would miss him.

I was caught up in a whirlwind of 'busyness.' On my to-do list I had to: make an appointment to see the dentist to have my teeth checked and cleaned; see the Pan Am doctor for a medical exam and make sure I had my smallpox vaccination certificate; close out my account at Barclay's Bank and convert my meager savings into US dollars to take with me. We were to bring a minimum of $300 to cover our living expenses, rental deposits and incidental expenses in New York until our first paycheck was earned.

My last day at JWT arrived. I was full of emotions facing all the heartfelt farewells and thoughtful gifts.

I was about to leave this easy, routine, comfortable niche in my life for the total unknown. After eighteen months of living and working in London it was especially difficult to start packing my clothes and belongings at the flat.

With a lump in my throat I bid a sad goodbye to my stalwart friend and roommate Linda, my special girlfriend Susan, the landlady upstairs and her maid, Nellie.

I left London, the big city chapter of my life, and went home to see my family for the final few days and another flurry of activity. My mother came shopping with me for a brand new suitcase. I had received instructions that only one moderately-sized case was allowed. In this we had to pack clothing and necessities to last a minimum of four weeks which seemed hardly room for more than basics. We could have one carry-on bag.

In those days most cases were soft leather or other similar materials; hard-shell cases with wheels came much later. I bought one aqua-colored suitcase and a matching smaller one. We had to shop for other necessities needed to last for the training period and beyond, keeping in mind it all had to fit into the one suitcase.

The anticipated departure day arrived on Saturday, March 21st. My parents and sister drove me to Heathrow Airport which became a very subdued two-hour drive. On arrival we parked the car and looked for the Pan Am Departures area. I checked in at the Pan American Ticket Desk for Flight 103 to New York (incidentally, Flight 103 was the flight brought down in 1988 by a terrorist bomb over Lockerbie, Scotland). We found our way to the Departure Lounge and waited.

My stomach was in knots, full of conflicting emotions. I was thrilled to see some of my closest friends who had come to see me off – my roommate and friend Linda, and my good friend Susan.

We heard the boarding announcement for my flight and I felt a deep sadness as we said our goodbyes. I was fighting back the tears, it was heartbreaking for me standing there watching my family walk away to get in the car and drive home – without me.

An airline staff member approached and escorted me to one side. I was led to the back of the boarding area and there stood three girls – all tall with short hair so I knew they must be heading to New York for Pan Am stewardess training. Interestingly, we were: one blonde, Kate; one redhead, Barbara; one honey blonde, Mary; and one brunette – me.

As future Pan Am stewardesses, we boarded the Pan American Boeing 707 Jet Clipper aircraft and were seated together in the rear of the plane. All four of us were quiet as the realization set in of what we were doing.

We started relaxing and began to chat and discovered that three of us had never flown in a jet plane before and here we were headed to a career of flying; we hoped we wouldn't experience any form of air sickness. The plane taxied down the runway and took off leaving London and dear Old England far behind.

A wonderful lunch of Chicken Veronique was served, and we felt special as the stewardess told us that a Mr. Girdler, who was the Chief of Icelandic Pan Am, arranged for us to have a celebratory glass of champagne with our meal. It was a good feeling to know there was someone on the plane who was looking out for us. He must have been in First Class and knew we were seated in the back of the plane. When the tables were cleared, the two girls in my row, Barbara and Mary, sat quietly and rested.

I was on such an adrenaline high of excitement I couldn't sit still and relax. I looked across the aisle and the fourth girl, Kate, was sitting alone in the window seat so I moved over and sat down in the aisle seat next to her. She was a very attractive blonde with a big wide smile. We talked for a bit about our backgrounds, our families and how she had been a librarian. (Unless we were super-brains, the few career options open to us in that era were being a teacher, nurse, librarian or secretary). Suddenly, while on the subject of our hiring experiences, Kate started telling me about her bust size. I was somewhat taken aback, but she chatted on about her buxom forty inches, and how surprised she was that she was hired with such an attribute.

I wasn't surprised at all!

5.

NEW YORK

After five-plus hours our plane started its descent and landed at Idlewild International Airport (now JFK), New York at five-thirty in the afternoon.

We had arrived in the United States of America!

We were agog with the thrill of it all as we were herded through Customs, where an especially gruff official seemed to take pleasure in brusquely telling us not to get carried away – as that 'one' suitcase was all we would be allowed in the future. What a dismal welcome.

After dragging through Immigration we were met by a smart, friendly-looking fellow who introduced himself as the Pan Am representative from the Flight Service Department, Harry Proia. He hustled us outside to the curb. Our cases and baggage were stowed in the back of a mini bus and we climbed in and were driven to the Forest Hills Inn for the first night.

The four of us approached the hotel sign-in desk and the bright young female receptionist smiled and assigned us our rooms – two to a suite. I was with Kate.

On entering the room we gasped with delight as we explored and found the luxury of an en suite bathroom, which actually had a shower and bath tub. And, seeing a television set in the room – we knew we'd arrived in America! Quickly the realization set in that the adventure of a lifetime was about to begin.

Mary and Barbara were rooming together. That evening Barbara left her shoes outside the bedroom door expecting them to be returned polished and gleaming in the morning as is the case in England. Mary was feeling homesick with a lump of apprehension in her throat and just went quietly to bed. In the morning Barbara opened the door to retrieve her shoes and was mortified as they were nowhere to be seen. In horror, the missing shoes, the only pair she had with heels, were reported to Housekeeping. That caused some frantic moments with staff searching all over for them, but fortunately they were soon retrieved from the trash bins outside. Evidently, in New York shoes were not polished and returned if left outside the door. The maid had picked them up and disposed of them in the garbage.

That morning we ate a hurried breakfast in the hotel dining room, orange juice, buttered toast and a cup of tea. We English girls were not used to tea bags and that is what was sitting on the plate alongside mini white tea pots. We opened the packets and weren't sure where to put the bag – in the cup or in the pot? We opted for the pot and hoped for the best but the resulting tea was disappointingly weak and lukewarm.

We were rushed and had to get back to our rooms to finish packing our cases and meet in the front lobby by eight o'clock. There we ran into another group of girls who were talking in languages unfamiliar to us. All of us were ushered onto a small Pan Am bus and told we were headed to our apartment building, The Forest Park Towne House on 118th Street, Kew Gardens, where we would be living during our training. Eagerly looking out the windows, we watched New York flash past as the bus sped by.

The new girls told us they had flown in from cities in Europe, Scandinavia, and the United States the evening before. We realized we were the next training class – all strangers, different nationalities, most of us tall, and with short hair.

The bus stopped in front of a high, older-looking red brick and stone apartment building and we were told to pick up our bags and proceed to the entrance hall. We were met and welcomed by a friendly matronly lady who introduced herself as Miss Dickson. She explained we were a class made up of girls from Norway, Sweden, England, Germany, and America.

We were assigned to Class 12 to live and train together.

At this point there were only fourteen of us. One American girl and a German stewardess from the Berlin base would be arriving later.

Miss Dickson explained that we were about to embark on an intensive course with long hours of study as Pan Am was condensing six weeks of training into four. She read out and checked off our names as she gave us the numbers of the apartments we were assigned, explaining that the arrangement was three girls to each apartment.

Everyone was anxiously looking around to see who had been given the same room number and hoping they would be compatible. I was assigned an apartment with a Swedish girl, Ann-Louise, and an American, Roberta. Ann-Louise was a stunning, tall, blue-eyed blonde. She had friends already in New York so she was telling me how she was looking forward to visiting them whenever she had time off.

I walked down the long hallway and was the first one to open our door which led into a small living room and from there into the one bedroom. There were three beds covered with soft green comforters. I was the only one in the room so opted for the bed close to the wall with another twin bed alongside and a small table in between. The third bed was across the bottom of the room and Ann-Louise, when she came in later, chose that one. It appeared to be very clean and airy but there was no television, for obvious reasons: they wanted us to study. Ann-Louise told me to call her Louise and that she'd heard our American roommate wasn't arriving until a few days later as she'd taken medical leave from an earlier class.

The apartments were completely furnished including linens, dishes, and cooking utensils. The cost to each of us was $80 for the four-week period. Miss Dickson introduced us to our resident supervisor, Miss Ayers, who would be living on the premises to take care of us and assist us with anything we needed.

An Introduction Party was held for us in the evening to get to know one another and to meet the graduation class ahead of us.

Most of those girls were striking blondes from Iceland and they were telling us their class was based in New York. Mary approached from across the room and she told me she was rooming with Tina (a Swedish girl), and Bonnie (an American of Lithuanian heritage). Barbara joined us and said her roommates were both from Sweden – Lilibi, and Karin a beautiful brunette who was a runner-up Miss Sweden.

Our early experience of New York life began the next morning, Sunday, when the small group of English girls decided to go out and find some breakfast. We roamed the street and ventured inside a small, local drugstore/café. We were ushered into a back room which appeared cozy and warm with red checked tablecloths on small square tables. The friendly waitress handed us enormous menus and it took us forever to decipher all the dishes offered; things we'd never heard of like hash browns, grits, and eggs over easy.

Finally, Mary and I played safe and ordered 'boiled' eggs. The eggs sounded like a good comfort food at a time when we were feeling unsettled and homesick. Barbara and Kate asked for fried eggs with hash browns, but they were surprised when the waitress asked them if they wanted the eggs 'sunny side up?' "What is that?" they both asked and the beleaguered waitress took the time to explain that the eggs weren't flipped over, just cooked on one side.

We thoroughly enjoyed the steaming hot coffee brought to the table before ordering and thought that was so generous. Even more extraordinary, the waitress came back and refilled the mugs without our even asking. That would never have happened at home.

When the waitress brought the boiled eggs and placed them in front of us, we were baffled as we were staring at two eggs, in the shell, in a bowl. We'd never seen anything like it before, being used to eggs in special egg cups with spoons. What were we supposed to do? "They feel warm so they must be cooked," said Mary hopefully.

We carefully cracked and removed the shell and with the spoon scooped the soft eggs into the bowl but they were broken and the yolks were oozing all over. Kate took one look and uttered, "Ugh! What a gelatinous mess - it doesn't look very appetizing." That comment cast a pall over our appetites but we were so hungry we bravely ate it all. This American breakfast was a very new and different experience.

We browsed the store and decided to shop for snacks. Mary and I noticed some bread-like things called 'English muffins' which looked like nothing we'd ever seen in England. So, out of sheer curiosity, we couldn't resist buying a packet.

At the apartment building Mary invited me into their mini-kitchen. We had some time to spare so we opened the package of muffins but didn't know what to do with them.

"Let's try toasting them," I suggested.

So we jammed them WHOLE into the toaster. We had no idea we were supposed to break them open and toast two halves. No wonder we thought they were inedible, doughy, and not English at all.

We had time to relax before training started in earnest, so we all crowded together in one of the apartments to get to know one another. Somehow we broached the subject of how and why were we hired – why us?

Tina spoke up and told us about her experience at her interview during the coldest December weather in Sweden. "It was so bitterly cold, way below freezing and with snow and ice on the ground, I wore thick knit stockings and boots to the interview. Sensible, right? So what a surprise I got, when at the end of the second interview, I was politely asked to return the next day wearing nylons and high heels so they could see my legs! Makes me feel they hired me for my legs not for my brains."

Gunnel chimed in with her feeling the same way as I had with thoughts of leaving prior to her interview. "I was surrounded by gorgeous Scandinavian girls," she said. "But I persevered and stayed. But the interviewers noticed I had an eye tooth that was discolored, and at the end of my second interview I was quite shocked when they told me, 'We would like you to see a dentist to have your eye tooth corrected. We cannot hire you for training until this is done and we see a positive result.' I was eager to become a stewardess and so complied and went straight to my dentist. I reported to the Pan Am Stockholm office two days later, showing off my new white tooth, and I was instantly accepted for training."

The English girl, Kate, changed the subject to 'hair' and told us that she was asked to have her long blonde hair cut short to the required 'one inch above the collar line' *if* she wanted to be accepted for training. She was instructed to report to the local Pan Am office in London the following day with it shorn off.

She told us, "I didn't hesitate and immediately called my hairdresser for an appointment. I sat in the chair and cringed as I watched my beautiful long hair cut off and falling to the floor – gone forever. When I appeared at the Pan Am office the next day, the supervisor was so pleased to see my hair cut short, she formally accepted me for training – just like that."

Another Swedish girl in our class, Reidun, said she could beat all our stories with her experience. "I had been a pharmacist for a few years and desperately felt like a total change and the chance to travel. I was very concerned because I was a year older than the twenty-seven-year age requirement."

We were stunned to hear that as she didn't look older, but Reidun continued, "After my initial interview at the end of the day, the American interviewer shook my hand and to asked me if I would consider going out to dinner with him that same evening."

We all gasped in disbelief!

"I was most surprised and a bit flattered too. I could see that it was still daylight outside so it didn't seem too daunting to go out with him, so I agreed to go. He took me to a special restaurant that was very famous in Stockholm. We were having a good time until, in the middle of the dinner, a photographer approached and wanted to take pictures. The Pan Am fellow made it quite clear he did *not* want his photo taken but the photographer took pictures of me anyway."

We were all flabbergasted and asked her, "What happened next?"

"Before the dessert appeared, he leaned across the table and took a piece of paper from his pocket and placed it in front of me with his pen and asked me to write down my name and age, minus one year. Which I did – there didn't seem any harm in that, after all. He then carefully instructed me on how to get by during the weeks in New York by telling me to always write my real age on all papers going to the Government."

We were full of questions and dying to know if he had made any advances.

"*No*, he was just very nice and I felt he somehow took care of me and promised I would make it into Pan Am despite my age!"

We were disappointed that nothing untoward had happened.

"When I showed up for the second interview the following day he was there, sitting at the end of the table with the other interviewers, and I looked at him and he winked at me. That made me more nervous but I thought I had better be careful not to make any sign of response as I didn't want anyone to know we had been out to dinner."

And, of course, she was accepted and Reidun insists to this day that he was just very nice. She never saw him again, not even on a flight.

Those of us who had survived the traditional interview process just couldn't believe these stories. And there were more when Edith burst in with her experience.

"I was a German au pair to an English family in London and one day a German friend and I took a bus to Heathrow to watch the airplanes taking off and landing. This was our entertainment. While we were sitting there on a bench, we started dreaming of the wonderful life of being an air hostess travelling all over the world. I was totally carried away and when I got home I sat right down and wrote letters to two airlines – Lufthansa and Pan American.

"In the meantime I moved to Portugal to au pair for an American family. A letter from Pan Am was mailed to my family home in Germany and it was a few days before my parents thought they had better forward it to me in Lisbon, and I'm glad they did. When I received the letter requesting an interview I was so excited. But I had to write back to let them know that I was no longer in London but in Lisbon, Portugal. I was hoping desperately that the move wouldn't go against the interview that I wanted so badly.

"After another week I was relieved to receive a response letter telling me to report at a designated hotel in Lisbon for an interview, where a Pan Am representative would meet me. At the same time there was a group of Pan Am interviewers in Lisbon interviewing some Portuguese girls but as I didn't speak Spanish or Portuguese fluently, I couldn't be thrown in with that group.

"I arrived at the hotel in plenty of time and had to wait in the spacious lobby. I was wandering around trying to control my nerves when I was approached by a fairly good-looking American fellow, with short dark hair and smartly dressed in a navy blue suit. He introduced himself and proceeded to ask me a few preliminary questions while we were standing in the busy lobby. This seemed rather awkward so he suggested, 'Would you mind coming up to my room to continue?'"

So I replied, "Well, yes, we really don't want to do it here in public do we."

We all laughed and Edith said, "He turned red with embarrassment but still led me over to the elevators and pressed the UP button. In that instant an official hotel concierge rapidly approached us, gently tapped him on the shoulder and admonished, 'Excuse me sir, but it is NOT allowed to take a lady up to your room.' The poor fellow became more embarrassed and turned even more red in the face. He said hurriedly, 'You're hired.' And just like that, I was accepted to stewardess training here in New York."

Bonnie was anxious to add yet another tale and told us, "I was living in Detroit, Michigan, and wanted to join my best friend in Europe and was looking for a job that would garner enough money to get me there for the summer. I happened to spot the Pan Am

35

advertisement in the local newspaper and called immediately. Amazingly, I was told to come the next day which happened to be the final day for interviews.

"I also felt the waiting room was filled with better dressed and prettier girls than me. But at the end of the initial interview I was asked to return in the afternoon – on condition I was willing to wear my hair down. I was wearing it up in a chignon. I did return for the second interview and made sure my blonde hair was hanging loose and well brushed. Lo and behold, I was hired."

Tina added a different story of arriving alone at the Arlanda airport near Stockholm, Sweden, with her one suitcase and one small carry-on bag in hand. While anxiously looking around feeling very lost, she spotted an elegant, attractive young lady struggling along carrying a suitcase and what appeared to be several hat boxes as well. And yes, that classy young Swedish girl was Lilibi sitting right there in the room with us all.

In this day and age none of these hiring practices would be tolerated. We look back and laugh at how naïve we all were, trusting everyone we met and how times have changed re ageism and sexism.

6.

TRAINING

O ur class was strictly told to report to our daily training classes
wearing conservative blouses or sweaters and skirts, with
medium or high-heeled shoes. Bulky sweaters, full skirts or flat-
heeled shoes were NOT permitted. In those days there were no
blue jeans and no pantyhose – we wore skirts and stockings with
garter belts.

Monday morning we had to be up early at six to get washed,
dressed, scrounge around for something to eat and be on the Pan
Am bus promptly at seven. Louise and I were lucky as only two of
us were vying for the bathroom; the other girls had to juggle three
trying to get ready.

Amazingly, we all made it onto the bus.

On arrival at the airport terminal, we were dropped off at Pan
Am hangar building number 14. We sat at desks in a small room
and spent the morning filling out official-looking forms – many of
them. It was during this time Reidun was a nervous wreck when
having to state her age, and with every form that was placed before
her, she dreaded filling in any personal information. Remarkably,
she got away with her deception.

At lunch time we were told to find the cafeteria and there we
were treated to American roast-beef hash for lunch. The chopped
up mixture of crispy fried meat and vegetables was very tasty and
reminded the English girls of Bubble and Squeak (fried leftover
meat and vegetables).

The afternoon was spent lining up at the Medical Office to receive our first and very painful shots for tetanus and typhoid. We weren't happy to see our upper arms burning red, throbbing and swelling. Later, the supervisor handed out copious reading material for us to study while back in our apartments.

Miss Dickson warned us when we vacated our apartments for the day that they would be checked to see if they were clean and tidy. Certainly today this would be considered an invasion of privacy but we thought nothing of it.

I was glad to have lots of reading to do. Louise had left to meet her girlfriends and the American girl hadn't arrived yet, which left me on my own. But I was able to study without interruptions and could concentrate on writing long letters home to my family and friends. No phoning, texting or email in those days and the air mail news took at least four days to reach its destination.

The following day we had an afternoon start so the English girls went shopping in the morning and stopped for a hamburger for lunch. What a difference from the Wimpy skimpy burgers in London. Americans were so generous with their portions. The burgers were juicy, delicious and filling – the best we'd ever eaten.

We started at three in the afternoon and endured training until ten at night. These seemed strange hours but maybe they were initiating us to the extreme work schedules we would have to adjust to when actually flying. Some of us found the early mornings and the late nights overwhelming.

Ushered into an office for our uniform fittings we saw the dreaded tape measures appear and our measurements were noted. We were shown the uniform ensemble and were told it was specially designed by Don Loper, a world-famous Beverly Hills couturier. The color was a Pan Am Tunis blue. The uniform jacket was fitted in style, with an over-the-knee sheath skirt, a white raglan short-sleeve blouse and a perky blue hat. We also had a cotton tunic-length pale blue smock which was to be worn for in-flight food service. The wrap-around blue winter overcoat with a tie belt was heavy and very long, almost to our ankles, and completed our outfits.

The skirt was a pencil silhouette with a deep-kick pleat for ease and comfort, but because we weren't allowed to show any panty or stocking lines, we had to wear thigh length, elastic-tight girdles. The explanation given to us was during flight the air pressure can make the belly swell and the girdle helped us keep a flat-tummy appearance.

Though it never happened to me, many girls suffered the embarrassing experience of having a supervisor approach them and lift their skirts to check they were wearing the mandatory girdle. We soon learned that the girdles would become miserably tight and uncomfortable, especially in the very hot and humid climates where we would be flying.

We were required to pay for our uniforms including a large and roomy uniform handbag in black calfskin with a fold-down cuff. The average cost of a complete uniform package was $288, which seems a pittance today, but was a huge expense to us then. We also had to buy our own shoes, a black leather pair with no higher than two-inch heels, and a pair of plain flat black shoes for working in the cabin. We had to buy gloves: a wrist-length white cotton pair for summer, and long, almost to the elbow, black leather ones for winter. We were given a white carry-on bag with the blue Pan Am logo on the front to carry our shoes, cabin smocks, and flight necessities.

Our first lesson was a Grooming Class on how to apply make-up. The female, German-accented instructor, Miss Hess, had placed umpteen jars on our desks including rouges, creams and foundations – all things most of us never wore and were not thrilled about having to start applying now. Most of us had good youthful skin anyway.

We were only allowed to wear ONE lipstick color and were shown a lush red shade – Revlon's Persian Melon. There were many audible sighs and moans about the rigid lack of choice, but that was the rule and we had to abide by it. Bonnie never wore lipstick and was not happy about having to start now and especially one with such a red color.

Miss Hess gave us a demonstration on how to apply eyebrow pencil and mascara. No dramatic or excessive eye liner or eye shadow was permitted.

Then she broached the subject of our hair. "You must maintain your hair short at all times and when pulled straight the length must be at least one inch above your collar line." She droned on, "No excessive back combing, or any style where the top half of the ear is exposed."

We were warned that no false hair coloring was permitted, and wearing a wig probably would have resulted in capital punishment. She impressed on us that, "You personify Pan American and we expect you to maintain a neat, attractive appearance at *all* times."

More quiet sighs followed, and Miss Hess wagged her finger at us, "Jewelry is forbidden! NO necklaces, NO earrings, NO pierced ears, NO bracelets, NO adornments of any kind. A watch is allowed and recommended, and one simple ring – nothing else."

She gave us a severe reminder that NO eyeglasses and NO contact lenses were allowed to be worn. We sat there in silence with serious faces.

The following evening some of the girls decided to take a break from all the rigid rules and mandatory studying. A plan was made to explore Manhattan and find the Rockefeller Center Ice Rink. I very gladly joined them, needing a change of scenery and a strong desire to see more of New York City. We clambered into a taxi and commented on how enormous everything appeared. High energy and constant hustle and bustle surrounded us. We spent time at the Rockefeller Center ice rink awed by the prominent bronze sculpture of Prometheus overlooking the skaters swirling and spinning on the ice below.

Farther along we stumbled upon an interesting bar called The Wheelhouse in Greenwich Village and wandered in. We were ushered to a corner table where we ordered drinks and settled in to enjoy the onstage show, a bluesy singer and a small jazz combo group.

To save some money we decided to take the underground back home. We were not impressed with our first experience in the New York subway system. On that bitterly cold March evening the carriages looked to us like steel cattle cars as they rattled into the station with outlandish graffiti splattered all over them. We had no choice at that point and huddled together watching intently for our station so we could jump off and hurry to the safety of the streets.

The next morning our American roommate arrived and we were finally a group of three. Roberta appeared shorter than most of us even though she was five foot five. She had honey-blonde, wavy hair and a sparkle in her eye. Full of personality, she seemed very friendly and chatty and told us her parents were recently divorced and she wasn't handling it well. Her home was in New Jersey, fairly close to New York City so she, too, had friends in town.

We resumed training at the hangar that afternoon and were initiated into our First Class Bar Service lecture. Bonnie wasn't holding up well from all the class drilling and many vaccinations and came very close to fainting, but this was a class she was looking forward to, and she struggled to pull herself together to participate.

We learned how to mix certain drinks, how to stock the bar, and how to take drink orders from the passengers, all served free of charge in First Class. For this service it was stressed we should memorize the passenger's name and drink order.

Preparing the popular cocktails of the time was fun even though we'd never heard of most of them: Bloody Mary, Manhattan, Martini, Vodka Martini, Screwdriver, Whiskey Sour and Mai Tai. Other mixed drinks we learned to concoct were the gin and tonic, Tom Collins, and Vodka Collins. We also had to familiarize ourselves with the full range of fine wines, cognacs and cordials – vintage Champagne, Burgundy Blanc and Bordeaux of the Premier Grand Crus to accompany the meals.

We envisioned nightmares of mixing up the cocktail ingredients – there was so much to remember.

On our flights we encountered requests for more unusual drinks that were unheard of and not even covered in class.

7.

EASTER

"In your Easter Bonnet with all the frills upon it,
You'll be the grandest lady in the Easter Parade."
Irving Berlin

Sunday, March 29th was Easter Day. We had the day free and
Roberta went home. Louise suggested the two of us go
downtown to see the famous Easter Parade. I felt so cloistered with
our intense training and studying that it was a joy to get out and
have the chance to explore more of New York. As the weather was
pleasantly warm and sunny outside, we dressed up in our best
suits.

When we hailed a taxi outside our apartment building a small
yellow vehicle pulled up and we had to squeeze into the backseat
of a regular sedan. The interior felt grubby and reeked of cigarette
smoke. The driver appeared to be older and foreign. His hair was
straggly and his clothing appeared well-worn. We told him we
wanted to go to Fifth Avenue and without any comment, just a
deep grunt, the driver sped away from the curb, swerving through
the heavy holiday traffic.

Not yet sure of the American currency, we nervously eyed the
mileage meter clicking loudly ever upward at alarming speed. This
was only our second ride in a New York taxi cab and we had no
idea it would be so costly for the two of us. We rummaged through
our purses to see if we had enough money between us to cover the

fare – and keep some in reserve for the return trip to the apartment. We frantically added up our dollar bills to find we had barely enough and then realized, with a twinge of alarm, that we would have to add a tip. We emptied our purses. When the vehicle lurched to the curb and abruptly stopped, we handed all the cash we had amassed to the driver. As we clambered out of the cab there was a loud muttering from the front seat and the next thing we saw was all our coins being flung from the driver's window and clinking onto the road as the vehicle roared off. We could only surmise that the driver was insulted by too small a tip. To make matters worse we were stunned to see our precious cash strewn all over the road and too much traffic to even think of retrieving it.

Standing on the sidewalk we were dumbfounded, crestfallen, and admittedly furious.

Trying not to let that experience dampen our spirits, we walked to Fifth Avenue where the sidewalks were clogged with people. An incredible spectacle appeared before us in a moving wave of the most colorful, elaborate, fantastic, beautifully decorated Easter bonnets we had ever seen. We saw hats with enormous pheasant-like birds sitting on top with long curving tail feathers, and large silk and paper flowers in the vibrant palette of Spring. There were baskets full of bunnies, and pet dogs wearing fancy little hats. Whole families, young children, even the elderly, all wore flamboyantly decorated Easter bonnets. The proud wearers were parading up and down both sides of the Avenue. We were thinking of all the time and effort and imagination that went into making these unique creations, and what fun it was to see everyone smiling and having a good time.

I'd never seen anything like it and I haven't since either. I just couldn't imagine the staid English parading up and down Oxford Street in such a fashion. That made the experience so much more unusual, different – and so American.

In the distance I caught a glimpse of the Empire State Building, the world's tallest building at the time. I'd never seen such an enormous skyscraper, and I was crushed to hear Louise say, "I hope you don't mind but I've been up there and really don't want to go again." My disappointment aside, we were having a marvelous time simply being a part of this spectacular parade.

We wandered onto a side street and just as we were wondering how to get back to the apartment, a Daimler car pulled alongside and a young man asked if he could give us a ride. Louise was a tall stunning blonde so no wonder this fellow was only too happy to have us jump in his car. He was very personable and quite good looking but when we reached our place, Louise invited him in for a coffee. I was wary and appalled as he was a total stranger. Naturally, he accepted readily and up he came to our apartment.

I left Louise to entertain him and retreated to the safety of the bedroom to study.

8.

FIRST CLASS

The following day we started training at three in the afternoon and continued until ten-thirty at night. We met in the mock-up of a 707 First Class cabin to learn the First Class food service. The model was complete with seating four abreast, two on each side of the aisle, and plenty of leg room to stretch out comfortably. The fully equipped galley looked intimidating. Our Galley Coordinator was Conrad Jacoby and he assigned me to be the cabin attendant with Karin working in the galley. Our classmates sat in the First Class seats and assumed the roles of first class passengers, but they were listening and watching as they knew their turn would come next.

Our instructor impressed upon us that Maxim's de Paris prepared all the meals, and told us that Auguste Escoffier, France's pre-eminent chef in the early part of the twentieth century believed, "Good food is the basis for true happiness."

Pan Am's First Class 'President Special' service was considered the ultimate in airline dining elegance. The more this was stressed upon us, the more pressure we felt for attaining perfection. We learned to set the tables, which were fastened to the forward seat and could be adjusted to the individual traveler. A large, white, continental-style tablecloth and napkin were placed at each table – the napkins even had a stitched buttonhole in one corner so they could be fastened over a shirt button. We were shown, and had to familiarize ourselves with the finest china, silverware and French crystal stemware. To complete the elegant effect flowers were added in small containers.

The girl assigned to the galley prepared all the food under the watchful eye of the supervisor. How stressful it was trying to remember where everything was stowed in that small galley space. There were so many hidden compartments, drawers, cubbyholes, spigots, dials, ovens, warming ovens, dry ice bins, four coffee makers which could provide freshly-brewed coffee for eighty cups every eight minutes, and multiple refrigerated tray carriers.

We learned how to heat the ovens to the correct temperatures, to cook the food without burning it, or ourselves, and present the dish on the plates or on the serving cart.

We familiarized ourselves with the menu by eating the dishes and could feel ourselves putting on unwanted pounds.

Below is a sample dinner menu handed out to our First Class passengers:

Hors d'oeuvre
Les Délices culinaires de la Voiture
Pinot Chardonnay

Fish
Les Filets de Sole au Vermouth
Pinot Chardonnay

Entrées
Notre Specialité: La Côte de Boeuf rotie
Cabernet Sauvignon

Le Coq de Bruyère farci au Riz sauvage
Pinot Chardonnay

Le Filet de Veal au Tarragon
Cabernet Sauvignon

Les Haricots verts au Beurre
Les Pommes Parisienne

Fromages
La Sélection de Fromages de Pays
Cabernet Sauvignon

Dessert
Le Flan à la Crème
Un Choix de Fruits des Iles et des Continents
Champagne

Café et Liquers
Café Americain   Café Sanka   Thé Orange Pekoe

Crème de Menthe   Bénédictine   Cointreau
VSOP Cognac   Drambuie

We started with the hors d'oeuvres course served from the rolling Clipper buffet. The challenge now was learning to serve these delicacies from the serving platter with a silver spoon and fork held in one hand – this procedure took lots of practice and we experienced many disasters. We persevered and eventually perfected serving pâté de foie gras and smoked salmon onto the plates in front of the mock passengers, taking extreme care not to fumble and drop anything in the process.

The second course could be a clear terrapin soup with Sherry, an oxtail soup, or a delectable cream soup. Learning to use the large soup ladle and not slop the hot liquid all over the cart was incredibly challenging. Many of us were wondering what would happen should we encounter turbulent weather during this course.

On occasion, fresh Iranian caviar would be offered on the menu. We were taught how to set up and serve this delicacy from a small crystal bowl placed into a tureen of ice. We mastered the arrangement of the accompaniments on the side – chopped egg with the yolks and whites presented separately, minced onion, lemon wedges, sour cream, and mini toasts. On the same cart we set up a frosted bottle of iced vodka and small glasses to offer alongside.

The fish course was usually Sole Meunière – a classic French dish of sole, dredged in flour, pan fried in butter and served with brown butter sauce and lemon. We heated this in the ovens and plated each serving in the galley to hand deliver on a tray to the tables.

The main course offered a choice of three or more entrees. The 'King of the cart' was the Roast Prime Rib of Beef. The roast beef was seared and cooked for fifteen minutes in the commissary and it was our responsibility to complete the roasting in the galley oven. We learned how to estimate the number of portions from each roast, figuring half-inch slices, and to prepare two roasts if needed. Thankfully, a thermometer helped us keep a watchful eye on the temperature, and when it registered 'rare' the beef was done. We were instructed to NEVER overcook it! When ready, the galley girl had to place the meat on a special carving board on the top of the cart and make sure the silver carving knife and fork were also on hand. The instructor showed us how to carve the roast alongside each passenger who requested it; this way they could choose which slice they preferred.

The vegetables were served from the cart with the serving spoon and fork in one hand – potato croquettes, snow peas, buttered green beans, or whatever was on the menu that day. Remember, always place the meat or fish at the two o'clock position on the plate, the vegetable at six and the starch, potato or rice, at ten.

We had to prepare and plate the other entrées most of which were prepared, cooked and frozen. These included: veal with tarragon sauce; lobster Thermidor (my favorite), consisting of a creamy mixture of cooked lobster meat, mustard, egg yolks, and cognac stuffed into the lobster shell and served with an oven-browned Gruyère cheese crust (this dish was a French specialty created to honor the opening of the play 'Thermidor' in Paris in 1894); Cornish game hen, a small succulent bird with short legs and a plump round breast, boned and stuffed with wild rice; grilled lamb chops; and other delicious dishes. It was drummed into us to never forget the all-important parsley garnish!

The Cheese Course followed. A selection of cheeses were offered including a soft cheese such as Brie or Camembert, a hard Cheddar cheese, and a Gorgonzola blue cheese. We learned how to cut or slice them and serve the passengers from the cart at their tables.

Remembering all the details was truly exhausting, so much to learn in so short a time.

Still another lesson was the Dessert Course, with the trainees' favorite being the Cherries Jubilee. The black cherries were laced with Brandy and slightly thickened before they came onto the plane. The fruit sauce was warmed in the oven before being poured into a warmed silver tureen and placed on the cart. We ladled it over the richest, creamiest, yellow French Vanilla ice cream served in an iced silver tureen using a special ice cream server. This was a wide fairly flat utensil used to slice the ice cream – no scooping. As the cabin attendant we again had to be very careful not to spill or splatter the warm cherry sauce right in front of, or onto, the passenger. For the passengers who didn't wish to indulge in dessert, we offered a fresh fruit basket.

Not yet finished – the final cart had to be set up with the coffee and tea pots, china cups, saucers, spoons, the cream jug and sugar. A selection of cordials and glasses were arranged on the cart to pour along with the coffee. This was an especially nerve-wracking time – trying so hard not to spill any scalding hot coffee on the passengers. We had to learn the liqueurs by the bottle shapes, not with sipping: Crème de Menthe, Bénédictine, Bénédictine and Brandy (B&B), Cointreau, VSOP Cognac, and Drambuie.

We sat in the mock-up cabin seats and enjoyed sampling all these very rich, delicious meals. Why, oh why, did they take our measurements *before* all these gourmet meal classes?

The galley service involved a number of training days, which allowed each of us to experience preparing the food, as well as working the cabin. There appeared to be a hundred things to remember working the galley but we were assured that in time cooking for forty guests would become as simple as cooking at home!

After these classes we returned to our apartments very tired, well fed and with expanding waistbands. Mary admitted to having nightmares about never remembering what all the compartments were for in the galley.

Mona, from Norway, was flummoxed because she had never heard of 'parsley' and had no idea what it was. Fortunately, Mona and Gunnel's roommate was a gorgeous blonde American girl and she was only too pleased to help them both with their English. She was extremely patient and went to great lengths to explain about parsley and what it was used for.

We were left with the comforting thought that we had accomplished the basic galley and service training. When on an actual flight, we could always turn to the experienced purser for guidance and help. And we did learn and pick up helpful hints from other crew members and pursers on subsequent flights.

In addition to the multi-tiered and exhaustive food service, we were taught to handle basic and advanced emergencies, such as attending a normal baby delivery.

The nurse-instructor tried to instill in us that on an airplane, "Ingenuity must be used with respect to the supplies to be used and the best location for the delivery." We were taking it all in and hoping we wouldn't have to cope with such a traumatic scenario. We could request a doctor's assistance over the intercom and were told that the odds were that we would have at least one doctor on board.

But, if not, it was up to us!

Not one of the girls in our Class 12 was ever faced with this challenge. I came close when I was informed that a baby had been delivered on a flight into Hawaii on the plane I was picking up to continue on to San Francisco. I remember being disappointed to have missed the experience by one flight.

We were instructed on how to warm baby bottles of milk or formula, and how to set up the baby bassinets. These had to be securely latched onto the bulkhead and were a joy for the mothers traveling with young babies.

After the long days of galley and cabin service training, and learning to deliver babies, the Water Experience classes that followed were the ones many of us will not forget.

9

EMERGENCY TRAINING

LIFESAVING SKILLS

Our class boarded a Pan Am shuttle bus and was driven to a local indoor swimming pool. On arrival we were led to the locker room where we changed into swimsuits, the ones we had brought from home, and donned our tight-fitting swimming caps to protect our hair.

The athletic-looking instructor introduced himself as Mr. Breitschwerdt. He told us to line up along the length of the Olympic size pool – the largest pool any of us had ever seen. We all wondered what was coming next when he shouted at us, "One by one, I want to see you *dive* into the water and swim to the other side of the pool."

Quiet mutterings echoed along the water's edge.

Most of us, me included, couldn't dive and Bonnie had a fear of water over her head. Everyone could swim but the American girls were the only ones who knew how to dive in head first. I had grown up swimming in the English Channel where diving was not part of the swimming scene. After much hesitation, those who couldn't dive, or were afraid to look bad, were allowed to jump in feet first. One poor girl couldn't even bring herself to do that, so two of us just 'pushed' her at the given moment. The American girls glided through the water showing off the 'crawl' while the rest of us (easy to pick out the Europeans) swam the awkward-looking breast stroke which is the only stroke we were ever taught.

Tall, red-headed Barbara gallantly jumped in feet first and valiantly swam her breast stroke across the pool. On nearing the other side she put her legs down to stand up, assuming she was in the shallow end, only to find she was sinking slowly under the water in the *deep* end of the pool. She came up gagging, spluttering, and most embarrassed, so two girls had to jump in and help drag her to the pool edge. We spent the rest of the pool time learning and being tested on lifesaving skills.

Needless to say, we were all relieved when that session was over.

WET DRILL AND DITCHING CLASS

The wet drill and ditching class was scheduled the following day and simulated being 'ditched' in the water and trying to man the life rafts. Luckily for us this was held at the pool. We were told some of this training actually took place in near-by bay or ocean areas, but this was March, and much too cold to be outside – how lucky we were!

Arriving at the pool, we were surprised and peeved to see the most unattractive, shapeless-looking black swimsuits and plain white caps being handed out to each one of us. Cringing, we headed to the changing rooms to put them on.

Our instructor was Mr. Breitschwerdt again. He told us to stand along the pool edge where we all warily eyed the huge orange life raft bundle. Mr. Breitschwerdt asked two of us to lift and throw this enormous raft into the water, which was not an easy task as it was *very* heavy. Once in the water the raft inflated immediately, whooshing open with quite a force, and filling up most of the pool. A female assistant handed each of us an orange life vest, and told us to put it on, tie it securely, jump into the water and then inflate it.

"Do not inflate them BEFORE you jump," bellowed Mr. Breitschwerdt.

One by one we jumped into the water with the limp life vests hanging round our necks. Inflating them while bobbing and flailing about in the water was a struggle, but eventually we managed to pull the right cords. We found out that once inflated they became an uncomfortable bulk around our torsos, greatly restricted our movement and hindered our swimming.

The instructor barked orders from the poolside and blew whistles for order as we struggled to swim to and climb INTO the enormous rubber raft.

We had to muster all our strength to clamber up and over the rounded edge. It felt like scaling an enormous bloated orange whale! The inflated vests squeaked against the rubber of the raft as we clumsily collapsed into it totally exhausted. AND this was in calm, warm swimming pool water. Whatever would it be like in the middle of the ocean, with high waves, in full uniform, freezing cold, and sharks thrashing around?

How could we save ourselves let alone other people?

Aboard the raft, we sat around the edge like drowned rats, dripping wet, and shivering. The instructor swam out to join us and showed us the life-saving equipment hanging over the edge in a huge bag.

Barbara was the one called upon to haul the emergency supplies into the raft. But, as she stretched and leaned over the side, she experienced a major swimsuit malfunction. Her shoulder strap *snapped* and she experienced a revealing problem. She groaned and struggled to hold her suit together. I was sitting next to her, saw her predicament and grabbed the two ends of the strap and hung on tightly. Barbara needed both her hands to grab the awkward emergency supplies kit and haul it into the raft – a difficult task with me hanging on to her and her broken strap ends at the same time.

Mr. Breitschwerdt pretended not to notice this calamity and was probably not amused by all the commotion. He calmly proceeded to take out the hand flares, medical kit, fishing gear, cans of water and food rations.

Although sopping wet, we tried hard to concentrate and learn about survival: how to use the drinking water kit to remove the salt from sea water, to wear outer garments to protect ourselves from sunburn, to stave off hunger by rationing candy, gum and vitamins to feed five or six people for one day, to treat sores by not opening or squeezing them, to protect eyes from glare, to treat seasickness, and for emotional disturbances there were phenobarbitol tablets to be used as a mild sedative.

When the instruction was over, we were told to remove our life vests and leave them in the raft. Happy to be free from their restrictive bulk we swam back to the pool edge with ease. Finished with our drill, we climbed out of the pool, showered under steaming hot water, toweled off and changed into our dry clothes.

The crew bus returned us to the apartment building and we all prayed we would *never* have to experience an actual ditching in the open ocean.

PLANE CRASH ON LAND

Another class extended survival training to a Plane Crash on Land. We were sitting quietly and attentively at our desks when Mr. Breitschwerdt entered the classroom, dressed this time in khaki slacks and a black shirt.

He had us imagine a plane crash in the snows of the Alaskan mountains. The lecture was about exposure to very low temperatures, when body heat can be retained by several victims huddling together, stressing to our disbelief that, "The best way to combat exposure to extreme cold is to take off **all** your clothing and huddle together." We had visions of huddling with the pilots and this brought on a barrage of, "Oh no," and "We'd never do that," while thinking of all the pilots who would absolutely love this scenario. "Warm your hands and feet against each other," Mr. Breitschwerdt continued in a serious tone. "Warm dry clothing is the best protection against cold and it is important to keep your socks and shoes dry. Remove shoes if your feet become swollen and do not rub any part which has become numb."

We were warned of frostbite, which is the localized freezing of tissues, and were cautioned, "Do not rub or massage the frozen part, and do not place a victim near a hot fire or open blisters!"

The instructor regaled us with his grim stories and continued with the case of 'hunger' telling us to, "Eat four ounces of solid food every two hours as this will increase your resistance to severe cold, that is, if food is available!" I think he was enjoying scaring us.

At the end of the class, Mr. Breitschwerdt left us with a personal piece of advice, "When flying I always tighten my seatbelt with an extra tug to be safe, especially on takeoff and landing." A habit I find myself doing to this day.

ESCAPE CHUTE AND FIRE EXTINGUISHERS

The Emergency Class continued yet another day when we were taken to a 707 cabin mock-up and shown where the life rafts were stowed in the cabin ceiling. We had to go through the grueling task of opening the compartments, dropping the heavy rafts down to the aisle floor and dragging them to the emergency exits. It was an advantage that most of us were tall as that helped in the laborious task of retrieving the cumbersome rafts from overhead. The instructor told us one story about some shorter Nisei stewardesses from Hawaii who experienced an actual emergency requiring the rafts to be used. The stewardesses' adrenaline was flowing so fast that they were able to drop the rafts and pull them down the aisle to the emergency exits over the plane's wings with no difficulty at all.

We were shown where the cabin fire extinguishers were stowed, and how to use them. It took lots of practice to twist open the seals, and aim and spray as fast as possible.

Being timed and tested on how fast we could pull out the emergency escape chute from the airplane door was another challenge. One by one we had to slide down the chute removing our shoes beforehand. It was all very well doing this on dry land, but again we all wondered – whatever would it be like sliding down the chutes and hurtling into life rafts thrashing about on wild ocean waves?

10.

HAPPENINGS

One evening I was home alone dutifully studying for the next day's tests. My two roommates were out visiting their local New York friends.

I heard a soft knock on our door and thinking it must be one of the girls, I jumped up and opened it. I was taken aback as there on the threshold stood a good-looking young man dressed in navy slacks and a white turtleneck sweater. I must have had a surprised expression on my face as, before I could open my mouth, he asked how I was and what I was doing. He then announced he was selling magazine subscriptions such as Vanity Fair, Harper's Bazaar, National Geographic and Life – but I didn't see any of the magazines. His big pitch, preying on the fact that I was alone in the apartment, was an offer to take me out to dinner if I paid cash for one of the subscriptions. This all sounded too glib and too good to be true so, despite the temptation, I told him I was sorry but I just didn't need a magazine subscription and didn't have enough cash to pay him. Fortunately that was the end of him.

The girls were talking about the same fellow the next day as he had tried knocking on their doors. They were laughing about anyone being taken in by such a line. Kate's roommates said they were lucky to have her with them as she reportedly kept guard and made sure any suspect males were told in no uncertain terms to, "Go away!" She had the advantage of being raised with brothers. But, we did wonder how he got into the apartment building and past our very strict Floor Supervisor.

Another afternoon during study time, there was great laughter and giggling echoing down the hall. I was curious to find out what was causing so much hilarity and ventured into the corridor. As I approached the wide-open door at the end, I could see a small group forming in Barbara, Karin and Lilibi's apartment. The girls were migrating to the bedroom and staring at one of the bed pillows on which was laid out a beautiful, woolen, hand-knit pale blue sweater. But, the sweater was so small it would have fitted a two-year-old! The concern and giggles from all around was however were they going to tell Lilibi that her favorite expensive cashmere sweater had been thrown in the washing machine and had shrunk (and, I mean, *really* shrunk) to this miniature size.

Poor Karin was the one who was doing her roommate the favor by including it in the wash. She assumed 'everything' could be washed in these new-fangled American washing machines. Most of us had never used a washing machine before and were accustomed to washing sweaters in bathroom basins or kitchen sinks. The now mini-sweater betrayed this innocent ignorance as it sat shrunken on the bed. Eventually, ever-stylish Lilibi returned and appeared in the doorway. We were all standing there very quietly in anticipation of her reaction. Well, with us milling around all she could do was laugh and shrug it off with, "Don't worry, I have many other sweaters I can wear!"

We did detect a slight hint of aggravation in her tone.

Interspersed with our training we had to endure painful visits to the Pan Am Medical Clinic to endure more immunization shots before flying to all corners of the world. The clinic was located at the airport in a small room with dazzling white walls. The doctor was a charming older gentleman clad in a white medical jacket and, with the assistance of a young cheerful nurse, he carefully vaccinated us against Yellow Fever, Typhus, Cholera and Tetanus. Again, our arms swelled and grew hot and red with all the vaccines they were pumping into us.

The vaccinations had to be noted in the bright yellow 'International Certificates of Vaccination' booklet. We had to keep this with us at all times in case it was needed upon entry to a foreign airport; and we had to have it readily available to record all our follow-up shots.

11.

AN EVENING ON THE TOWN

My fun-loving American roommate, Roberta, wanted me to experience dining New York style. I was elated to have the opportunity to get away from all the studying, and see more of exciting New York City. Roberta invited me to join her and her girlfriend Patsy for dinner at Trader Vic's. London had a lot of ethnic restaurants but I'd never heard of a Polynesian one, so I was looking forward to the experience. I dressed up in my red and black knit suit, and Roberta looked very smart in a dark blue velvet dress. We hurried into our overcoats, rushed down to the lobby, and hailed a taxi in front of the building.

Nighttime in New York was a sea of sensory input. Neon signs were ablaze in all colors, traffic lights flashed red, amber and green at every city block and endless lines of red taillights and yellow headlights lined the street. The taxi eventually dropped us at the Savoy Hilton Hotel where we met Patsy who rushed toward us and welcomed me with a big hug. She was vivacious and pretty with long dark wavy hair. I saw no sign of Trader Vic's but Roberta explained it was inside the hotel.

I was elated to see the most enormous restaurant with bamboo everywhere, soft green upholstery, exotic flowers, tiki carvings, giant shells, and odd tribal masks covering what seemed to be every square inch of wall and ceiling space. I had an immediate feeling of being in the Polynesian islands.

A charming waiter ushered us to a table in the middle of the dining room. There was so much to see all around us, and the atmosphere was alive with all the chatter of diners having a good time. We were seated in comfortable soft-cushioned chairs and the waiter handed each of us a large red-covered menu. The foods and dishes sounded foreign to me and I wondered about the ingredients of Pu Pus, Bongo Bongo soup and Beef Cho Cho.

Fortunately, Roberta had an air of confidence about her as she had visited the restaurant before. She and Patsy consulted the menu and ordered drinks first.

After a short while, the waiter presented each of us with round clay bowls filled with a drink which had the most beautiful creamy-white exotic flower floating on top. I was speechless. I'd never seen such a presentation before. The intoxicating scent of a gardenia is not something often experienced in England – especially floating around on a drink! Roberta had ordered Scorpions for the three of us. She leaned over and warned me, "Enjoy this concoction but sip slowly, don't gulp it down, as it contains two rums, brandy and Triple Sec....Cheers!"

Roberta took charge of ordering from the menu. We had ample time to enjoy our drinks, chat happily and take in all the tropical ambiance of the dining room before the food finally arrived. We shared a huge serving of crispy fried spicy prawns followed with platters of Wasabi Filet Mignon and sticky white rice. The beef was the most delicious and tender I had ever tasted, spiced with wasabi (strong and hot like horseradish) and soy. I was comfortably satisfied but Roberta insisted we indulge ourselves and ordered Polynesian Snowballs for dessert. The presentation was beautiful with very large balls of creamy vanilla ice cream rolled in toasted fresh coconut, sitting in a pool of warm bittersweet chocolate – true decadence.

I wondered if I would ever fit into the Pan Am uniform that was being made to my 'arrival' size.

The whole evening was an incredible American dining experience. What impressed me the most was at the end of our evening, when the waiter presented us with the bill, Roberta insisted on paying for the entire meal and all our drinks. She adamantly refused to have either Patsy or me contribute a thing, and I was beginning to realize what a special young lady she was. I had never before had a friend affluent enough to offer such generosity.

Before we left the table, I was wishing out loud as to what a memento it would be to take a menu home with me as a reminder of such a thoroughly enjoyable evening. Why didn't we just ask? But the menu was huge, multi-paged, and in such a beautiful cover that we assumed they'd say NO. So, what did we do? Proper as always we conspired to secrete one under Roberta's loose-fitting overcoat. We stood from our chairs, donned our coats, and left our table with great care, walking sedately toward the main lobby.

Unfortunately we had to descend some steps on the way. We were light-headed with the after-effects of our tropical drinks when Roberta suddenly stumbled and tripped down a stair, crashing in an unladylike heap to the floor. The hidden menu flew from her coat like a dove freed from its cage, spinning through the air before hitting the carpeted floor with an audible thud. Patsy and I rushed to help Roberta, thankful that she seemed unscathed and helped her up and brushed her off.

Our cheeks flushed red with embarrassment. We were so nervous at being caught in petty menu thievery that we left the menu laying there on the floor and rushed for the door. Helena and I jumped into a waiting taxi and were whisked off to our apartment.

This grand hotel was demolished just a year later in 1965 to make way for the General Motors building and the Trader Vic's restaurant moved to the Plaza Hotel.

12.

TRAINING CONTINUES

PUBLIC SPEAKING SKILLS

Public speaking skills were considered essential. Our assignment was to prepare a speech to deliver to the class and instructors. The topic had to be about a country we had visited or wished to visit someday. I chose Switzerland as I had recently returned from a memorable, college trip to Interlaken for mountain hiking. Living in the south of England, I had never seen a snow-capped mountain, and with that holiday, had fulfilled yet another dream.

Despite being uneasy at the prospect of public speaking, we wrote out our speeches, made brief outlines and practiced. The class day arrived and we all forged ahead, taking our turns standing in front of the group and delivering our talks, hearts beating fast, and mouths turning dry. The German girl, Edith, told us she was terror stricken but somehow found the courage and got through it. She told us later, "Public speaking is definitely not for me."

We learned microphone techniques for delivering in-flight announcements, and made the announcements in English but then also delivered them in our secondary foreign languages. Kate told me, "You spoke French very well, but with a decided British accent."

We were tested on everything we had learned and were constantly threatened with being sent home if we didn't pass all of the exams.

FIRST AID EMERGENCIES

For the First Aid class we had to study the standard course of instruction in 'First Aid to the injured by the American National Red Cross.' We were expected to pass a test in order to receive a certificate of completion.

Our instructor was a formidable older nurse who introduced herself as Miss Lavallee. She began each session with a stern look at each one of us young, eager, stewardesses-to-be, shook her finger and intoned, "Life is NOT a bowl of cherries." This was seared into our brains, and how very right she was.

Miss Lavallee instructed us with great patience in aircraft common emergencies: aero-itis (irritation of the middle ear due to pressure, colds etc.), sinusitis, anoxia (oxygen deficiency), heart attack, seizure, fainting, hyperventilation and motion sickness. And more dire and intense situations such as asphyxiation, hemorrhage, shock, fractures, wounds, burns, scalds, and eye injuries.

By this time we were over-deluged with information but had to continue with a long session on Health Hints for the Tropics. In this environment we must become water conscious, food conscious, heat conscious re sunstroke and severe sunburn, and insect conscious. We had to cover many icky skin diseases especially prevention of fungal infections.

Our brains were at bursting point.

PASSENGER SERVICE

More days were filled with classroom study to learn about passenger service: making our passengers feel at home from take off to touchdown, recognizing the problems brought aboard with so many different passengers, and that we were the ones they turn to for help, improving customer relations – an air traveler who is more enthusiastic at the end of the trip than at the beginning. We learned to anticipate little things – like noticing the passenger unable to fill out customs and landing documents, and the ones worried about making connecting flights.

Other required studies included US Customs and Passport regulations; theory of flight, navigation and communications; currency conversion; time conversions from local standard time, Greenwich Civil Time, the 24-hour clock, and familiarize ourselves with all the aircraft documentation.

We also had to learn how to interpret and plan our monthly flight schedules by filling out our flight preferences for the month – what countries we wished to fly to and when. The Flight Scheduler would grant the requests by seniority but being brand new stewardesses we would be at the bottom of the list to those who had years of flying before us. Most schedules had girls flying about fifteen days per month with trips ranging in length from four days to as many as twelve days. All lodging and transportation expenses while on trips were covered by Pan American, and we were paid per diem at each layover base to cover meal costs. We soon found out the per diem was surprisingly generous.

MODELS FOR THE DAY

Some members of our class were honored to model the Pan American uniforms and dress through the ages for a dinner banquet honoring Pan Am employees and their families. This was an annual event and coincided with our training class. Not all of us were selected and I was thrilled to be included in the model group.

I was assigned to wear the new in-flight pale blue smock, Mary donned the original Pan Am uniform which had a longer front-pleat skirt, Kate wore the current uniform, Barbara was costumed as Queen Elizabeth I, and Roberta dressed as an American cowgirl (complete with hat and boots). Mona, Louise and Bonnie wore the native costumes of Norway, Sweden and Lithuania.

It was quite an occasion in a huge banquet hall full of people. At the end of the parade we were bombarded by photographers, and then were expected to mingle and chat with the guests. The evening was a lot of fun and definitely helped break the monotony of study.

13.

FINAL DAYS

The days and weeks were passing rapidly and at last the day was upon us for our final class. That morning we were given a tour aboard a real 707 Pan Am jet aircraft. We were told, and expected to remember, that in 1958 Pan Am entered the Jet Age with the Boeing Clipper, a plane that could fly at 35,000 feet at 658-plus miles per hour, carry as many as 150 passengers, and was the first passenger jet to fly across the Atlantic. We had to familiarize ourselves again with the placement of emergency equipment, the cockpit, and the galleys, and generally experience the confined size and space in which we would be working.

The worst part of the day was in the afternoon when we had our dreaded uniform fittings. After so many days sitting and feasting on all the rich First Class food, every one of us had gained weight. We were squirming into our skirts, sucking in the added pounds, and appalled that we were bursting at the seams.

That embarrassing experience was a good incentive to lose the unwanted weight. I immediately decided to stop adding sugar to my hot tea and coffee and haven't added any since.

Jenny was depressed at her weight gain and total inability to lose any pounds despite all her attempts to reduce. Gunnel and Mona instinctively felt sure the poor girl was pregnant, but Jenny denied such a possibility and was adamant that she had *never* 'done it' with her boyfriend. Nevertheless, her weight spiraled upwards and all in her belly area.

We now owned our uniforms and felt official. We were responsible for buying our own gloves so Louise, Kate, Barbara, Edith and I, went on a shopping trip downtown. We found the glove store Pan Am had recommended and after much trying on and peeling off, we bought our long black leather gloves for wear during the winter months, and the wrist-length white cotton ones for summer.

Further down the street we found a shoe shop and tried on many flat black shoes which were required for in-flight wear. With much parading up and down we were all able to find pairs that looked right and fit comfortably.

After our shopping spree we cruised down the street and stumbled upon a small European-style bakery. The sight and smell of delicious-looking fresh-baked pastries staring back at us in the window was too much to pass up. We had little will power between us and indulged in some wonderfully decadent and fattening éclairs – full of yummy thick cream with chocolate icing on top. They tasted so good and were a much-needed energy boost.

So much for losing weight!

Finally, our graduation day arrived. It was announced that we *all* passed and were now Pan Am Stewardesses. We were told to go downtown to Lucien's Beauty Salon on Fifth Avenue to have our hair cut to the official length and set to the acceptable style. We made our appointments and set off in groups. After an hour of shampooing, cutting, and drying in curlers under huge dryers, we emerged from the salon looking identical – our hair the same length, same back-combed style and curled around the ear. The only unique thing was our different hair colors. It had been explained to us that all our haircuts were tax deductible as a uniform requirement!

Now coiffed and outfitted in our full uniforms we were transported to the airline terminal for our graduation photographs. This was an incredibly exciting day, and we paraded though the airline terminal with all eyes upon us – 'the Girls in Blue.' We were escorted to a steep curving staircase and told to line up by height on the flight of stairs with the tallest girl on the topmost step and on down by height to the shortest one at the bottom. As tall as I was at five feet eight inches, I ended up in the middle of the group.

After the class photos were taken, we were guests of honor at a graduation ceremony. We had to line up again and as our names were called we stepped forward to receive our well-earned diplomas and gold Pan Am 'wings.' It was impressed on us that we represented three out of every hundred applicants interviewed and were about to join other girls from thirty-seven different countries around the world.

The senior Pan Am official, Mr. Viola, congratulated us and announced, "You are Pan American," and "the image of a Stewardess is the image of Pan Am." We felt truly honored and were offered a glass of champagne, told to relax and enjoy the graduation party that followed. One of our instructors, Mr. Proia, entertained us singing Italian love songs on Roberta's guitar.

Our euphoria was dampened slightly when we were reminded that we were on a six-month probation period. During this time there would be supervisors checking us on our in-flight appearance and service performances – and with no advanced warning! Too many non-compliance occurrences would result in employment termination.

14

SAN FRANCISCO

Great, Wide, Beautiful, Wonderful World
William Brighty Rands, 1800s

After weeks of intensive training, constant examination, and a final graduation ceremony, the suspense was not yet over. We were left wondering *where* we'd be based – in New York or San Francisco – the only two major bases Pan Am had at that time in the Overseas Division. Each base flew Round the World flights half way around the globe and met in Bangkok, Thailand.

The morning after the graduation party the announcement was finally made that our Class 12 was being assigned to the West Coast San Francisco base. Sadly, two of the Swedish girls were told they had to stay in New York as they spoke Italian (as well as English and their native Swedish), but they didn't seem to mind. Louise was one of the girls and she had a boyfriend in Italy so she was happy at the prospect of seeing him more frequently. The other was the sophisticated city girl, Lilibi, so it suited her too.

The rest of us were left in a state of consternation thinking about a major move to far away San Francisco on the other side of this enormous country and a lot farther away from our homelands. We didn't know exactly where San Francisco was and it was stressed that it was a coveted base and usually only those with high seniority were lucky to be assigned there.

We learned later that the class of girls which trained before us, and the one after, were both based in New York.

Tina admitted she thought she was good at geography but as soon as she got back to the apartment she searched for her world map and looked up San Francisco. She had absolutely no idea where she was going and seeing it marked on the far west coast of this vast country didn't really make it that much clearer.

Now the next dilemma was who would be rooming with whom in San Francisco. Those who lucked out with compatible roommates during training had formed close friendships and were staying together – Gunnel and Mona, and Barbara and Karin. There was a lot of anguish as these girls teamed up and others were left out.

Of my two roommates, Louise was staying in New York and Roberta told me she had a good friend in San Francisco and would be sharing an apartment with her. I had a sinking feeling hearing they had plans of their own.

I didn't agonize for long as Mary, who had been rooming with Tina and Bonnie, approached me and asked if I'd consider sharing an apartment with her. I didn't hesitate and readily agreed. We were both English which was comforting, and Mary and I felt happy that the decision was made.

The irony of this relocation was that Pan Am did not fly across the United States, having no domestic flights or routes. It was solely an international airline and to get to San Francisco from New York we had to fly to London, and then from London on to San Francisco. This revelation roused the English girls' thoughts. If we were landing in London, maybe we would have time to see our families.

Sad farewells were showered on my parents only a month before, having no idea when I would be seeing them again. Now I was writing excitedly to tell them I would be back in London in just a few days. I was elated at the thought of seeing them so soon, but for them I'm sure my visit would be bittersweet. How long before we would be together again – especially as I was on my way to live and work on the far west coast of the United States, thousands of miles further away from home in England.

73

The day for departure arrived and I packed my few belongings into my one aqua suitcase. We said our goodbyes to the two girls staying behind. Louise said she would keep in touch, and Roberta promised we would be seeing each other in San Francisco as she gave me her new address and phone number. How lucky she was to have a roommate and apartment already waiting for her.

I felt an immense sense of pride dressed in my brand new Tunis blue uniform, with my hat on, wearing long black leather gloves and the well-earned stewardess 'wings' on my jacket.

I was a Pan Am stewardess.

With my suitcase in one hand and my bag and purse in the other, I set off on the Q10 bus for the Pan Am Departures Building to check in for my flight to San Francisco via London. Some of us, including me, were assigned to work the London flight while others deadheaded in the back of the airplane. Then we would reverse and those working to London would be deadheading on the flight to San Francisco, while the other girls worked the cabin. Deadheading meant we were given empty seats on the plane SUBLO (subject to passenger load), and traveled as regular passengers.

On arrival at the airport I headed for the Briefing Office to sign in on the Crew Schedule Sheet for the Round the World, Flight 2. It was just before five-thirty, my check-in time for the seven p.m. flight departure.

The entire crew was there looking smart in their Pan Am uniforms, yet they were all strangers to me. We had been told that we would seldom fly with the same crew members. The older captain introduced himself as Captain Harris and introduced me to the crew as the newly graduated stewardess. He chatted with each one of us before explaining the flight conditions expected and he estimated the flight time to be six-and-a-half hours. The senior purser introduced himself as Bill, and the other purser was Betty. Purser Bill told us we had fifteen passengers in First Class and a full load aft. He went over the cabin and galley assignments and special passenger information, and told me to work in the First Class section but to spend time in the Waiting Lounge first.

Normally one stewardess was assigned to the airport Waiting Lounge to meet and greet the passengers. We were to introduce ourselves, calm nerves, allay first flight jitters, and generally chat with the travelers. This was especially difficult as I had just been informed that the flight was delayed for one-and-a-half hours due to a ninety-degree heat wave. The passengers' nerves were getting ragged when they heard all the cargo was being unloaded. I had to explain it was to compensate for the lower density altitude of the hot outside air. This is what they meant when they told us we had to be quick to adapt to new situations.

When I finally reported to the plane, I helped the First Class passengers get comfortable by handing out magazines or the day's newspapers. I offered playing cards, coloring books, and crayons to the children. We also carried writing materials, paper, and pens, for those wishing to write letters while aloft. Most importantly I checked all their seatbelts to make sure they were securely fastened.

Flying was an elegant experience. Most travelers used their hard-earned savings for international tickets and made efforts to dress up for the special occasion. Looking smart and well groomed was the travel style. There were no bulky carry-on bags filling up the overhead racks or stuffed under the seats – *all* baggage was stowed in the cargo hold and only hats, coats and light packages stowed in the open overhead shelf. Most passengers were extremely appreciative of every little thing done for them.

Purser Bill looked very smart in his crisp white jacket, black tie and black pants, and he told me to prepare for the lifejacket and oxygen mask demonstration. I was trying hard to remember the sequence from training. I heard him start the welcome announcement and he continued while we positioned ourselves to go through the emergency procedure.

I was standing in front of the First Class passengers and concentrating hard on keeping up with the announcement. Bill was explaining the drill for lifejackets and at the right moment I tugged down on the blue tab – but I must have pulled it too firmly as it snapped off with a 'ping' and sat in my hand! I was mortified and felt very conspicuous standing there with the tab clutched in my now hot palm, hoping that no-one noticed. I felt like I was standing on stage with all eyes upon me, and I had to think quickly. I simply placed the tab on the floor and carried on with the rest of the demonstration as my face burned red with 'new girl' embarrassment. We had to endure these little incidents and get through them, and they felt magnified when happening for the first time in front of the watchful eyes of the passenger audience.

After take-off Purser Bill told me to hand out the menus to each passenger. The front cover of these menus bore a reproduction of an authentic Currier & Ives clipper ship print. Each print was one of a series reproduced through the courtesy of The Museum of the City of New York.

I walked down the aisle and asked for each passenger's drink preference. As I approached each one, I tried hard to memorize their names. Bill mixed the drinks at the bar and I carried them to the passengers on a small tray.

Purser Bill was very considerate, which I appreciated in my 'newness,' and he took the time to show me special ways of folding the napkins into fantastic shapes as holders for the different serving dishes we would be placing on the dinner cart. He created rectangular shapes to hold serving utensils and flower shapes into which he placed the sauce bowls. I was so impressed and thankful to be learning new techniques to improve the presentation of our service. It was these little touches that set the Pan Am service apart from many others. I helped Purser Bill set up the seat tables with crisp white cloths, set out the silverware and crystal wine glasses, the square glass salt and pepper containers, and placed the small flower arrangement in the center.

We then began the multiple-course dinner. I served the hors d'oeuvres while the purser poured the wine choices. The training was coming back to me as we progressed to the entrées. 'Remember to place the entrée plates with the meat at two o'clock' was the mantra in the forefront of my mind as I placed them in front of the passengers. Meanwhile Purser Bill carved the roast beef from the cart for those who had requested it. After the cheese course and then the dessert, which this evening was the familiar Cherries Jubilee, I carefully poured the coffee while Bill offered the after-dinner drinks.

When everything was cleared away and the passengers could put up their tables, we handed out ample white cotton-covered pillows and warm blankets which were stowed on the shelf above the seats. On went the provided eye masks and the passengers settled comfortably to sleep.

I was asked to check the restrooms and spent time replenishing the paper and soap supplies, wiping down the sink area and picking up any dropped debris on the floor. The bathrooms were *supposed* to be pristine at all times.

The purser then sent me to the aft Economy section where I helped set up the many breakfast trays for the full load of passengers. My energy was flagging by this time but there was always work to do. I had been on my feet for many hours at that point but the adrenaline of a first flight was keeping me in motion.

As we neared London, Purser Betty asked me to hand out the Customs and Landing forms. I was brand new, bright and eager, and after the passengers had completed the documentations, I walked the aisle and proceeded to collect them. Betty approached me and with a look of consternation on her face asked, "What are you doing?" I felt rather foolish as she explained to me that the passengers had to keep the customs and landing forms to get through the Immigration and Customs areas at the airport. Oh dear, I should have remembered that. She then told me to hand them all back. What a task that was and it took up lots of time as I had to ask each row what their names were to return the correct forms.

There were so many things to remember on one flight, but I hoped that with time it would all fall into place.

After seven long hours we finally arrived at Heathrow, London. I stood by the purser and said goodbye to the passengers at the doorway. When the last passenger left the cabin the flight was officially over.

Nine in the morning and, no surprise, it was raining. The crew boarded a coach which drove us to the hotel in central London. We checked in, received our per diem, and most of the crew scurried off to their rooms to get some much-needed rest. Pan Am provided first-rate hotels for our layovers and accommodations were usually in the town center to make it easy for shopping and sightseeing. Instead of rushing to my room to sleep, I excitedly called home and made arrangements to meet my parents at the Victoria Railway Station later that morning.

Seeing my parents sent me into an emotional turmoil. It seemed surreal as we took a taxi to Knightsbridge and enjoyed a light lunch at Harrods Department Store. I felt the atmosphere was strained due to me leaving the next day for far away San Francisco. My parents were putting on happy faces but deep in their hearts they must have felt a profound sadness. The hours ticked by and we had to face another heartbreaking goodbye. With an aching heart I jumped into a passing taxi to return to the hotel, and they left for Victoria Station to catch the train home.

On entering the hotel I had an uplifting surprise. There in the lobby stood my class friend Tina who had arrived from New York on a later flight. She looked very tense so I suggested we sit in the lounge so she could tell me what was troubling her. We sat in the comfortable armchairs and Tina told me how nervous she was at the start of her flight from New York. She was working aft and her brain was so full of all the rules of what to do and what not to do brainwashed into her head that she started off with a massive headache. After the meal service was over and the lights were turned down she was shocked to see most of the crew resting in the empty seats while the passengers slept. To her this was a definite no-no according to our training.

"Not me," said Tina "I patrolled that cabin every fifteen minutes or so and, when not walking up and down checking on the passengers, I drank lots of coffee to keep awake. By the end of the flight, I was literally jumping from all the caffeine, and when we had to sit for landing, the *jump* seat had a whole new meaning."

She was beginning to unwind and felt better for sharing her experience but she was exhausted and took off for her room to try and get a good long sleep – if that was possible after drinking so much coffee!

The following morning I left on the crew bus for Heathrow Airport. After checking in my suitcase, I left the crew to wait in the passenger lounge as I was deadheading and this was going to be an eleven-hour-long flight.

It was exciting to fly over Greenland and see the mountains, the icebergs, Labrador, and then the vast mountain ranges of the Rockies. I was lucky to be in a First Class seat and I watched the crew to learn more from their service. We landed in Los Angeles first to allow some passengers to disembark before the plane flew up the Pacific Coast to San Francisco.

On landing we passed through Customs and Immigration, and I joined the crew on a Pan Am bus which took us to the local Holiday Inn by the airport. Some of the girls from my class had arrived already and it was a welcome sight to see their familiar friendly faces in the lobby.

We started chatting and Karin wanted to tell us about the trauma of her first working experience. She had been assigned a flight to Frankfurt in Germany, not London, and told us, "During the service I was asked to warm a baby bottle. That wasn't difficult but when I returned and handed over the warmed bottle to the mother, who was sitting in a window seat with a child on her lap, I managed, somehow, to spill some of the formula on the man sitting next to her. The one thing we dreaded doing. I apologized as best I could but he was furious and yelled at me! I ran back to the galley devastated but he got up out of his seat and came after me. I was taken completely by surprise when he faced me in the galley and said, 'It is all forgotten - *if* you go out to dinner with me in Frankfurt.'"

"Well, did you?" we asked incredulously.

Karin grinned and answered, "Sorry to disappoint you, but I didn't even stay over in Frankfurt. I was immediately scheduled on a flight to London, and from there to another plane deadheading to San Francisco – and here I am."

We were given instructions to meet in the hotel lounge at six o'clock that evening. A Pan Am representative came in and introduced himself as Mr. Al West. He welcomed us to San Francisco and told us we had *three days* to find a place to live and to let the Pan Am office know of our new addresses as soon as we were settled. That was it. He bid us good evening and left.

We sat there in a daze for here we were in a totally unknown part of the United States and had no idea where to start. We were distressed with the urgency of finding a place to live in such a short time, before setting off on our first flight assignments.

Six of us, Gunnel, Mona, Barbara, Karin, Mary and I, huddled together and made a decision to stick together and hire a car to start our search in San Francisco. We learned that Gunnel was the only one with an American license as she'd been an au pair girl on the East Coast working for the Volvo family before applying to Pan Am. She offered to do the driving which was a huge relief to the rest of us.

Early the next morning we met for breakfast and the hotel reception desk called for a taxi to take us to one of the airport car rental companies. We chose a large car to seat six and signed all the paperwork. Piling in the big Buick car, we set off for the streets of San Francisco. All of us could easily fit in one car as the huge American sedans could seat three in the front seat and three in the back and there were no seat belts to worry about.

We enjoyed the Highway 101 drive north and on rounding a deep curve there it was – the famed city of San Francisco looming in front of us. What an incredible sight. Tall buildings amassed together in a picture of architectural splendor as the morning sun sparkled and danced off the façades. We turned onto Market Street, parked the car and stepped out full of expectation.

The Emporium department store was nearby and took up almost a full city block. We couldn't resist the temptation to explore and eagerly entered the massive building; however, we didn't stay for long and came out feeling rather glum as it appeared rather old fashioned and gloomy inside. This was not what we had expected and collectively wondered if this was all San Francisco had to offer for shopping? To boost our morale we saw a coffee shop across the street and decided to take a break to discuss our next move.

Upon closer inspection the small café also appeared dingy and dismal, but we entered anyway. The coffee was disappointingly weak. If this was San Francisco we weren't impressed and opted to get in the car and head right back south to a little town called Burlingame.

We were so naïve we had no idea there was more to San Francisco beyond Market Street.

After a long drive south we spotted the Burlingame exit. Our spirits lifted as it appeared to be a delightful, small town. We slowly drove around the streets looking for apartment buildings hoping to see 'Vacancy' signs. We did see some, but they didn't have anything available furnished – especially for six of us needing three separate apartments.

By now we were concerned, worried that we weren't going to find anything. But as our hopes were plummeting, we took a turn down a side street named Floribunda and there we saw a building with a big sign out front stating in glorious black text "Furnished Apartments for Rent."

Gunnel steered over and parked outside the building and we eagerly climbed out onto the sidewalk. The building appeared fairly new and promising. We rang the Manager's bell and waited at the entrance doors – six young, brand new stewardesses all eager to find a place to live.

After some minutes the manager appeared and introduced herself as Mrs. Reeves. She was short, middle-aged, with wavy grey hair and a sweet, welcoming smile and warmly invited us into a vast entry hall. We explained we needed three, possibly four, apartments and they had to be furnished as we had not a stick of furniture with us. Mrs. Reeves told us this was a brand new building and there were several two-bedroom furnished apartments available and she showed us the available ones on the two levels.

She led us outside to see a small shimmering blue swimming pool and we all gasped as that to us was sheer LUXURY.

We were so ecstatic with the building, the rooms, and the pool, that we signed on the requisite dotted lines right then and there, selecting three one-bedroom apartments on the second floor with balconies overlooking the pool. Mrs. Reeves was thrilled to rent out so many at the same time.

After the dark, old Victorian flat in London, the apartment Mary and I rented seemed like a dream. It was brand new, spotlessly clean, and with lots of windows to welcome in the California sunlight. The floor had plush beige-colored carpeting throughout, and a very modern-looking kitchen with a huge (to us) harvest-gold refrigerator with a large freezer section on the top. What a bonus that was as most refrigerators in England were half the size with no separate freezer space. The single bedroom had two twin-size beds, a side table between them with a large lamp for ample light. The spacious bathroom had a shower in the bathtub and a huge mirror stretching across the entire wall above the washbasin.

No more sharing a bath with the landlady, restrictions to two baths a week and sharing the toilet with her maid.

All six of us were thrilled the all-important housing matter was decided so easily and it was a big worry off our minds. Mary and I were together, Gunnel with Mona her roommate in training, and Barbara and Karin would share another apartment as they had been roommates in New York. Later Tina and Kate joined us and rented a fourth apartment down the hall. Our training group was becoming a close family of friends.

Back at the Holiday Inn the receptionist greeted us with a message. We had instructions to meet in the lobby the following morning and board a Pan Am bus to the airport.

John Hale and Al West, the San Francisco Supervisors, met us and led us on a tour of the San Francisco International Airport, showing us the before-flight briefing rooms, the passenger lounges, and the scheduling room. We met the schedulers who had the job of assigning each stewardess her 'lines' of flights each month.

We all hoped we would find our way around when on our own.

On the third day, Mary and I checked out of the Holiday Inn and hired a taxi to drive us to Burlingame. We were anxious to organize our brand new apartment before we received our first flight assignments.

The motherly Mrs. Reeves greeted us and let us into the apartment and handed over our two door keys. We told her we didn't know where to start. She must have seen the perplexed expressions on our faces and was only too happy to tell us how to find the utility offices downtown and explained that first we had to look into getting the electricity turned on, and then get hooked up for a telephone. What a good feeling to have a manager who cared enough to explain all this to us.

The apartment had a light and airy feeling, and had all the basic furniture. The living area had a beige sofa, two wooden end tables with a lamp on each, one brown upholstered armchair, and an oval coffee table; there was a small rectangular kitchen table with a pearly white Formica top and four basic chairs.

However, we needed to shop for the necessities as we were arriving with absolutely nothing to furnish a place for living. Mary and I walked downtown to the local Woolworths department store, feeling fortunate there was one on the main street of Burlingame. There we shopped for blankets, sheets, pillows and bathroom needs and looked for necessary kitchen supplies. We proudly opened bank accounts at the local Bank of America. Shopping done, we lugged all our purchases back to the apartment.

In the lobby we chatted with one of the other tenants who introduced herself as Maggie, and she very sweetly offered us a coffee pot, plates and a tea pot which she insisted she wasn't using. She also invited us over for some warm apple pie and coffee and we happily accepted. Mrs. Reeves stopped by later to see how we were coping and offered us some extra blankets. Everyone was so welcoming and friendly.

The final group of girls from our class arrived at the Holiday Inn. They had the same reaction on seeing San Francisco (the south end) as we did and drove to Burlingame as we had done. But Floribunda didn't have any three-bed apartments. The manager told them to try a larger building not far away and there they rented an apartment for all of them – Edith, Bonnie, Reidun and Jenny.

Eight Pan Am girls from our Class 12 were sharing apartments in the Floribunda building. That evening I joined Kate, Karin and Barbara for a walk around the neighborhood and we were surprised at how cool it had become late in the day but, after all, it was mid-April.

Next morning Gunnel stopped by and said she had the rental car for one more day and asked, "Mona and I thought we'd use the car for one last drive back to San Francisco, would you and Mary like to come with us?"

"Yes! What a super idea and let's see if there really is more to the city than Market Street," we answered.

Mary and I quickly changed and put on our dressy city suits and gloves. We had learned that San Francisco had a custom for women to wear white gloves in summer and black gloves in winter and NEVER be seen wearing white shoes after Labor Day. Appropriately dressed, the four of us slid into the car and drove up the freeway toward San Francisco.

Thanks to advice and directions we had garnered from our new friends in Floribunda, we did find the famous San Francisco hills and gasped at how steep they were. Gunnel bravely drove us slowly through the bustling streets of China Town and around Nob Hill. We were fascinated with the old fashioned cable cars and so many wondrous sights at every turn.

Gunnel was tiring from the driving and we were getting hungry so we wound our way down to Union Square. We parked the car in the underground garage, and found the I. Magnin and Macy's Department Stores and couldn't resist looking around both. We were impressed and relieved to see that they were so much more sophisticated than the Emporium on Market Street.

We asked a store clerk for a casual place to eat and she suggested the popular San Francisco cafe, Blum's, which was right outside facing Geary Street. It sounded the perfect place for what we had in mind and we rushed out to find it.

What a place! And what a menu!

We saw happy diners eating the most delicious-looking enormous ice cream sundaes. The waitress offered us a menu full of tempting dishes but we went straight to the dessert section. We ordered three to share among us and the waitress encouraged us to try the famous Coffee Crunch Cake, a vanilla cake frosted with coffee flavored whipped cream and lots of coffee caramel crunch, the Coffeesta Sundae which was rich vanilla ice cream covered in hot chocolate sauce with coffee crunch and whipped cream on top, and the Goshawful Gooey – a sundae with thick hot fudge sauce poured over rich ice cream, covered with whirls of whipped cream and a big red cherry on top.

When they were placed before us, we had never seen anything like them before. Not one scoop of ice cream, but two and three ample scoops, piled high in clear glass goblets. We couldn't believe the huge portions but enjoyed them all!

Again, we were all hoping we would fit into our uniforms after such indulgence.

We retrieved the car and crossed the famous Golden Gate Bridge over the Pacific Ocean entrance to San Francisco Bay. We were beginning to understand how fortunate we were to be based in this beautiful city. Breathtaking views were everywhere. Turn a bend in the road or drive to the top of a hill and there was yet another stunning view stretching before us. All around the city the buildings glistened in the sunlight. The scenery was so different from anything in England, Europe and Scandinavia.

Mary and I settled into our apartment. We invited the girls over to our new home to sunbathe on the small balcony. It was very hot for mid-April, and in England we'd have been shivering and bundled up in sweaters and coats. Looking longingly down at the swimming pool, we decided to put on our bathing costumes and head down to the pool where there was more room for us all to stretch out. Coming from Europe and Scandinavia we were all obsessed with having suntans.

The temperature soared and the water looked so inviting some of us plunged in to cool off. The others who didn't have swimsuits with them just stripped to their underwear and, looking all around making sure no-one was watching, in true European style, jumped in too. We didn't worry about getting our hair wet as none of us had flights that evening. This was utter luxury and so California – to be swimming outdoors in April.

The single young men who were living in the same building were lauding their luck with so many young, foreign stewardesses moving in at the same time.

15.

UNKNOWN HORIZONS

Mary received her first flight assignment and was elated to see she was going to Honolulu on the island of Oahu in Hawaii. A day later I received my flight assignment and saw, with dismay, that I was flying to the arctic cold and snows of Alaska. I have to admit I was disappointed as I hate the cold. How did this happen? However, I didn't despair for long as I knew I'd be seeing a lot of Hawaii in the weeks and months ahead. Kate announced she was also scheduled to Alaska and she wasn't thrilled either.

For our first flights we had to look our very best and make sure our hairdos were not touching our uniform jacket collars. Barbara and I thought we both needed a haircut so we asked Mrs. Reeves for a recommendation and she mentioned the hair salon in downtown Burlingame – The Pink Palace. We raised our eyebrows at the name and after our last hairdos coiffed in Manhattan in New York City, we just hoped this small town beauty shop knew what they were doing.

We walked to the salon and on entering the open front door we were struck with how very 'pink' it was inside. There were pink walls, pink towels and the staff wore pink aprons. I took a deep breath of unease as a Miss Agnes approached with scissors in hand and proceeded to cut my hair. True to the styles of the day, it was cut short, curled up in huge rollers, dried to a crisp under the tall floor-standing hairdryer and then brushed and backcombed mercilessly for lift.

A haircut and set for only seven dollars and I have to admit Miss Agnes exceeded my expectations.

I methodically packed the warm clothes I would need for my short flight to Alaska and back. I was debating about calling a taxi to get me to the airport for the ten p.m. departure flight as I had to be in the Briefing Room two hours ahead and "Don't ever be late" was ringing in my ears. We were threatened with forfeiting our entire line and put on a Call List, if we were just two minutes late. And that meant no plans as we had to be by a phone on standby in case we were needed at very short notice, at any time of day or night, for the rest of the month.

I was in luck as Maggie, who lived on the floor below, offered to drive me to the nearest bus stop. We were quickly realizing that without a car we were dependent on buses, taxis or friends. Dressed in my uniform, wearing my hat, long black leather gloves, carrying my black purse, the burdensome overcoat, and my one, now heavy, suitcase, I was left at the bus stop in the approaching dark of evening.

I had to wait twenty minutes for the bus – and froze! I was finding out that the evenings became very cold in this part of California at this time of year.

What a late time to start work. I wasn't used to this crazy schedule yet. The bus dropped me off at the airport and I lugged my baggage to the Maintenance Base. I found my way to the Flight Briefing room and met the crew members already there: the captain, pilots, pursers and the other stewardesses.

Captain Everett introduced himself, a younger than usual, military-looking captain, and explained that only the crew members were flying to Travis Air Base as this was a MATS flight (Military Air Transport) from there to Alaska. I was happy the purser was also an English girl, named Pamela. She was friendly, warm, relaxed and very understanding of my being brand new and that helped immensely. Pamela introduced me to Junior Purser Margo and the Swedish stewardess Alda who would be working with me on the flight. As we entered the empty airplane, it seemed strange seeing all the vacant seats in a darkened cabin but we buckled ourselves into our crew seats and the plane took off into the pitch black skies.

We were enjoying this no-passenger flight to Travis when the captain's voice announced we were experiencing landing gear trouble. The flight engineer shot out of the cockpit, charged down the aisle, bent down on his knees in the middle of the cabin and was, I was told, checking the gears. This activity didn't help me relax, especially when I heard this was the captain's very first flight in a 707 jet.

However, the engineer must have fixed the gears as we continued on and arrived safely at Travis at eleven-thirty p.m. We had a brief layover and the captain told us to get something to eat in the cafeteria before boarding the passengers and setting off again at one-fifteen.

We boarded all the passengers and I worked in the front of the cabin with Pamela and Alda was assigned the galley. After take-off and a short snack service, one of the servicemen came up to the lounge area and started chatting with me and told me he was from Miami and was interested in this being my first flight. After awhile he returned to his seat. I was surprised when he came back shortly and very sweetly presented me with a little paper bird that he'd made sitting at his seat.

After an uneventful flight, with no gear problems resurfacing, we landed at Anchorage at three in the morning their time. It was *so* icy cold and bleak and I could see dark menacing mountains looming all around us. We left the plane in the hands of a maintenance and clean-up crew. Our bags were loaded onto a crew bus and we took our seats and were driven to the hotel where the crew headed straight to the bar for drinks to get warmed up. This was the last thing I wanted to do as I was so tired, probably from 'new-girl' nerves, but thought I'd better stay with the group. I finally got to bed at five-thirty in the morning!

Ten days before our arrival, the largest earthquake in North American history had struck Anchorage, Alaska, on Good Friday,

March 27, 1964. Tectonic shifts had thrust sections of the ground thirty feet skyward. We had landed right in the middle of all the devastation and destruction.

My roommate Alda and I slept in and woke up at noon. We dressed as warmly as our suitcases allowed, and headed downstairs for something to eat. The waitress was still agog with the deadly earthquake news and encouraged us to walk downtown to see the aftermath. We thought that would be quite a sight to see and after a sandwich and coffee, we donned our warm coats and ventured off toward the main street.

The sight before us was deeply disturbing. Never before had I paid attention to earthquakes. In England they just didn't happen, especially at this horrific never-before-recorded 9.5 magnitude.

We walked slowly along the main street and it felt eerie and bizarre to look down and see the roof tops, broken, bent and buckled – level with our feet. I could feel goosebumps rising all over me as I saw where the ground had opened wide like a gigantic jaw and swallowed up two-story buildings. It looked so horrific and surreal.

Even stranger, on the other side of the street, the buildings were still standing but the fronts had vanished, crumbled away to piles of rubble on the ground below. The interior rooms were exposed to the outdoors with dining tables and chairs still intact, living rooms, even bedrooms totally unscathed and open to the elements and every passerby. It was like staring into a giant doll house.

What a stroke of fate to be on the right side of the street at that sickening moment of the ground opening up and devouring everything along the fault line. An apartment house on one side of the street was completely flattened with the elevator shafts sticking out of the ground at stark, hideous angles surrounded by piles of debris that used to be homes. On the opposite side a Catholic Hospital had hardly moved. It was unnerving to be witnessing this devastation so soon after it had happened. Walking down the street we shivered, feeling a sinister quiet all around us. We felt so distressed that it seemed wrong to get out a camera and take pictures of other people's misery.

The following day a group of crew members, me included, thought it would be interesting to go on a van tour of the earthquake trail. The driver explained to us the area soil was glacial silt which is very stable until shaken. As we drove by the McKinley building he told us it had swayed a staggering *ten feet* in each direction and was now condemned. Trees were ripped in half, huge trunks divided in two by deep chasms. The amazing thing was that only nine people were killed and the quake lasted a good five minutes at five-thirty in the evening. Most unusually it was the more affluent area in Turnagain Bay, so called by Captain Cook in 1711, where the worst damage occurred. Enormous luxury homes just slid down into the sea and disappeared into its icy murky depths.

The locals were thankful the catastrophe happened on Good Friday meaning all the children were home from school, and we did see school buildings jutting out of the jagged ground with rooflines folded like concertinas. The Government Hill Grade School had collapsed into a deep fissure but strangely no windows were cracked or broken.

It was an unforgettable day.

We went to bed early at eight o'clock to get three hours sleep before getting a wake-up call at eleven the same evening for the return flight back to Travis. We were told to expect a hectic flight as there were lots of children on board. I worked in the back and offered hot chocolate to those who wanted it and later handed out menus before serving a hot breakfast of cheese omelets with sausages and warm rolls. I walked the aisle pouring coffee with one hand while balancing a tray of sugar and cream in the other. We landed in the morning and I was asked to stand at the bottom of the ramp to help the mothers and children who were disembarking first. The crew stayed on board and when the last passenger left, we flew the plane back to San Francisco arriving at ten. We had been working all night long and I was so relieved and thankful to have Pamela offer to drive me home to Burlingame.

I had survived my first flight out of the San Francisco base and was left with the daunting memories of the worst-ever Alaskan earthquake.

Mary arrived home from her Hawaii flight a day later. She was enthralled with the magnificent tropical vistas, the powder soft sand, clear blue surf, and the balmy warm air. I told her about the freezing cold of Alaska and the horrors of the earthquake devastation.

Later I called Roberta and she invited me to visit her and her roommate Terry in San Francisco. The following morning I dragged myself out of bed, still tired and catching up after the Alaska experience, and caught the bus to San Francisco. I found my way to Roberta's apartment in a building stretching up a steep hillside with cars parked sideways at alarming angles. It was a spacious old place with fantastic views from the windows right above Leavenworth Street.

True to Roberta's generosity, she offered to take me for a tour of the City. I slid into the custom leather passenger seat of her shiny new navy blue Corvette sports car. She fearlessly snaked the car down Lombard Street telling me it really was the crookedest street in the world. We then headed up a very steep hill to Coit Tower in the Telegraph Hill neighborhood. The tower is a two-hundred and ten-foot-high monument built in 1933. I took lots of photos of the vast city views from so high up and wandered inside to see the many fresco murals. I had very little knowledge of local history but the colorful paintings depicted the struggles of working class Americans from the Depression era period.

Back in the sporty Corvette we wound our way down and up another steep grade to Nob Hill and the Mark Hopkins Hotel. We parked the car and Roberta led me inside. I learned that the original mansion on the site was a dream home for Hopkins' wife Mary. It was destroyed by the fire that followed the 1906 earthquake but was later built as the luxury hotel it is today. Roberta took me up the elevator to a rooftop bar area which was surrounded by glass on all sides and showed off more fantastic views. Roberta insisted we take a break and order a drink, so we sat at a table by one of the vast windows and enjoyed Whisky Sours while absorbed in the breathtaking vistas.

The Fairmont, another magnificent hotel, was across the street. We walked through the massive doors into an enormous lobby with huge marble columns seemingly holding up the ornate ceiling. There was an impression of gold in every direction. Gigantic palm trees were growing out of equally enormous ceramic pots.

Roberta loved to see my reactions to all these new experiences and she grabbed my arm and led me to the elevators. I had no idea what I was in for until the elevator door opened. It appeared to be hanging out in space, glass sides from floor to ceiling. I was speechless as we stepped inside, hanging on with a tight grip as we sped up the 'outside' of this tall building. We could see more truly unbelievable views stretched out all around us. We reached the top with a jolt and the other visitors got off leaving Roberta and me to feel the stomach-lurching ride all the way back down again. After all this stimulation we were happy to relax and enjoy lunch in the hotel restaurant.

Back at the apartment I met her roommate Terry who had just come in from work. The three of us had a long visit and a glass of wine before I had to return home. What joy when Roberta insisted on driving me all the way to Burlingame. How could I say NO? She loved driving her Corvette and when we arrived at Floribunda, she wouldn't even come in – dropped me off and turned right around and sped back to the City. The drive was a good forty-five minutes each way.

I let myself into our apartment feeling elated from an exhilarating day.

Mary and I had a few days off before our next flights so we soaked up the sun around the pool and met some of the young men who lived in the apartment building. They readily offered to drive us to the airport when we needed, which was very decent of them. Mary mentioned she was off to Bangkok the following day and Fred, a suavely good-looking fellow who lived on the floor below us, agreed to drive her all the way to the airport terminal.

Gunnel, Karin, Barbara and I were enjoying a few more days off before our next flights so we decided to rent a car and visit San Francisco's Golden Gate Park. It was a beautiful clear sky day when we set off and we explored the extensive park, walking around Stow Lake and Spreckels Lake where we marveled at the unusually large tree ferns. We ended our day having our photo taken in front of a giant Buddha and enjoying tea in the tea house of the relaxing Japanese Tea Garden.

We were becoming more and more enamored of this intriguing City.

16.

AUSTRALIA

I received my flight line for the following month and was thrilled to see I had a flight to Hawaii en route to Sydney, Australia. I was deadheading to Honolulu and meeting my flight crew there.

When the day arrived for my departure, Ed, a young Naval Officer living on the ground floor of the apartment building, kindly offered me a ride to the airport. Standing and waiting forever at the local bus stop was becoming a dread – especially on cool evenings. I was so appreciative for his thoughtfulness when he dropped me off and was even more impressed when he carried my suitcase into the building for me.

At the Crew Briefing I met the captain and pilots, the pursers and stewardesses. One was a German girl, Hilda, and two Nisei girls, who were the second generation born to the Japanese who emigrated from Japan. Senior Purser Larry told me that as I was deadheading I had been assigned a seat in First Class for the first leg of the Round the World flight as far as Honolulu. That was a pleasant surprise and I boarded the plane after the passengers and sat in my assigned seat by the window. I watched how the crew performed, always intent on learning anything new.

I relaxed in my seat and enjoyed a wonderful lunch of fresh shrimp salad, beef carbonnade (a hearty French beef stew with caramelized onions), followed by a rich chocolate mousse and champagne for dessert.

This was truly living the high life.

After a five-hour flight the plane landed on the island of Oahu at the Honolulu International Airport. When I stepped off the plane I immediately felt enveloped by the welcoming warm air. A portly Hawaiian lady, dressed in a cool full-length muumuu carrying an armful of tropical flower leis and a huge flower in her hair, approached me, lifted her arms and placed a lei garland around my neck. She welcomed the stewardesses with her leis and sang a heartfelt 'Aloha.' We eagerly climbed into the crew bus which immediately filled with the exotic scent emanating from all the leis and were driven to our hotel.

I was lucky to have my own room in the Royal Manor Hotel which was the Pan Am crew hotel that stood alongside the Royal Hawaiian. I threw open the windows, turned off the chilling air conditioning and luxuriated in the heavy balmy air. I had time to find the beach for a swim in the Pacific Ocean and quickly changed into my swimsuit and cover-up dress. In training we were told to never walk through a hotel wearing a towel, to always cover up with a dress.

I wandered down to the famous Waikiki beach and was awed by the curved bay of soft white sand and azure blue water with the famous Diamond Head off in the distance. Diamond Head I learned was a huge volcanic mountain and the name was given to it by British sailors in the nineteenth century as they had mistaken the calcite crystals embedded in the rock for diamonds.

I enjoyed my first lazy swim in the ocean and felt refreshed and energized, but I had to return to the hotel and rest before being called at ten p.m. We had to be at the airport to prepare for the Sydney flight leaving at one a.m. These were crazy working hours but being young and full of enthusiasm they didn't seem to bother us – the benefits far outweighed the long hours, drastic time changes and all-night flights.

This was my first flight to Australia, on the other side of the world, and I was very excited. At the crew briefing I met Captain Andrew. His hair was so short it looked shaved but he had a benevolent demeanor and reminded us that this was 1964 and we were flying one of the first Pan American South Pacific jet services offered between Honolulu and Sydney on the new Boeing 707. He then introduced the pilots and cabin attendants: Elke from Germany, Cindy from the US and another English girl named Lesley. This was going to be interesting having two Lesleys on the same crew.

I was assigned to work the galley in the back and the nerves started in as this would be my first time working the rear galley. I didn't need to worry as Purser Fred told us the passenger load was very low with only thirty passengers aft.

When the passengers were boarded, all the announcements had been made and the plane was airborne, I put on my blue smock and in-flight flat shoes, and tackled the galley. It was almost two a.m. and we were only offering juice and coffee with finger sandwiches as the majority of the passengers just wanted to be left alone to get some rest. Most of them stretched out on the three seats with the armrests pushed up; with a pillow and blanket they were comfortable and soon asleep. Those were the days!

I was in the galley setting up trays with glasses and was in the middle of pouring the cold guava fruit juice when the plane suddenly lurched. We must have hit some turbulence as the plane was shaking hard. I was caught unawares as I hadn't experienced turbulence this violent before; I was becoming a little concerned but was trying bravely to keep calm.

The plane hit another serious jolt and this time the sticky juice flew all over the galley and me, leaving trails of cold pink liquid across my pristine smock and down my legs. Thankfully, Cindy came back from First Class to help me while the purser walked the cabin to assure the passengers it was only turbulence. Hanging on to steady ourselves was difficult enough let alone mopping up the messy spills at the same time.

In the middle of all this upheaval I felt something odd happening and glanced down. I was momentarily shocked and embarrassed to see the flat heel had fallen off my shoe and lay there in the middle of the mess. I stood there in my sticky wet smock, staring at the wretched heel, and said to no-one in particular, "Whatever next and what am I going to do now?" I tried pushing the heel back on but it refused to stick. Cindy could see my dilemma and very kindly offered, "Why don't you look for your other pair of shoes while I start the clean up process."

I had to excuse myself to rummage through my carry-on bag to find my street shoes, the high heel pair to be worn when wearing our uniform hat and jacket. I had no choice and hurriedly put them on to get me through the rest of the flight. I found out that it's not easy working the galley and walking up and down those aisles repeatedly wearing high-heeled shoes. With the turbulence finally subsiding we had to continue our late night supper service – minus the juice.

The plane had to make a scheduled stop at Nadi, (pronounced Nandi) Fiji, to refuel. The island of Viti Levu looked beautifully lush and green as we came in to land but we were asked to stay on the plane even though the passengers were allowed off. The clean-up crew arrived and they had extra work to do to mop up the sticky surfaces left by the juice incident in the back galley.

The huge Fijian men grinned with wide friendly smiles showing broken brown-stained teeth and they seemed incredibly happy people. They wore long white wrap-around skirts to their ankles and were totally barefoot showing the biggest brown feet I'd ever seen.

I was lamenting to one of the male passengers that the crew wasn't allowed on the island because it was just a fast half-hour re-fuel stop. What a lovely surprise I had when he returned to the plane and offered me some beautiful postcards which he had bought in the little airport shop – a thoughtful gesture from a total stranger.

The one bothersome thing about these stopovers when we weren't allowed to disembark, was the horticultural officials coming aboard and spraying pesticides all over the cabin – up one side and down the other, along the floor and high along the ceiling. The smell was quite unpleasant and we had no choice but to gag and breathe in all the fumes. We tried to hang out at the open doorways as much as possible and gave no thought to the medical implications resulting from all the chemicals, but that's the way it was.

With the passengers re-boarded and all accounted for, the menus were handed out and I had to start preparing the breakfast service for the aft cabin passengers before our arrival in Sydney. The task before me was to make the coffee, warm the rolls, reheat the omelets in the ovens, cook the ham and pineapple, plate everything individually, add the parsley garnish, and then place the plates on the trays before being presented to the passengers. Thank goodness it wasn't a full load.

After the service all the trays came back to the galley in good time for me to stow everything away in the allotted racks and drawers. Then I had to clean up the work surfaces and lock everything down ready for landing.

We touched down at eight forty-five in the morning. We said goodbye to our passengers and then stepped down the ramps ourselves.

I had arrived in big, wide, vast untamed Australia.

We collected our bags and were bussed to the Hampton Court Hotel where Captain Andrew invited the crew to a de-briefing party. Being Australia there was lots of beer and the group became quite raucous, not what I was used to. I stayed for a short while but was exhausted after the long flight and excused myself to find my room.

Cindy was my roommate and when she came through the door she announced she had visited Sydney many times before and wanted to sleep. I was very tired too but that was the last thing I wanted to do. Here I was in Australia for the very first time in my life and it was only noon. I yearned to explore and see as much as I could. My spirit sank on hearing her words as I wanted a companion to share the sights with me. I hoped someone else on the crew wanted to do the same but they were mostly old-timers and all retired to bed. How boring!

Being the young new girl on the crew I was too excited to sleep. I changed out of my uniform into a cool sundress, grabbed my bag and ventured out on my own. I had no idea where I was in relation to downtown so I concentrated on all the street names and started walking. It was a hot autumn afternoon, but I walked down William Street and through some beautiful parks. Crossing through Hyde Park I was fascinated with a group of young schoolchildren wearing their straw panama hats and navy and white school uniforms. The scene reminded me so much of home in England.

I spied some quaint little shops down a side street and spent some time perusing through the different stores. One was an excellent book shop where I found a heart-rending book of poems with beautiful illustrations. A little further on I stumbled on an Australian artifacts arcade where I fell in love with a little fuzzy koala bear and bought it just for me.

Keeping an eye on my watch I backtracked to the hotel and arrived just in time. When I entered my room, Cindy told me to clean up fast and join the crew for another party in the captain's room to be followed by a dinner excursion. I had no idea this was being planned and now understood why everyone had gone to bed to get some rest – except me.

What an interesting flight crew after all. The captain knew of a great restaurant called The Hunter's Lodge overlooking Sydney Harbor. There the whole crew indulged in the most Australian meal imaginable. The pilots ordered many drinks for us including beer, whiskey sours and wine. Captain Andy ordered a fantastic feast of seafood – succulent oysters, huge king prawns, lobster and steamed mussels – all fresh from the local water. I had never before eaten so much seafood. After this sumptuous feast Captain Andrew ordered Crème de Menthe and Tia Maria for everybody. Luckily we didn't have to fly the next day as we had a three-day layover.

Over breakfast in the morning the crew organized a trip to the Sydney Zoo. I was elated to be with such a fun group and was only too happy to join in with whatever they were planning. How had I ever thought they were *boring*?

The Taronga Zoo was on the shores of Sydney Harbor where we enjoyed extensive views across the water. At the zoo we saw the many strange animals of Australia – wombats, platypus, kangaroos, and lots of koala bears in the eucalyptus trees.

Oohing and aahing while leaning over the Koala enclosure fence, the young, friendly, dungaree-clad keeper invited us in and actually offered us the opportunity to hold the adorable furry creatures. We ventured through the gate and he explained to us that 'koala' is thought to mean 'does not drink' as they only drink when ill or there's not enough moisture in their favorite food – eucalyptus leaves. The zookeeper reached into a tree and pried off a cuddly looking koala and very carefully placed it in my arms. I sank down with the unexpectedly heavy weight of this adorable creature. I almost dropped the poor thing and it slid down from my grasp, and, probably as scared as I was, curled its long claws into my hip and clung on tightly.

"Oh gosh, what do I do now?" I gasped. The koala wouldn't let go – its sharp claws were dug in for the long haul. I desperately wanted to get the heavy animal off my hip. The koala might be cute but its claws were becoming painful, they were for clinging onto tree trunks and branches, not my soft flesh! A long time passed before one of the keepers noticed my anxiety and the plight of the koala clinging precariously onto my side. Thankfully, he came to the rescue and very cautiously managed to pry the large claws away from my waist and slowly lift the weight off my hip.

"Thank you," I gasped in relief and rapidly escaped from the enclosure; regaining my composure, I joined the crew and wandered the winding trail.

We stopped at the Emu enclosure intently watching the tall soft-feathered brown birds when another friendly zookeeper invited us into their pen. I was rather hesitant after the koala experience but went anyway. Instantly the birds approached and their long thin necks craned toward us. Standing face to face with their large heads and menacing big beaks was quite unnerving. They can reach up to six feet and more in height and as tall as we were we felt somewhat dwarfed by them. And then, silly me, I reached into my pocket for a tissue. Oops, what a big mistake that was! The birds heard the rustling of the paper and came bounding over, their huge three-clawed feet sending clouds of dust in the air as they dived at me trying to get at my pocket, which, according to the amused keeper, they hopefully thought was full of food. I stood there momentarily paralyzed envisioning a scene of *the bloody attack of the emus*. The keeper came over in the nick of time and shooed them away. He then told me emus are watching all the time, are unusually curious and have incredible hearing and eyesight. And I found all that out in one small gesture.

This was becoming a nightmare day at the zoo.

The platypuses we watched from *outside* the fence. A big red WARNING sign told us of the poisonous stingers on their rear feet. No touching these animals – I was keeping a safe distance. The sign went on to inform us they are an Australian mammal mix of duck, beaver and otter – what a quirk of nature.

Further along the path we saw the wombats, which looked relatively harmless – their fun name coming from the original inhabitants of the Sydney area. They are the largest herbivorous burrowing mammals in the world and are about forty inches in length with short tails, rodent-like front teeth and huge powerful claws. With short stubby legs and little ears they were ugly looking and did not have the appeal of the cute koalas.

After seeing all these unusual creatures and having the afternoon heat bearing down on us, our group decided to leave the zoo and take a boat ride out on the Bay to help cool off. We walked down to the water and boarded a tour boat. What spectacular views. I had to admit it was almost more stunning than San Francisco as homes were perched on the hillsides and the gardens stretched down to the water's edge.

Off in the distance we could see the beginning building stages of the famous Sydney Opera House with half-constructed 'sails.' It was sitting on the Bennelong Point close to the Sydney Harbor Bridge and a fellow tourist informed us it was largely conceived and built by a Danish architect Jorn Utzon. Feeling refreshed from the Bay breezes, we wended our way back to the hotel. Another exhilarating day.

The following morning the first and second officers, Clyde and Al, offered to take me and Elka to Doyles on the Pier for lunch. We accepted happily and climbed into a taxi for the short ride to the restaurant which was situated on the Fisherman's Wharf hanging over the water. We were seated on the deck facing the views and the waiter told us we had to try the pan fried John Dory, a deep sea fish native to the Australian waters. We took his advice and were glad we did as the fish was so mild, delicate and delicious. We were following flight rules and not indulging in any beer or wine this time as we had a five-thirty pick up that afternoon. Nevertheless, we enjoyed yet another meal of Sydney's wonderful fresh local fish.

A taxi dropped us at the hotel and we rushed to clean up and pack for our departure. Cindy wasn't in the room so I showered and washed my hair and started packing for our long flight back to Honolulu. I had a start when the door opened and in walked Cindy – but not alone. She was followed by a fellow she introduced as Carl who calmly sat down on the bed drinking a bottle of beer.

I was not amused as I was wrapped in a towel, my hair was sopping wet and I wanted to get dressed. I grabbed my hair dryer and part of my uniform and locked myself in the bathroom. When I cautiously crept out, there was no sign of Carl and I continued with my packing and dressing. Time was fast approaching our pick-up hour and I didn't want to be late because I was on probation.

At the airport briefing I was assigned to work the First Class cabin but there were only five passengers. The purser asked me to open the wine bottles and uncork the Charles Heidsieck champagne. True to Pan Am serving only the best food and drink, this French champagne was one of the most prized and most awarded in the world.

We served a light late dinner of fresh Australian oysters and prawns before landing at the Pago Pago International Airport in Samoa for refueling. Even though it was midnight we could see crowds of natives sitting around the airfield enjoying the cool night air and the entertainment of the planes coming and going.

For the continuing flight we picked up six new passengers and now had eleven in First Class. I was thrilled when one of the passengers, laden down with beautiful shell leis hanging from his neck, took them off and presented them all to me. They were tiny shells from the local beaches in all colors of pinks, browns and white intricately woven together. I felt quite honored and thanked him profusely but I couldn't wear them so stowed them away in my carry-on bag. (And I still have them).

We served a full hot breakfast and then I went aft to help in the Economy section. The crew appreciated the help as they had eighty-one passengers to feed and it was a very straightforward flight to Hawaii.

I was not continuing on with the Sydney crew so I said goodbye and checked in to my own room at the Royal Hawaiian Hotel. As I unpacked my suitcase, the phone rang unexpectedly and I was surprised to hear the Pan Am Scheduling Office telling me there was a change in my flight plan. I would not be deadheading that same evening back to San Francisco but had to stay in Hawaii until the following afternoon to *work* a flight back to Los Angeles instead and from there fly on up to San Francisco.

Our schedules were frequently changed at the last moment; this was part of the job and any plans we'd made back home just had to be put on hold.

I had an extra day in Hawaii and a room to myself which was always a joy. I spent more time leisurely sunning on the beach and swimming in the ocean. After a welcome good night's sleep, I awoke to the chattering of Mynah birds fluttering about in the trees outside my window. Totally rested and relaxed, I felt ready that afternoon to join the new crew for the flight to Los Angeles. I didn't know any of them but this was a relatively short flight of five-plus hours. Purser Blanche asked me to work the Economy galley but we had a light load of only eighteen passengers which made the task far less stressful. I had to prepare a light dinner of Chicken Bordelaise with Oriental Rice.

When the service was over, a young man from Saudi Arabia very graciously asked me to play cards with him. He had been given a pack of Pan American playing cards which we always had on board for anyone who asked. He wanted me to play a two-person Patience game, so we played and chatted and he expressed his desire to return and settle in Sydney and become a writer. I wonder if he ever did. I always enjoyed the chance to meet and spend time with our interesting passengers.

We arrived in Los Angeles at eleven-thirty p.m., a little later than scheduled. We had to race to the San Francisco-bound plane, which was being held for us as we were deadheading on the flight. We landed in San Francisco at twelve forty-five a.m. Much to my dismay, none of the crew lived on the Peninsula to give me a lift home. At that time of night there were no busses so I had to call and wait for a taxi to come by the terminal and take me to Burlingame.

I was half asleep in the back of the cab but the friendly, middle-aged American driver in front was plying me with questions. He was genuinely interested about my being English, countries I was flying to, and how was I liking America? I struggled to stay awake to talk with him. When he pulled up in front of the apartment building in Burlingame, the most wonderful thing happened. I leaned over the front seat and handed him the fare money plus a generous tip, and he turned to me and insisted I take back the 'tip' saying, "You're new here and I know you need this more than I do."

I was flabbergasted – this was California and people cared – compared to the experience in New York where our precious coins were rudely tossed out the window.

17.

ALASKA, TOKYO

I had four days off to relax at home before my next scheduled flight. Mary and I were settling into our new apartment, happily adjusting to the unbelievably large refrigerator, the brand new electric oven and stovetop with four burners, the huge stainless steel sink and in that sink a mysterious metal circle around the drain hole with the words 'garbage disposal.' Mary and I wondered what this was and figured that it meant just that – a disposal for all our garbage – with a press of the magic button it all disappeared. So, being the novices we were, we tossed everything down and thought how ingenious these Americans are.

Needless to say, the inevitable happened and one day the disposal didn't whirr anymore as we pushed our teabags down the hole. With dismay and annoyance we hunted down the building maintenance man and asked him to please come and figure out what the problem was. A short, stocky little man clad in grey overalls came in weighed down with his heavy toolbox. He fiddled around and climbed under the sink and opened the drain pipe and before our eyes he fished out lots of used shredded tea bags with strings attached. He shook his head enough to say 'these foreigners.' But he very patiently explained to us that ONLY discarded food was to go down the disposal. Mary and I stood there feeling rather embarrassed and a trifle foolish.

"Please, young ladies, remember - no bones, no tea bags, nothing with metal or strings attached. No, No, No." So, after the fact, we were educated into the ways of American kitchen conveniences.

The following day we met Ed reading by the pool. He was very quiet but put his book aside to chat with us. Later, he invited me back to his studio apartment and after a glass of wine asked, "If you don't have any plans for this evening, would you like to go to San Francisco with me for dinner?" I loved the suggestion and readily replied, "Yes."

I was excited to be going out for the evening especially into the big City. I changed into a navy blue dress and took along a white cardigan, just in case. Ed picked me up and we drove into San Francisco. He treated me to a casual dinner and later we drove over to the Red Garter on Broadway. This was a well-known beer palace night club and we spent an enjoyable evening listening to the lively Banjo Band music before heading back to Burlingame.

Ed stopped by again the following afternoon and asked me to dinner at the Domino Club in San Francisco. I explained that I would love to go but I had to get back early for an eleven forty-five report time at the airport. Not accepting that reason to forego the evening Ed decided that we could leave straight away. It did seem a crazy thing for me to do when I had a deadline the same evening, but I figured I would be safe with dependable Ed. We drove into the City and entered the Domino Club on Fillmore Street. All around the room were racy oil paintings of nude women – San Francisco in the Sixties. After dinner Ed suggested going on to the Gold Street nightclub. Once there though, I couldn't relax and enjoy myself knowing I had to get back for the close-to-midnight Briefing deadline and I kept looking at my watch. I finally told Ed we needed to leave and he half-heartedly agreed and drove me back to Burlingame as fast as he could.

I ran up to my apartment and hastily flung on my uniform. I threw extra-warm clothes into my case for an Alaska layover and rushed down to Ed's apartment. He felt badly getting me home so late and offered, thank goodness, to drive me to the airport. Barbara was with me as I rapped on his door. She was deadheading on the same flight and had been ready all evening wondering where I was as we'd agreed to go together – she didn't want to bear the consequences of being late either.

On arrival at the airport, Ed screeched to a stop, we grabbed our bags from the trunk and tore off leaving him standing there. We walked as fast as 'ladylike' would allow through the terminal and just made it to the Briefing Office with a minute to spare. The captain raised an eyebrow at us as we lunged breathlessly through the door.

Captain Roberts briefed us to expect a routine flight and I was happy to see Pamela again as the senior purser and she assigned me to work the First Class galley. The service was easy with only five passengers and being so late at night we served hot chocolate and mini sandwiches to those who wanted them. We handed out blankets and pillows and allowed the passengers to rest.

We arrived in Anchorage at two a.m. and were surprised to see the sky so light at such an early hour. It was summer and Captain Roberts told us this northern area could have as much as fourteen to nineteen hours of daylight. The crew bus pulled up at the Traveler's Inn Motel and we checked in for our room numbers and received our per diem.

The following morning we awoke late to a surprisingly warm sixty degrees. Barbara and I met for breakfast and our waitress insisted that we see the earthquake damage downtown. I had been horrified by many of the scenes on my previous trip but this was Barbara's first time so we decided to explore together. We wore suit jackets and matching skirts as the weather was so mild and headed downtown. Barbara was speechless at the devastation surrounding us everywhere. We were seeing whole city blocks flattened with nothing but rubble from collapsed buildings in all directions. Anchorage was by far the worst hit area.

Returning to the hotel, we met some of our crew members who told us they had signed up for a tour of Mt. Alyeska just twenty-seven miles from Anchorage. They told us to come along so we added our names to the list and had just had time to run up to our rooms, freshen up and dash back to the lobby.

Ron, the young rugged-looking driver, ushered the six of us outside to his van. He showed us more earthquake damage as we drove toward the mountain where we saw massive landslides and deep fissures. And there it was looming before us – the then-biggest ski mountain in Alaska. We had the thrill of flying up the mountainside on a ski lift, two of us to a chair. I couldn't believe here we were in Alaska, yet it was so warm shirtless skiers were racing down the mountainside showing off tanned bodies. The sky was a cloudless blue, the sun was brilliant and the snow everywhere was a blinding sheet of glittering white.

After that exhilarating experience, we climbed back in the van and Ron drove us on to Turnagain Bay, an arm of Cook Inlet. Here we saw large areas of landscape that had dropped and disappeared into the gaping ground as deep as eight feet. There were massive rock slides evident along the roads and we stopped to take photos of these dramatic scenes. Far off in the distance we could see the backs of Beluga whales in the water.

Back in town Ron advised us to try the local Red Ram Café for an early dinner; we were all hungry and headed straight there before checking back at the hotel. We ordered a meal of Alaskan King crab for everybody. What a feast it was – and quite an initiation for me learning how to eat it. The plentiful crabmeat was so fresh and delicious especially dipped in the warm melted butter. There was so much good food and for only four dollars a person!

I retired to my room by eight to get some rest, sleep if I was lucky, as I had to be up at one in the morning for a pick up at two to prepare for the next flight on to Tokyo. Barbara said goodbye as she was leaving on a different flight.

We had to pass through many time zones in our travels but being young we were taking it all in stride. With the constant jet lag, we did appreciate the long layovers in between our flights.

On the flight from Anchorage to Tokyo I worked in the aft cabin with Purser Pamela, and Charlotte, a Nisei girl, was in the galley. I was forewarned that a Pan Am Supervisor, Jane Gottschall, was sitting in the back of the plane and was probably taking notes on our service, especially mine as I was still on probation.

There were only forty-five passengers to take care of. We served a hot breakfast after take-off and then, as we prepared to serve the hot lunch, the plane started lurching and shuddering and I knew we'd hit turbulence. We had to anchor everything down and wait for the shaking to subside. Precious time was lost but we but proceeded with haste to serve the lunch of Cornish Game Hen stuffed with Wild Rice. I smiled sweetly at the supervisor and at the end of the flight she approached me and told me I had done very well. What a relief to have passed that inspection!

We landed in Tokyo at five-thirty in the morning and were driven in the crew bus to the Hotel Japan. I was rooming with the Swedish stewardess Marit. What a surprise when we opened the door and saw inside an unusual Japanese-style room! The beds were on the floor and beautiful white kimonos were laid out in place of robes. We were astounded to see a Japanese style sauna in the bathroom but were too tired to take it all in so we changed into our nightdresses and tried to get some sleep. On waking we put on the kimonos and ordered the Room Service Japanese breakfast as we were in such an oriental setting.

The maid arrived with a large black tray which she carefully placed on the low coffee table. Thereupon sat several dainty bowls filled with the strangest looking food I'd ever seen. We sat on the floor, Japanese style, and Marit and I sampled small tastes of everything even though we had no idea what we were eating. I was longing for some toast and tea but the whole breakfast was only 680 yen each, about two dollars.

Marit found a card advertising an in-room Japanese massage, and said, "We're in a Japanese room, we've just eaten a Japanese breakfast, and now we should try the Japanese massage."

"I'll give it a try, Marit," I said reservedly as I had never experienced a massage before so I was a bit hesitant. She quickly called down to the Reception Desk and ordered a massage for two in our room.

As I was wondering what to expect there was a gentle knock on the door and in came two cute little Japanese girls who didn't look much older than we were. They bowed low and said "Konichiwa" the Japanese hello. They spoke as little English as we could speak Japanese so there followed a communication comedy. We could understand that we were to disrobe and lay on the big white towels on the beds. I felt very self-conscious laying there with nothing on and they tried to show us to lay face down while they massaged and pummeled our backs, all the way down to our toes. The girls were using generous amounts of exotic oils which added to the mystique of the experience. I have to admit to a fit of giggles while all this was going on and the two girls were giggling too and we had no idea what they were telling each other. I felt exhausted as much as relaxed when they were done. We paid them in Japanese yen and they bowed to us grinning widely and with little steps shuffled their way out the door. We thanked them with an "Arigato!"

Pamela called our room and asked us if we'd like to experience having our hair styled at a local beauty shop called Komachi's. Always ready to try anything new, we said "Yes." It was perfect timing as our hair was looking flattened and oily after our massages. We hurriedly showered and dressed and met Pamela in the lobby. She suggested walking as it wasn't too far away.

Komachi's was a tiny little place down a narrow alley in the Ginza district. There were three fascinating Japanese girls working there and they were surprisingly dressed in a Western Sixties 'mod' style. They introduced themselves as Aiko, Yazuki and Cho. There was only one sink so we took turns having our hair washed. There were no hooded hair dryers, and Aiko used a hand dryer in one hand and a big round brush in the other to style my hair, brushing my bangs against their natural way.

"Why brush that way?" I asked out of curiosity.

Aiko explained in her broken English, "It help straighten curls and waves." And it did. We were impressed with our haircuts and styling and were charged only 500 yen which was only one dollar and forty cents.

Pamela, who had visited Tokyo many times, led us to the Imperial Hotel where Pan Am crews had stayed in the past. This was the grande dame of Tokyo's hotels and was designed by Frank

Lloyd Wright in the Maya Revival style. Pamela wanted us to see the famous arcade of shops, and we were awed by the quality merchandise of beautiful pearl jewelry, woodblock prints, porcelain and oriental antiques.

We came to a stop outside a wonderful Kimono shop, enthralled with the exquisite silk kimonos. They had the most beautiful intricate embroidered designs adorning the sleeves, and huge striking colorful designs covering the backs. We couldn't resist entering the store and wandered through the racks of these incredible garments. Up close we could see the intricate embroidery stitched in brilliant colors. I was smitten with their beauty and chose a black one with a white lining to buy. The exotic colors of reds, oranges, yellows, blues and whites of the floral designs glowed against the jet black background. I had visions of it hanging on a wall someday.

After hairdos and shopping we were feeling hungry so Pamela took us to Suehiro's Restaurant in the Ginza for an authentic Japanese meal. We sat on the floor on square grey cushions and ordered the rice-wine Sake which arrived on a tray in a beautiful small grey-blue ceramic flask with a narrow neck. It was poured into tiny, dainty, ceramic handle-free cups called ochoko. Pamela explained that we should hold the ochoko in one hand with the other hand under the cup. Following her directions, we held the cups and did a Japanese toast of "Kampai."

Pamela ordered Japanese dishes the waiter recommended for us. He was wearing full kimono-style dress and brought us a platter of Sashimi which he explained is raw fish. We did raise an eyebrow on hearing that but in fact it was absolutely delicious, especially dipped in the soy and wasabi sauces. We were having fun mastering the chopsticks and finding out it wasn't as easy as it looked. We tried the Sukiyaki which was enoki and shiitake mushrooms with wafer thin slices of beef brought to the table arranged like an oil painting on a large white platter. We struggled to pick up each piece with our chopsticks and cook it in the pot of bubbling soy. We left in a daze after a full day of new sights, sounds, smells, foods and more likely the sake rice wine. What a uniquely Japanese day.

I was sorry to leave Tokyo but knew I would return many more times.

On the returning flight to Honolulu I was assigned to work the First Class galley. I was managing very well until the coffee service. I was struggling to pour coffee from the very heavy and very hot container into the small serving jugs. Suddenly the scalding hot coffee spilled all over the floor barely missing me as I jumped back, quietly cursing. I had to clean up the mess and start all over again to brew a fresh batch. This job was touted to be so glamorous but behind that façade lurked a lot of frustration and hard work.

We arrived in Honolulu at six-thirty in the morning and, after signing in at the hotel, I went straight to bed to get some sleep and woke up at noon. I went to the beach and met some classmates. Karin, Edith, Mona and Roberta were sunning themselves on the Waikiki sands.

Roberta had ear trouble and wasn't happy as the Pan Am doctor had told her she was grounded in Hawaii and couldn't fly until it was better.

Edith told us the sad story that Jenny's increasing weight gain forced her to see a doctor and she heard the devastating news that she was in fact pregnant, as we had suspected. She had been forcing herself into the tight girdle but now knew she couldn't get away with it any longer and despondently gave in her notice to quit (maternity leave was unheard of). She left for home devastated and sadly we lost track of her.

Karin had flown in from her very first flight to Bangkok. She excitedly told us she had been working in the First Class cabin on the way there. A charming young American gentleman sitting in the lounge spent time chatting with her and said he knew a lot about Bangkok. Toward the end of the flight, he asked if he could have the honor of taking her sightseeing. We weren't surprised.

She told us, "We had a really good time together as he toured me all over Bangkok. Later in the day he told me he was going to a Charity Ball that evening in the presence of King Bhumibol and Queen Sirikit and he really wanted me to go with him! My dilemma was not having a full-length dress. I explained to him that I had only packed a formal *short* dress but he insisted that would be acceptable. And so I dressed up and donned the short dress. Amazingly, with his connections, he managed to get us there before everyone else arrived. He told me to sit down at a floor-length tablecloth-covered table and to sit there all evening so no-one could see my legs under my dress. I didn't dare get up. But I'm glad I went as it was a wonderful evening and the King entertained everyone by playing the saxophone."

We sat there envious of Karin having been in the presence of Thai royalty.

All afternoon we lazed in the sun and swam in the ocean covering ourselves in baby oil and iodine – the sun lotion of the day. Karin leaned over and asked me, "Please walk over to the Reef Hotel with me as I want to see Gerry. He told me to come over when we were finished on the beach."

"Who's Gerry?" I asked.

"Oh, he's a guy I met here on a previous layover," she replied casually.

This sounded like a loose arrangement but I said I'd join her for some support. Gerry was an Army officer but not really Karin's type I thought when I met him. We didn't stay long but he told us to meet him and his friends on the beach to join in some folk singing and dancing later in the evening. That sounded relatively harmless so we agreed to go and it was a lot of fun singing and dancing in the moonlight with the surf rolling in around our ankles.

The next day we had a rare, almost civilized, pickup time of nine-thirty in the morning. We checked in for a flight headed to Los Angeles and were informed that we had a full load of passengers in the Economy section but only thirteen in First Class. Mona, one of my classmates, was scheduled to join our crew as an extra to help in Economy.

We walked the aisle serving drinks from the cart: cocktails and liquors cost $.50, the wines, beer and cigarettes $.25, and a split of champagne was $1.00. After handing out the menus we began the hot lunch service. Anne, a tall blonde English girl, was working the galley and was very organized – she needed to be to produce all those plates of piping hot dishes, and remember to add the all-important parsley garnish, warm the rolls, prepare the hot coffee and boil water for tea.

In the middle of this hectic service, and not the best of times to see it, the Stewardess Call Button began flashing its red 'help me' signal. I could see the purser was busy so I walked down the aisle to see what the problem was. Arriving at the row of seats I found an elderly white-haired lady who looked deathly sick. She struggled to tell me in embarrassed hushed tones that she had a heart condition. The alarm bells went off in my head, and seeing how sickly pale she looked. I dashed back to tell the purser who quickly took control of the situation.

She made an announcement asking for a doctor but there was no doctor on board. The plane was full but we couldn't leave the ailing passenger where she was sitting against the window with two passengers sharing the row hemming her in. Luckily we had the extra stewardess, friend Mona, to continue with the food service while we moved the now very weak lady slowly up the aisle to one of the empty First Class seats. We gently sat her down where she had more room. I rushed forward to unlatch the walk-around oxygen bottle from its galley location, and brought it to Pamela who deftly hooked it up to our patient while I covered her with a blanket and made sure she was comfortable.

We hoped she'd make it to Los Angeles. We were two hours out and asked the First Class cabin crew to keep a watchful eye on her as we had to retreat to the aft cabin to help finish the meal service. In the meantime, the cockpit called ahead to make sure we had an ambulance waiting on landing. Fortunately, the lady held on, probably thanks to the oxygen, and as soon as the plane doors were opened the ambulance crew rushed up the ramp and carefully carried her off the plane.

We stayed at the Pen and Quill hotel overnight and I slept late. I called Mona but her room phone rang with no response so I ordered and enjoyed a room service breakfast. I eventually found Mona sunbathing by the pool so I joined her to soak up more sunshine. She had me in stitches with her story about a first class passenger who had approached her on a flight and asked, "Where is the john?" Mona told me, "Well, I had never heard of this American expression and answered, 'Oh, I have not seen him.'" We had to be fluent in our languages but many American expressions confused me too!

She left soon after that as she was deadheading to San Francisco on an earlier flight and I had a later five-thirty pick up time.

On the last leg of this trip from Los Angeles to San Francisco we were picking up a flight that had come in from London. Most of the passengers had disembarked, but a few stayed on board to continue on. At the Crew Briefing I was assigned to work in the First Class cabin.

A Pan Am representative rushed in and advised us to prepare for a very special passenger – Ringo Starr! Was this the one and only Ringo of the Beatles? We were told that it was, and that Vivien Leigh (Scarlett O'Hara in the 1939 smash hit Gone With The Wind) had also flown in from London but had disembarked to stay in Los Angeles. She was the beautiful British actress once married to Sir Laurence Olivier.

We boarded the aircraft to prepare for the short flight home and there on the passenger list the purser saw the name 'Ringo Starr.' It was around this time, mid-1964, that the young new group from Liverpool, England, the Beatles, had rocked America, the world, and me with "Beatlemania" and their Number One hit songs, "I Want to Hold Your Hand" and "All My Loving." No wonder we were all jittery with excitement. There were only four passengers in First Class and sure enough there was Ringo, the last to board the plane with his manager Brian Epstein. The purser ushered Ringo to his seat 4A. Brian Epstein sat and chatted with him for awhile and after take-off, moved up to the forward lounge area.

I never before had such a celebrity in our care. I was the only English girl in First Class so the crew gave me a lot of encouragement and prodding to go and talk to Ringo. I was petrified at the thought of talking to such a rock star but the cabin crew wouldn't take 'No' for an answer and practically pushed me down the aisle in his direction. I did reason he was the same age as me, actually just two years older, and we were both English.

Hesitantly, I leaned over the aisle seat. He was sitting quietly in the window seat and I introduced myself and told him I was from England too to start up some kind of conversation. I plucked up the courage to sit down and could tell he was as nervous as I was and just as shy. He probably wanted to be left alone. I persevered and asked why he was travelling alone without the other Beatles. He told me how upset he was as he had become ill and had to stay behind in England, missing half the Tour. The rest of the group had been performing throughout the Scandinavian countries but now he was happy to be catching up with John, Paul, and George who were already in Australia.

He rather apologetically told me he couldn't get his razor to work, so I was only too happy to go and look for one from our Pan Am travel kit supplies. When I returned and handed it to him he was genuinely thankful. For some reason he momentarily glanced out the window and asked me what the mountains were called that we were flying over? My mind was in a euphoric fog and I had no idea. I'd only lived in California for two months, and in my star-struck daze, I said the dreaded words, "I don't know." We were told in training to make something up rather than utter those words and I couldn't believe I had said them. I quickly changed the subject and asked him to please autograph a menu for me and one for my sister which he happily did.

When I slowly succumbed to reality, I realized he was just as human as I was.

After about ten minutes I excused myself as it was time to leave the young man alone. Having flown all the way from London he must have been extremely tired. In training we were told to not pester or engage in conversation with celebrities unless they invited it. Ringo Starr was a major exception.

I had actually met and talked with one of the famous Beatles and had his autograph to prove it. When we landed in San Francisco, Ringo was the very last passenger to leave the plane and as he exited down the ramp, we could see him swallowed up as he disappeared into a frenzied mob of reporters and photographers. That date is imprinted on my mind – June 12, 1964 – two months after I started flying.

My head was in the clouds and I felt I was floating all the way home. I ran along to our apartment and threw open the door. I was bursting to tell my story but was met with silence and darkness. I rapidly deflated finding no-one at home – Mary and Roberta were away on trips. Oh, what a letdown!

I dropped my bags and turned back down the hall and knocked on Barbara and Karin's door but no-one answered there either. I couldn't believe they were away too. What utter disappointment to be so full of news and not a soul to tell. I couldn't sleep that night. I tossed and turned thinking about the thrill of meeting and talking with one of the Beatles.

Next morning, I sat down and wrote a long letter to my sister telling her all about Ringo, and she wrote back straight away to tell me that her college girlfriends were bowled over with the news that I had actually chatted with him and had his autograph.

Mary came home the next day from Hawaii and the poor girl was bombarded with my news before she'd even had a chance to get in the door. She wasn't as Beatle crazy as I was so she didn't react with the same overwhelming enthusiasm.

Mary changed out of her uniform and we decided to go to the Pan Am Scheduling Office to fill in our bid lines. We were so junior on the seniority list but there was always the hope that we'd draw at least one of the lines we requested. In a way, it was like mapping out a vacation for a whole month. Shall we go to Tahiti or maybe Paris via London, or Bangkok, with a few short trips to Hawaii and on to Australia? We picked up our Line sheets and filled them out while there, handed them back in, and returned to the apartment.

We changed into our swimsuits and relaxed by the pool. Kate was there with Tina and a group of guys and girls from the building. We were soaking up the sun, our suntans growing ever darker, which was considered the 'glamour' look. Kate, the extrovert, shocked us all by removing her bikini top. Admittedly, she was laying face down but even so the girls were stunned and I think the guys were too but it didn't stop them from gawking.

And, Kate got her all-over tan.

18

TOKYO, CLARK, TACHIKAWA

P amela, one of the pursers on the Tokyo flight, had agreed to pick me up at nine-fifteen in the evening.

At the appointed hour I was patiently waiting in the lobby. But there was no sign of Pamela. I was becoming frantic with every minute that passed, anxious to get to the airport so I wouldn't be late for the important Flight Briefing. I didn't want to forfeit my line for the entire month and go on Standby, and I was still on probation and didn't want being late on my record.

Joe, one of the apartment residents, leisurely strode through the entry doors. He stopped in midstride when he saw me and asked what I was doing there looking so perplexed. I explained I was waiting for a ride that hadn't turned up and it was getting very late. He saw my plight and readily offered to drive me himself – except he didn't have a car.

Undeterred, he sped up to Fred's apartment and, on hearing the story, Fred actually let Joe borrow his car to drive me to the airport. It really was amazing that we'd become one big family in that apartment building – all helping one another out or at least the guys were always eager to help the girls.

Joe was driving erratically, not being used to Fred's car, but I closed my eyes and hung on as I just wanted to reach the Briefing Room before it was too late. I thanked Joe when he braked at the curb with minutes to spare and dashed off lugging my suitcase in one hand and carry-on bag and purse in the other. I arrived at the Briefing huffing and puffing and explained my rather harried appearance. The captain was relieved to see me but Pamela was aghast and apologetic as she had clean forgotten to pick me up!

Once again, we were ferrying an empty plane to Travis Air Force Base with no passengers on this leg. At Travis the crew disembarked and Captain Storkan told us to eat something in the cafeteria as we weren't leaving there until two in the morning. I enjoyed a warm slice of cinnamon apple pie with vanilla ice cream, good comfort food which helped to calm me down.

Back on board the plane and after all the passengers were seated and belted in, I felt honored as Captain Storkan invited me into the cockpit to experience the take-off. I strapped myself into the observer seat which is behind the captain. What a thrill it was to listen in on the information passed from one pilot to the next. A pre-flight check and double-check of every instrument, dial and switch was made, according to a printed checklist. The engines were started one by one and the jet taxied to the edge of the runway. Captain Storkan called the Control Tower for permission to take-off. I could feel the power of the taxiing and the take-off began. That experience certainly gave me a better understanding of what goes on in the cockpit during the take-off procedure. We were fortunate to have these experiences offered as part of our initiation process.

Once aloft I excused myself from the cockpit to work the front galley. At that late hour we offered warm pastries and hot chocolate or coffee. It was a routine flight all the way to Alaska and most passengers slept. On arrival in Anchorage, it was five-thirty and we were plunged into freezing cold rain.

At the hotel my roommate Inge, a brunette Swedish girl, and I hunkered down in our room and slept into the early afternoon. It was still raining heavily when we awoke and as the cafeteria served breakfast till three, we ordered room service and ate in our room. We each enjoyed a big bowl of steaming hot oatmeal with brown sugar and cream, lots of whole wheat toast with honey and plenty of coffee. The weather continued grey, wet, and gloomy and looked bitterly cold outside.

Pamela came by to watch television with us. We had a long, lazy day in the hotel and it felt good to unwind and relax for a change.

The next day the weather was still icy cold and raining heavily so we ventured down to the restaurant for an early lunch and then prepared for our pick-up at two-fifteen.

At the Briefing we were told to prepare for a General Electric Charter flight to Tokyo. We greeted the GE employees onto the plane and were appalled to see them decorating the cabin with colorful streamers. It was an unusual sight, but we left them to it and dreaded that this could become a raucous party flight. Fortunately, the passengers weren't too noisy and seemed appreciative of our service

After the meal service the passengers were excitedly holding a company charter raffle, and they insisted the stewardesses join in and buy a ticket. We couldn't see any harm in it and each bought a twenty-five cent ticket. I forgot all about it until the plane landed. While walking the aisle I halted in surprise as I heard my name announced over the intercom, "The winner of our GE raffle is *Stewardess Lesley Peters* with the number 45." I couldn't believe it – out of all those people on board – I was the winner. And, when we arrived at the Palace Hotel the prize money had actually been delivered to the hotel in a large manila envelope with my name on it.

In the morning Inge and I hailed a taxi to the Oriental Bazaar at 5-chome Jingu-mae Shibuya-ku on the outskirts of Tokyo. We had learned from other stewardesses that this was the place to shop as it had so many unusual oriental artifacts on display and all reasonably priced.

The cab pulled up and stopped in front of a rickety two-story building. Undeterred we paid the taxi driver and stepped inside. There was a sense of cramming and crowding on the shelves and on every inch of floor space. We spent a long time looking at vases of every shape and style in glass and delicate porcelain of the Kutani, Imari and Satsuma styles.

I was fascinated with the miniature Japanese dolls. They had exquisite pale porcelain faces and were dressed in the full Geisha style. They were about eight inches tall and I studied them all. I took my time and selected one dressed in a dusky blue silk kimono with a beautifully painted expression on her fragile porcelain face. Her head was covered with the Geisha black hair and headdress and even her dainty hands were exquisitely shaped. She was protected in a square plastic box. I carried her to the counter and watched the shop girl wrap it with care and place it into a big paper bag which I held onto tightly.

There was an upper level to explore and we climbed the open, narrow, wooden steps to the second floor. We took our time perusing even more fascinating Japanese crafts.

Our concentration was abruptly halted when the whole building shuddered and shook violently. Inge and I gasped and grabbed onto each other. We didn't dare move, rooted to the swaying floor.

An earthquake?

We were alarmed by the shattering noise of fragile vases and heavy objects toppling off the narrow shelves and crashing to the floor. Shards of once-exquisite handiwork lay scattered around our feet.

We had experienced fearful turbulence in the air and now we were in the middle of a horrendous earthquake on the ground.

"What should we do?" Inge pleaded.

I peered through the narrow window space and my eyes opened wide as I saw a telephone pole swaying back and forth. That sight was extremely disconcerting and I blurted out, "It's dangerous outside because of downed electric lines but it looks safer than staying up here. Let's follow everyone else as they must know what they're doing."

We were trapped on the upper level as the shop was becoming more and more unstable. The other shoppers were rushing for the narrow staircase, the only way out, so we followed them in a desperate hurry to get to the street. It was a fragile stairway so we were praying it would handle this crush of bodies rushing their descent to the unstable ground floor.

Once outside in the open, we stood for a moment to calm ourselves, as far away from the swaying telephone pole as possible. After the mayhem, the street became deserted as everyone fled in all directions. We couldn't stay there stuck to the sidewalk, and decided to find a taxi to take us to the safety of our hotel. A cab drove by at the top of the street and in that moment we lost our fears and raced up the block to flag him down. Mercifully, the driver saw us and stopped to pick us up.

We hurried into our hotel and felt safe and secure in the spacious lobby. I was still clutching the shopping bag with my delicate geisha doll inside and was happy she had survived the adventure unscathed.

Later that day we learned an earthquake had rocked Tokyo at eleven twenty-one that morning on Monday, June 20th. Luckily for us the quake was a minor one with no casualties or serious damage reported. This was my first earthquake experience and it was the suddenness I found so unnerving.

In the morning I had breakfast with my roommate Mary, who had flown in the night before. We exchanged news and spent the day together.

A taxi took us to Fuji-Torii Japanese antiques and art store. The front window displayed the most elegant decorative Japanese screens and we ventured inside. A kindly salesman explained that the folding screens were called 'byobu' (meaning protection from wind) and could be from one panel up to six or even ten. We wandered the store and were fascinated with the subtle, effortless artwork and ink calligraphy on gold-colored silks. (Centuries ago the backgrounds were gold leaf.) Many depicted single flower branches, luscious fruits and misty landscape scenes.

I was mesmerized by an elderly wiry gentleman with wispy white hair and a graying beard. He was sitting cross-legged and hunched over on the hard wooden floor deftly painting a single screen. He held a long brush in his hand and applied the paint with delicate touches and the utmost precision.

I had enjoyed oil painting when in England and I stood there enthralled and watched him for a long time. When he was finished he looked up and grinned at me. I noticed wide gaps between stained teeth and he gestured with his long fingers at the screen and at me. I assumed he was asking if I would like it.

The burnt orange and deep red colors of the ripe and bursting pomegranates hanging from a delicate branch on a soft-gold background appealed to me immensely. I decided to use my raffle winnings toward the purchase. I was so thrilled to own this incredible piece of artwork having watched it come to life in the hands of the charismatic elderly artist.

Back at the hotel I had to pack and have my uniform at the ready. I was hoping to get some sleep before being called for a three-thirty a.m. pick-up. Mary was leaving the next day for San Francisco.

The crew bus arrived at the Tokyo International Airport where we saw a heavy fog curling across the airfield. The captain assured us we could take off with no problem, so we boarded the passengers heading for Clark Air Base in the Philippines. I was working the front galley and prepared a hot roast turkey dinner. We landed at Clark and when we opened the cabin doors we were instantly enveloped in sizzling heat.

We stood there melting on the tarmac and were aghast when an official-looking fellow approached and told us to climb into the back of an *open* military truck that was standing just feet away. We clambered in as ladylike as we could, in that muggy stifling temperature and wearing our full uniforms, hats, white gloves, hose and tight girdles. We had to sit on our upended suitcases under the searing sun as we were driven over a dusty, bumpy road to the base hotel.

We scrambled down looking damp and bedraggled, but the life-giving, cooling fans inside the small hotel lobby helped revive us. A pleasant surprise was an invitation into the Officers' Mess for breakfast. We were treated to a huge gourmet meal of steak, scrambled eggs, crispy hash browns and lots of coffee – a huge meal to digest when most of us felt sick from the heat.

We were assigned rooms for the short layover. Some of us tried sunbathing but that didn't last long as it was just too hot, even the water in the pool was uncomfortably warm. We retreated inside keeping cool under the ceiling fans until the mid-afternoon pick-up.

Captain George flew us to Tachikawa Air Base in the western part of Japan. On arrival I was informed that I was to leave the crew. That was a surprise and I wondered 'why?' Funnily enough it was Karin, from my class, who was taking my place. I only had time to say hello and wish her well in passing. I was chauffeur-driven to the hotel wondering what flight I was assigned to next. I had a room to myself, but not for long, as I was told to be ready for a six-thirty in the morning pick-up to join a brand new crew.

At the Briefing I met Captain Stickler and was delighted to see my roommate Roberta and classmate Mona on the same crew. The captain explained we had to ferry a plane to Misawa which is north of Tokyo in the Tohoku region of Japan. On arrival the crew disembarked and enjoyed a Japanese-style lunch in the Snack Shop. Refreshed and fortified, we loaded the new passengers and flew to Anchorage, Alaska. We had to go through customs and I wasn't happy paying duty on my newly purchased Japanese screen and porcelain doll.

From Anchorage we deadheaded on Pacific Western Airlines to Seattle where we picked up a Pan Am flight from London and deadheaded on that to San Francisco. It was always a bonus not working the flight and being able to relax and mingle with the passengers. Roberta drove home to San Francisco and I caught a ride with Mona as her boyfriend Mike had come to pick her up.

I learned from Scheduling that I had been taken off my original schedule to accommodate a London flight I had coming up next on my line. We had to have a certain number of hours at home base before being eligible to leave again on another trip.

19.

ENGLAND

L ondon and Paris scheduled for June 29th would land me in
England on my birthday the next day. I was very excited about
going home again and packed my suitcase, put on my uniform –
white gloves now for summer – and was ready to leave. The report
time was eight forty-five in the morning and I called the
Burlingame Cab Company for a taxi instead of waiting for a bus.

At the Briefing for this Round the World flight taking the Polar
route, we met Captain Everett, the pilots and cabin crew: the senior
purser, Bill, the second purser, Jill, and the stewardesses: Leatrice
from Honolulu, Laila from Norway, and Candy an American.
Purser Bill assigned me to the First Class galley.

There were only five passengers to Los Angeles and we served
champagne, fresh warmed sweet rolls, orange juice and coffee. In
Los Angeles we picked up seven more First Class passengers
making twelve in all. Among them was the fifties star Dorothy
Dandridge who had been nominated for an Academy Award for
her role in Carmen Jones and had a starring role in Porgy and Bess.
(Just one year later she died at the young age of 42). Shirley
MacLaine's secretary also boarded as a First Class passenger.
(Shirley MacLaine had received Academy Award nominations for
the movies The Apartment and Irma La Douce).

From Los Angeles it was an eleven-hour flight. After take-off
Purser Bill handed me the announcement booklet and asked me to
make the French announcement as we were flying on to Paris after

London. I welcomed the passengers and gave information re the flight time, arrival time and the services offered.

I changed into the blue cabin smock and secluded myself in the galley steeling myself for preparing the food for the long cart service. The President Special menus were handed out and there were five courses for a formal luncheon service:

Hors d'Oeuvre
Le Homard en Cocktail
Lobster Cocktail

Entrées
Le Filet de Boeuf grilléMaître d'Hôtel
Grilled Fillet of Beef "Maitre d'Hotel"

Poulet au Muscadet
Breast of Chicken with Muscadet Sauce

Les Suprèmes de Sole Bonne-Femme
Supreme of Sole "Bonne Femme"

Les Petits Pois à la Française
Buttered French Peas

Les Pommes Parisienne
Parisienne Potatoes

Fromages
La Sélection de Fromages de Pays
Selection of Cheeses

Dessert
Le Flan à la Crème
Custard Pie

Un Choix de Fruits des Iles et des Continents
Fruit Basket

Café   Thé
Café Americain   Thé Orange Pekoe   Thé Vert Japonais

The entrées for this service were plated from the galley but the other courses were offered from the cart. It took about four hours and I was exhausted and hot from the oven heat in such a confined space.

There was a lot of emphasis on presentation – both of the food on the plate and placement on the cart. The purser was quite fastidious adding to the pressure of getting everything perfect. There are so many things to remember working the galley but the training and subsequent in-flight experiences were making the service more routine. Best of all the passengers were happy and appreciative.

Once the long service was over and all the used dishes put back in the racks, the trash bin emptied, and the galley spotless again, there was a welcome break. But I daren't leave the galley, even though the cabin was quiet and most passengers were reading, resting or settling in for sleep. I wanted to begin preparation for the early breakfast service. We were offering:

Orange Juice
Fresh Fruit
Assorted Cereals with Fresh Cream
Eggs Benedict
Eggs Any Style – fried, scrambled, boiled
Rolls, Butter, Jam
Coffee, Tea, Chocolate

When the purser announced the service, the egg orders were taken and I was happy to see most of the passengers wanted the Eggs Benedict. Oh joy, this meant only three requested eggs 'any style' and they all wanted 'scrambled.' This made life in the galley so much easier. One infant needed a milk bottle warmed.

While we were offering the Charles Heidsieck champagne and orange juice, I had time to start warming the rolls, pour cereals into bowls, heat the coffee and cook and plate the eggs. The service progressed smoothly. The passengers were now wide awake and eager to be landing.

We arrived at Heathrow Airport to a crisp sunny morning and clear blue sky. We picked up our bags and headed straight to the crew bus to be driven to the hotel. This day was my twenty-second birthday.

In the hotel lobby I approached the captain, smiled sweetly, and asked him to please consider letting me off the Paris leg of the flight so I could go home to visit my parents for my birthday. He considered a moment and said, "As the passenger load is so light flying on to Paris and back, I think we can certainly manage with one less stewardess on the crew." He looked at me sternly and added, "With one provision, make absolutely certain you are back here at the hotel in time for the pick-up crew bus to Heathrow!" I was elated and thanked him kindly and rushed off to use the hotel phone to call home.

Without even checking into a room, I hauled my case outside and hailed a cab to Victoria Railway Station to catch the first available train south to Chichester. It was an hour-and-a-half ride in those days on the express train. I was still wearing my uniform as I hadn't wanted to waste time by checking into a room to change.

On the train I entered an empty carriage and collapsed into the seat and hoped to close my eyes and rest. I should have known better as before long a young man opened the door and asked if I'd mind if he joined me. He sat down in the seat opposite and said he recognized my Pan Am uniform and told me he was an American from Chicago. And, no surprise, he wanted to talk all the way to Chichester. I was having a hard time keeping my eyes open having been up working all through the night but I tried to be civil and answer all his questions. Oh, how I just wanted to close my eyes and sleep.

It was a very special birthday being home with my parents. They had planned a family get-together tea party to celebrate. Aunts, uncles and cousins arrived in the afternoon and we enjoyed mini ham sandwiches, my favorite fresh strawberry trifle and home-made birthday walnut cake with coffee frosting. It seemed bizarre being surrounded by family when, only a matter of hours ago, I had been on the west coast of the United States of America.

How thoughtful and trusting of the captain to let me off the crew for that one leg to Paris, and how special the Pan Am 'family' became for these considerations. It was a whirlwind two-day visit and I did make it back to the hotel for the third night, in time for the next day's pick-up. The captain was very happy to see me!

On the return flight to San Francisco I was working the cabin in the Economy section. We had many Europeans on board. I worked the drinks cart and the passengers paid with cash for their liquor drinks and we had to contend with English pounds, French francs, German marks, and other foreign currencies. What a headache that was trying to calculate the correct American currency change and we didn't have the convenience of calculators.

By the time we'd walked briskly up and down the aisle multiple times, serving afternoon sandwiches and cookies with coffee or tea, my arms were about to drop off. There was no time to take a break. Once the tea service was cleared away we had to go right into preparations for the dinner and had to contend with an added hour-long stop at Winnipeg in Canada for re-fuelling.

We were preparing for this unexpected landing when the 'red' stewardess button blinked on sending out its 'Please help me' plea. I followed the purser down the aisle toward the lighted seat row. The passenger sitting in the aisle seat hoarsely whispered his name - Levi Guiseppi. He appeared to be in his early sixties and looked sickly pale and agitated. He tried to explain with limited English in a raspy voice, words we could hardly understand, that he didn't feel well and pointed at his throat gasping the word 'cancer.' He was becoming weak and I was upset to see his head lolling forward onto his chest.

Fortunately, Winnipeg was just minutes away but when we tried to help him off the plane, he adamantly refused to be taken to the hospital and with a burst of adrenaline energy he managed to shout at us that he wanted back on the plane and into his seat. So, what could we do as we couldn't force him from re-boarding the plane. We led him to the last and empty row in the First Class section and by lifting the armrest we were able to lay him down. I was told to sit with him all the way to San Francisco. I kept him comfortable with pillows, warm with blankets and, when he became heated and feverish, placed ice towels on his flushed forehead and face – sending up a hasty prayer that he wouldn't die.

The flight was scheduled to land at Seattle to unload passengers and yet again at Portland, and refreshments were served in between each flight section. All those landings and take-offs were tiresome and exhausting especially taking care of a sick and stubborn passenger. By the time we finally landed in San Francisco at ten-thirty at night it had been fifteen hours since the plane left London. Thankfully our sick passenger survived and was taken off the plane first, quietly this time, down the ramp and into a waiting ambulance.

It had been a grueling trip and I had to call and wait for a taxi to take me home as no-one on the crew was headed my way to offer a ride. On arrival at the apartment, I staggered through the door, dropped my bags, and went straight to bed.

20

CRAZY SCHEDULE – CRAZY PASSENGER

I had an early report time for a trip to Hawaii. Ed offered to drive me to the airport in the morning as it was on his way to work. I was only too happy to have a ride and gladly accepted. Ed was punctual and dropped me off at the curb at seven-thirty in good time for my eight a.m. report.

I walked casually through the airport to the Briefing Office and signed in. Looking around I wondered where everyone was – I was the only one there. On asking the lone scheduler, I was told the report time for my crew had been changed to nine forty-five. How had I missed the notification? Annoyed, I consoled myself with the thought that it was far better to be too early than too late. Now I had two long hours ahead of me to wait so I headed to the nearest restaurant and ordered a cup of coffee.

As the new report time neared, I wandered back to the Briefing Room and met the crew, among them a Dutch girl, Martje, one Norwegian girl, Siri from Sweden, and the two pursers. Captain Rogers didn't look very happy and apologized for a further delay until one o'clock. We all groaned, me especially, thinking of how long I'd been waiting already. However, we were treated to a free lunch which helped the time pass and gave the crew time to chat and get to know one another.

Due to the delay, I was assigned to the Airport Passenger Lounge where the passengers had also been waiting for hours and were growing edgy. I introduced myself, explaining that I would be one of the stewardesses on the plane with them as far as Hawaii.

I tried to calm their irritations which helped put my own frazzled nerves into perspective.

Finally, we heard the welcome announcement to board the plane. Despite a nearly full load of passengers, we managed a good routine flight all the way – until just before landing.

Nearing our arrival into Honolulu we were walking the aisle checking seat belts and were surprised to notice an unkempt, haggard-looking woman sitting in the window seat in the last row of the plane. During the flight this strange person had repeatedly asked for iced tea and we dutifully kept filling her cup. But as we started our descent she appeared to be acting drunk. She stubbornly clung to her cup and refused to let me take it when we were clearing the cabin for landing. We became more disconcerted when she began shouting loudly and incoherently. Worst of all, she insisted on smoking a cigarette during the landing which was strictly forbidden. We were close to touchdown and the captain was ordering the crew into their jump seats to prepare for landing, so we had no choice but to leave her. At the time, the cockpit crew had their hands full landing the plane.

After all the passengers had disembarked, this obnoxious woman was still obstinately sitting in her seat muttering and mumbling utter nonsense and refusing to leave the plane. The purser tried reasoning with her and soon realized he needed help to remove her from the seat. As a last resort he called the cockpit to come to the rescue.

She remained doggedly in place. She was becoming increasingly rowdy and agitated, and to me it was a disturbing and unpleasant sight. We were relieved to see one of the pilots marching down the aisle but even his presence and insistence were to no avail. The only option left was to call Pan Am Security on the ground.

Three big burly guards appeared in the rear cabin doorway. We were astounded to watch these three strong muscular young fellows struggling laboriously to lift this hostile female up and out of her window seat, and then carry her flailing body down the ramp and off the plane.

The cup was found and it reeked of alcohol – she must have been pouring her own spirits into the iced tea during the entire flight and we were so busy with the heavy load of passengers, we didn't notice anything unusual. Why didn't the passenger sitting in the aisle seat say anything as he must have seen what she was doing? But then, maybe he didn't notice either.

We were so relieved to leave the plane, step into the fresh air and walk away from that ugly scene. On arrival at our hotel and in my assigned room, I quickly changed and escaped to the warm, relaxing Waikiki beach.

21

THEATER

On the third leg of this trip flying from Los Angeles to Hawaii, the senior purser assigned me to work the First Class cabin and Siri to cover the galley. There were few passengers and after the formal lunch service I had time to chat with one of them, a Mr. James Doolittle, who was relaxing on his own in the First Class lounge. He was a charming gentleman in his forties and he requested a black coffee and a liqueur which I served on a small tray. He seemed eager to talk and launched into the topic of ballet.

I enthusiastically told him I had seen the unforgettable Rudolf Nureyev dance with Dame Margot Fonteyn in Swan Lake at the Royal Opera House in London. At the end of the performance, I had been spellbound as they returned to the stage for at least ten encores. Dame Margot was presented with an enormous bouquet of deep red roses and ever so slowly, with such a romantic flourish, she graciously plucked one long-stemmed bloom from the mass and offered it with a curtsy to her magnetic partner Nureyev. Mr. Doolittle appeared quite enthralled with my telling of the experience and explained that he was a theater producer and director. Unfortunately, at that point I had to apologize and leave him to continue with our cabin service.

Toward the end of the flight, Mr. Doolittle, who was still seated in the lounge, beckoned me and Siri to join him. We were so surprised when he invited us to accompany him to a ballet performance at the New Theater in Honolulu that same evening. He told us he was involved with the production. Siri and I were thrilled to have the invitation and told him we'd be honored to see his ballet. We were glad the two of us were going together with this relative stranger.

Siri and I were sharing a room at the Royal Hawaiian Hotel. I emptied my suitcase onto the bed and realized I hadn't brought anything special to wear, not expecting any invitations of this magnitude. Siri had an appropriate dress but my short sundresses just wouldn't do. I took a deep breath and let out a sigh of distress – momentarily – as I remembered hearing about the stylish dress shop in the hotel arcade called Carol and Mary's.

And that's where I headed. After trying on an armful of dresses, I stepped into a full-length, deep-pink shift dress with a long slit up the side. This was the one, and I didn't hesitate to buy it. With my confidence restored, I ran up to the room with a happy smile.

I felt very elegant wearing the new long pink dress and Siri looked stunning in a beautiful bright blue Thai silk dress she'd had made during a layover in Bangkok. At six o'clock we eagerly walked down to the hotel lobby and waited for Mr. Doolittle. He arrived shortly looking very dapper in a black evening suit and greeted us warmly. He led us down the hotel steps, one on each arm, into the sheer luxury of a waiting limousine (limos weren't as commonplace in the Sixties as they are today).

Siri and I relaxed into the plush seats and Mr. Doolittle entertained us with many show business stories. On arrival at the theater, the chauffeur opened the door and Mr. Doolittle came around and escorted us, again on each arm, into the theater. He led us to the front-row-center seats of the Loge and we felt very special as he sat down between us.

Mr. Doolittle explained to us that the star Zizi Jeanmaire was a French ballet dancer from the Paris Opera Ballet and was married to Roland Petit, who was a choreographer and dancer with the same company. He added that Zizi had also appeared in several Hollywood films. We were enthralled with the whole performance and the exquisite dancing, and felt saddened when the extraordinary evening came to a close. We were chauffeured back to our hotel and Mr. Doolittle accompanied us into the lobby. We thanked him very much for a memorable evening and he thanked us in return for joining him, and departed to his waiting limousine.

What an exceptional, unexpected experience with a charming, gracious gentleman.

The following day Siri and I decided to go swimming and sunbathing in front of the Royal Hawaiian. We smothered ourselves in baby oil and iodine and now, years later, we're all suffering the consequences. We never heard the words 'skin cancer' and there were no warnings, so we soaked up the sun every chance we had. After an hour Siri became uncomfortably hot and returned to the hotel to prepare for an early flight back to San Francisco.

I stayed on the beach near the water's edge for awhile longer and eventually succumbing to the heat, I picked up my things and walked along the sand to the cool of the hotel. As I strolled through the lobby, clad only in my swimsuit with a short muumuu cover-up, I was shocked to see Mr. Doolittle waving at me. I smiled as he approached and stopped to chat. All I could think of was the awful timing with me standing there covered in oil and sand and feeling most unkempt. Obviously that didn't deter Mr. Doolittle as he surprised me by politely asking if I would accompany him to see a Japanese Kabuki performance that evening. This was a little more intimidating as I would be alone with him but I told him I would be honored. He said he would be waiting for me at six o'clock in the lobby.

I rushed upstairs to my room, grabbed the phone and called the beauty salon for an immediate appointment to have my unruly hair washed and set. I then showered off all the baby oil, sand and salt. My next dilemma was 'what to wear?' I had worn the sleek pink dress the evening before and couldn't justify buying another one, so I reluctantly made do with one of the dresses I had with me – a soft yellow-colored one that was more formal albeit short. I just had time to pull everything together and make it down to the lobby by six. And there he was waiting, as promised. Mr. Doolittle took my arm and led me down the steps into the waiting limousine.

We were ushered into the same Loge center seats and I was eagerly looking forward to seeing this unusual performance. Mr. Doolittle leaned over and told me that Kabuki is the classical Japanese dance drama. When the performance began I could see it was vastly different from anything I had seen before. I sat back in my seat and was totally fascinated with the unique, elaborate make-up and stylized wigs the actors wore; their faces painted stark white with exaggerated black lines elongating their facial expressions and especially their eyes. I was intrigued to see male actors playing both the male and female roles, and seeing the sophisticated costumes displaying such exotic colors, detailed oriental designs and styles. I was enchanted.

After the performance Mr. Doolittle casually invited me to join him backstage. The evening was becoming even more intriguing with this wonderful surprise and I was honored to be introduced to the Kabuki actors, meeting them in person and seeing up close their over-stated make-up and magnificent ornate costumes. Their ebony black wigs were enormous and covered with the most intricate and colorful adornments. Seeing how many costume layers the actors wore, and the heavy wigs on their heads, I was ever more amazed that they moved with such grace and agility on the stage.

I was so grateful to Mr. Doolittle for giving me the opportunity to see such an unusual performance and especially the unique chance to meet the actors.

On exiting the theater, Mr. Doolittle politely asked me to join him for a Chinese dinner at Tai Chin Lee's. Of course I said, "Yes." And we had another thoroughly enjoyable evening and more so because there were no expectations. He was attentively charming in every way.

These experiences were part of the 'glamour' side of being a Pan Am stewardess.

22

HAWAII, GUAM, PHILIPPINES

B ack on line again I had a flight assignment to Hawaii, Guam, and on to the Philippines. On the leg from San Francisco to Honolulu I was working the First Class cabin and the purser, Fred Wagner, asked me to pass out the dinner menus and follow up with the entrée orders.

I eagerly obliged and approached a charming, middle-aged American couple, Mr. and Mrs. Brown, sitting in the front row. They were dressed smartly and intently studied the fancy menus. When I politely asked them for their entrée preferences, I was taken aback and left momentarily speechless as Mr. Brown pointed to every wine suggestion listed *under* each entrée and then tried hard to pronounce the French verbiage. He must have thought the wines were the dishes! Now how do I explain this 'faux pas' without embarrassing a very dear gentleman?

They appeared to be the typical hard-working couple who had saved up their entire lives for this trip of a lifetime to Hawaii. I took a deep breath, smiled sweetly and asked them if they would enjoy the Sole, Lamb Chops or the Sweet and Sour Pork with Pineapple. I was so happy when they both responded with "the Sole."

On the leg from Manila to Guam, I was assigned to work the First Class cabin. We had twelve passengers on board which in First Class, in those days, was considered a lot. The purser asked me if I would like to work the Roast Beef cart. I took a deep breath as this would be my very first time in charge of this special presentation. I calmed down after taking entrée orders and getting to know the passengers as I had been trained to do. Purser Fred helped me set the cart with the crisp white cloths, and, when it was ready, he placed the huge roast prime rib of beef sedately on its serving board. The vegetable tureen, containing potato croquettes and buttered green beans with slivered almonds, was positioned at the other end of the cart.

With a big smile on my face I set off down the aisle. It did feel good to put our training to use. Not every passenger had ordered the beef, but I had a very sharp carving knife and was able to carve slices to the individual's preference – from rare to medium to one request for the well done end piece. The purser was right there to help if needed as he was serving the vegetables onto the plates. It was quite a feat but made easy by having a very calm, no turbulence flight.

On arrival in Guam we were driven to the very basic Cliff Motel. At that time it was the *only* hotel on the entire island. Except for the military bases, we felt we were on a deserted island. I was exhausted and it was very late in the evening so we retired to our rooms. My roommate was Brigitte who had been working the First Class galley while I was carving the roast beef.

As we opened the room door and turned on the electric light switch, we went from sleepy to fully alert.

"Eek!"

Huge black, evil-looking cockroaches were scurrying around our small room and into the bathroom. What a nightmarish scene. We chased the little monsters all night. Neither of us had the nerve to squash them so we found some soap powder under the bathroom sink and tried pouring this over them. That was to no avail as, much to our dismay, the creatures just crawled out from under the soap dunes and scurried off again. We did manage to get some fitful sleep but, in the light of morning, we immediately reported the problem to the management and thankfully they somehow got rid of the pests.

Brigitte wasn't feeling well probably due to the lack of sleep, and she went back to bed to recuperate. I spent most of the day lounging around the pool to stay out of her way. I was quite happy sunbathing and swimming when a pilot from another flight sat down on the lounger next to mine and started up a conversation. He was one of the better-looking younger pilots with a crew cut and unusually pale blue eyes. He told me his name was Chuck and after chatting for a while, he asked me if I'd like to have dinner with him. I figured 'why not' especially as Brigitte was ailing in bed. I explained my predicament to him so he told me to knock on his door when ready. After quietly changing into one of my sundresses, and trying not to disturb my sleeping roommate, I casually walked over to Chuck's room just off the swimming pool.

I tapped lightly on the door to announce my arrival and instantly the door opened – wide.

I gasped.

I stood there momentarily frozen to the spot.

He was standing there – stark naked – much to my utter surprise, and horror.

This was not what I was expecting at all!

On the spur of the shocking moment, I didn't know what to do. I didn't want to garner attention by turning back shrieking past all the sunbathers around the pool, heaven forbid that I make a scene! So… I entered the room. I hoped to hide a major breakout of embarrassment by acting totally unfazed.

I did a fast look around and sat awkwardly on the edge of the bed closest to the door, in case I needed a quick getaway. There was nowhere else to sit. Not knowing quite where to look, or quite what he had in mind, I told him flatly, "I think you'd better get dressed!"

With that, he did, probably disappointed, but I just wasn't about to give in to an advance like that. I didn't even feel attracted to him! My mind was racing. This was an invitation to dinner and with my roommate asleep in bed, I had no other option to get anything to eat.

We did go out – albeit to the local A&W for a hamburger! Of course, in Guam there were very few other choices of restaurant anyway.

After that discomforting scenario I made a point of avoiding him, easily done as he was off on another flight the next morning and I never saw him again.

Two mornings later we left for the airport and this time I worked aft with one hundred and fifty nine sailors on board from the Polaris submarine USS Stockton. We served them roast beef sandwiches after take-off and a full dinner service before landing in Hawaii. They were having fun and were so happy to be returning home.

One of the officers organized a pool to see who could guess the nearest touchdown time and that kept them busy for a while. Then, much to our dismay, one of the Lieutenants walked the aisle and handed out big fat cigars to everyone. As the sailors indulged in lighting them and blowing clouds of obnoxious smoke into the air, it didn't take long before the cabin filled with a thick, pungent smoke screen. It became a heavy, brown fog by the time we reached Honolulu and was so dense we couldn't see one end of the cabin from the other. Smoking in the cabins was allowed and taken for granted.

We reeked of smoke when we stepped off that plane, our uniforms were permeated. We had breathed all the acrid smoke into our lungs while walking up and down that aisle in the enclosed cabin and no-one thought a thing about health hazards from second-hand smoke.

The sailors were oblivious as they had been out on patrol for sixty-five days. All they cared about was disappearing into the massive crowd of riotous, passionate hugs and welcomes from their waiting families – wives, children and girlfriends.

On arrival at the hotel we rid ourselves of the cigar-infused uniforms and sent them out for dry cleaning. What joy to have that service so handily available.

23

STORIES AROUND THE POOL

B etween flights we recuperated at the apartment. We lounged at the pool, enjoyed casual dinners with friends and delighted in exchanging our illustrious flying stories. One day a group of us was sitting around the pool dangling our legs in the cool water and having a good chitchat session.

Tina was lamenting about her latest flight to Hawaii and was telling us, "I sat down on the jump seat in the First Class section, trying to get a moment's rest and catch my breath. To my dire annoyance a young man sidled up, sat down and tried to engage me in conversation. I just wanted to be left alone. I wasn't even attracted to him – he wasn't that good looking. I told him to leave but he persisted. In desperation, I got up, grabbed the coffee pot in the galley and started walking down the aisle pouring coffee for the passengers whether they wanted it or not.

"Later that same day, when the crew was at a layover party, I asked them, 'Who was that irritating guy on the plane in First Class?' They were astounded I hadn't recognized him or didn't know he was from one of the wealthiest families in Hawaii. I had absolutely no idea, and, oh well, I missed another great opportunity," said Tina with a shrug.

Mona was sitting with us and she was excited about having survived an emergency 'chute' experience and fortunately for her not into the sea but onto an airport tarmac. She told us the story about her Round the World flight from San Francisco to Los Angeles and on to London.

"The plane had an almost-full load of passengers. Soon after take-off from Los Angeles something went very wrong with one of the engines. The captain's voice was heard on the intercom and he announced with apologies, that due to engine malfunctions, the flight had to return to Los Angeles.

"He explained that since the tanks were FULL of jet fuel, they had to fly out over the ocean and fly around and around to dump most of it. This procedure took a very long time and the crew, especially me, and most of the passengers, were in a state of nervous tension hoping that during this time the malfunctioning engine didn't catch fire or worse, drop off. The captain explained to the concerned passengers that the fuel didn't just gush down into the pristine ocean below, but as soon as it hit the atmosphere, it broke down and blew away.

"When the cockpit was satisfied that most of the fuel had been dumped, they began the descent to land at the Los Angeles International airport. It was rather scary looking out the plane windows and seeing the airport in full emergency mode with fire trucks and ambulances at the ready everywhere," said Mona. "But we did make it down and thanks to the experienced pilots they landed the plane safely with no mishap."

That wasn't the end of it as the crew still had to take emergency precautions to get the passengers off as fast as possible. Mona and the crew had to put into practice all they had learned about lowering the emergency chutes from the cabin doors.

"The adrenaline was flowing. The orders were given for all shoes to be removed and the passengers thankfully stayed relatively calm and complied, glad they were at least on solid ground and not bobbing about on the open ocean. We had Leslie Caron as a passenger in First Class who was the film actress famous for her role in the 1958 musical Gigi. In the midst of all this chaos, she dashed back to retrieve her mink coat. I don't blame her for not wanting to leave that behind," Mona said.

"One by one, the shoeless passengers slid down the chutes to the welcoming ground below. The crew came down last and miraculously there were no casualties. The shaken passengers were escorted to an airport lounge and the crew was driven to a nearby hotel.

"That's when the aftershock of what we'd survived set in and I started shivering all over and turned very pale. The captain decided that we all needed a Cognac to recover and ordered one for all of us. That was the first time I'd ever drunk Cognac and it didn't taste very good, but it sure did help a lot," Mona laughed.

"In the meantime a new plane was flown down from San Francisco and about four hours later we all boarded this plane and welcomed back the same passengers – minus only three or four who opted, for obvious reasons, not to show.

"Of course, the cockpit crew was replaced with a fresh group of pilots. But, after that long, harrowing ordeal, we, the same cabin crew, had to carry on. We stewardesses went back to work and started all over again with the long eleven-hour flight ahead of us. We worked all the way over the Pole to London, with an added fuel stop in Winnipeg, making the trip even longer. What a long, exhausting day and almost a twenty-four hour work day!" Mona exclaimed.

Gunnel and Bonnie appeared in the middle of this story and we moved over to the loungers to join them. Gunnel was excited to share her recent encounter with a famous film star.

"I was working in the First Class cabin leaving Saigon for Hawaii and couldn't believe I was seeing Robert Mitchum coming up the ramp."

We were envious she had met such a famous star who was one of America's screen legends. He had starred in many movies but most notably in The Sundowners, Cape Fear and The Longest Day in the early Sixties just before Gunnel met him. She continued with her story.

"He had been entertaining the troops in Vietnam and after take-off he left his seat and moved up to the lounge. He grinned widely and asked me for a Martini. He was so much fun and I was very generous with the Martinis," she smiled, "and when he got off the plane in Hawaii he gave me a big hug and a big kiss and said, 'You're a doll!'" Gunnel laughed with a twinkle in her eye.

We were all oohing and aahing over Gunnel's good fortune, when Bonnie changed the subject to unbelievable turbulence on a flight from Hawaii to Los Angeles.

"At the beginning of the meal service, I walked the aisle serving warm rolls. We hit a downdraft and the rolls took flight, as did everything in the open overhead compartments. At the same time, the bar and galley areas emptied all over the floor. It was utter chaos!

"I was stunned and felt the strange sensation of elevating off the floor toward the ceiling. This was followed by an even stranger sensation when a male passenger leaned over, grabbed me tightly around my legs and pulled me down into the seat next to him. Just in time, as he saved me from going airborne and possibly hitting my head. The rough turbulence continued jolting the plane in every direction for the remainder of the flight, almost three more hours, and it was impossible to continue with any kind of service. The captain ordered all crew personnel to remain belted in their seats. Can you imagine, a few people walked off complaining there was no food served."

What extraordinary experiences we were encountering in the course of our working days.

24.

TAHITI

My bidding line showed my first flight to Tahiti in the middle of the month. Tahiti sounded so tropical and romantic and distant. Known as the Pearl of the Pacific it is the largest island in French Polynesia, annexed by France in 1880.

After flying to Hawaii we left Honolulu working a five-and-a-half hour flight to Papeete. We had Miss Tahiti on board in First Class. She was exotically beautiful with shiny black long hair and big black eyes.

I was working the aft galley preparing meals for fifty-six passengers. We were serving Wild Rice stuffed Cornish Game Hen and Chinese Pea Pods. The game hens I had cooked in training but although I had prepared many vegetables, the Chinese Pea Pods evaded my attention. I was busy preparing and plating the hens laying them artistically on the special sauce. BUT when I removed the pans of Pea Pods from the oven and lifted the lids, I went hot all over as they looked a sickly color of yellow-green. And, just my luck, at that very moment the ego-driven purser strutted into the galley adding to my agitation. He was a perfectionist about his service. When he eyed the yellow pods lying limp and lifeless in the pans, his face turned red with fury. He began ranting at me about ruining his service by carelessly overcooking the only vegetable.

I stood there devastated but I wasn't about to let this egomaniac reduce me to tears and, awful as I felt, I apologized. He just grabbed the plates and served them to the passengers with a lone stuffed game hen sitting in the middle of the plate on its bed of sauce – minus the vegetable.

I learned the hard way that Chinese Pea Pods need the absolute minimum of cooking time – and will never forget!

I was thankful when the plane landed at the Faa'a International Airport at seven o'clock in the evening and the sun was sinking behind a beautiful orange-streaked sunset sky. Walking through the airport into the warm tropical air, we were bombarded with plump jolly Tahitian ladies carrying armfuls of shell leis. They draped these unusual leis around our necks – lots of them and they were quite heavy. There were shells of all shapes, sizes and colors, some incredibly tiny and intricately woven together.

A little crew bus shuttled us to the Bel Aire Hotel and when I saw the grass-roofed huts on stilts hanging out over the darkening blue lagoon, I gasped in awe. It was so incredibly beautiful and looked just like the tropical paradise of dreams.

The four stewardesses were staying in one bungalow sitting over the calm water. It was spacious with two two-bedroom suites. We were all fairly new girls and we were amazed to see a large part of the living room floor was a panel of thick glass. We stood there fascinated watching the water beneath our feet and mesmerized by the tiny, tropical, colorful fish swimming below us.

We chose our beds, cleaned up, changed into cool dresses and met our crew in front of the lagoon to watch the evening Tahitian dancing show in the moonlight. The air was warm and relaxing, almost sensual as the dancers entertained us. They were wearing beautiful palm frond and grass skirts adorned with shells and beads at the hips, bright floral bikini tops and exotic flowers or shell crowns in their hair. They were shaking their hips at such a pace it was exhausting watching them.

The show ended and two of the pilots suggested we go along to a bar called Quinn's. No-one hesitated so we piled into the crew bus and off we went. The girls weren't sure what to expect as the pilots told us that Quinn's was a notorious bar in Papeete, and I could see why when we arrived. It was packed full of strange people of all types drinking, smoking, dancing, wild and carefree. I was a little apprehensive at first but happily secure in a group with the pilots and girls from the crew. Many alcoves were full of sailors from the yachts anchored in the bay, all smoking and drinking with young, and not so young, local women. Most of the women, some young and attractive, and some quite unattractive, were wearing traditional loose Tahitian dresses of colorful floral fabrics and wore beautiful flower leis everywhere even around their hair.

We were jostled and cramped but the pilots managed to find a small table and we all crowded around and ordered drinks – a Tahitian Mai Tai for everyone. The Tahitian word Maita'i means 'good' and the drinks were delicious, especially with the fresh sweet pineapple chunks and colorful tropical flowers adorning each glass. A small group of local men played pulsating island music on wooden drums, ukuleles and a guitar and we soon lost our inhibitions and joined in the wild dancing and had a fun time. Too soon the evening came to an end and we returned to our hotel. We were tired from the long day and tumbled into our beds and drifted into deep Tahitian slumbers.

We woke early the next morning, amazingly with no headaches from the night before, and could appreciate the beauty of this French Polynesian paradise. The water was flat and glassy calm right up to our door. There were beautiful streams, little wooden bridges and sandy paths all around us. From our bungalow we could see the greater lagoon and beyond where the ocean stretched out to the horizon. The sun was rising and sending rays of blinding light across the water which sparkled as if sprinkled with tiny diamonds. This truly was an Eden.

Some of the crew members suggested taking a tour, so we boarded an open jitney bus for a drive around the island. We chugged along through charming villages where the most adorable children played in the dust along the narrow roadways. They all had jet black hair and beautiful dark eyes and were always smiling and happy to see us, running and shouting behind our little bus until we turned the corners and disappeared.

We bumped along the rough dirt roads through villages where the homes were simply made of cinder block or wood with rusty corrugated aluminum roofs, other huts were covered by palm frond thatch roofs. The yards were cleared of brush but we saw many banana and fruit trees growing wild and in abundance amongst the luxuriant vegetation, and behind stretched the ever lush rainforest.

The locals grinned at us showing their gaping smiles and the driver explained to us they love to pour sweetened condensed milk on *everything* and the sticky sugar ruins their teeth. Well, that would do it! Everyone we passed waved happily and I couldn't help thinking of Gauguin's vibrant colors in his exotic paintings of the islands with its beautiful women. We enjoyed the tour immensely and were so disappointed when we returned to the hotel much too soon.

We had to fly out the next day so the crew met for breakfast alongside the deep turquoise lagoon. We enjoyed bowls of fresh local fruit, the sweetest deepest yellow pineapple with papaya and bananas, hot flaky croissants and fresh pots of strong coffee. After that tropical morning feast, we headed to the airport.

The magical layover re-energized us for the flight back to Honolulu.

25.

WATER SKIING

On one of her flights Mary had met a Pan Am pilot, Norman, who invited us both to go waterskiing. He wanted to take us to the San Joaquin river in the Sacramento River delta north-east of San Francisco. Neither of us had experienced waterskiing before and we made this quite clear to Norman. But he insisted on taking us anyway. What were we letting ourselves in for this time?

It was another beautiful sunny warm day and Norman was happy, with Mary beside him, to drive us to the river in his big convertible with the top down. His ski boat trailed merrily along behind us.

We reached the boat ramp at the river's edge and helped Norman unhitch the boat and launch it in the water. Norman left to park his car nearby and Mary and I climbed in. When he returned we went for a long ride speeding down the river and enjoyed the hot sun on our skin and the cool wind blowing through our hair.

Norman steered the boat to a reedy bank, slowed to a stop and asked Mary, "Are you up to putting on the skis and giving it a try?"

Mary reluctantly agreed, "Okay, I'll go first and see how I do. Please don't laugh though if I fall in."

They both plunged into the water and Norman helped Mary put on the skis and told her to hang on to the tow rope tightly between her knees. He jumped into the boat and slowly started the engine.

The boat surged forward and I was thrilled to see Mary lift up out of the water. But, I gasped as she took a sudden nosedive and disappeared from sight. What a relief when she surfaced, and I could tell she was frustrated but she gallantly agreed to give it one more try just to please Norman. She hung on tightly while rising out of the water but regrettably nosedived again. That was it. She'd had enough and wanted to get back in the boat.

She encouraged me to have a try next. These were the days of elaborate rubber swimming caps to preserve our hairdos. I put on my favorite cap covered with white ruffles and Norman helped me put on the skis. As instructed I hung onto the rope, my hands clenched tightly and white knuckled.

I was deep in the water with the skis vertical, and as the boat took off I felt myself slowly pulled up out of the water. It was quite a thrill. I expected to follow this feat with an inglorious nosedive but instead was faced with the reality of actually standing up on the skis skidding along the water and hanging on for dear life. The sheer exhilaration of speeding across the water was intoxicating. I could do this!

After zooming along at breakneck speed, I was beginning to wonder how to stop. My arms were aching and I simply couldn't let go of the rope – it was a lifeline to the boat. And there I was waterskiing down the river feeling pleased with myself yet at the same time scared to death.

Norman was getting carried away and was upping the speed, much to my utter dismay, and it was all I could do to hang on to the rope as the boat veered one side and then the other zooming down the river. I just wanted to stop and had no idea how. My arms felt like they had stretched another inch with my holding the lifeline in such a tight death grip. I couldn't hang on a minute longer, my arms were numb, and in a flash, my fingers unwound and I let go.

I fell forward and sank deep into the river – head first. I miraculously and frantically swam up to the surface gasping for air and that ungraceful maneuver had cost me my precious ruffled white swim cap.

I clambered back in the boat happy to be out of the water. Norman searched all over in the thick reeds and bushes along the bank, but my prized swim cap was nowhere to be seen. I had to leave it behind buried in the mud at the bottom of the river – my hair was sopping wet!

Mary courageously tried another turn, buoyed by my crazy stunt, and she managed to pull herself up and out of the water but staying upright eluded her and she sank yet again into the depths. She begged off and we went for a boat ride instead of tormenting ourselves. We offered to drive so Norman could ski but he was adamantly against it. He probably didn't trust us with his treasured boat but he did take us out on other occasions.

26.

LONG TRIP TO SINGAPORE

This was a scheduled ten-day trip but due to unusual circumstances it turned into fifteen.

Fred kindly offered me a ride all the way to the airport. Again I deadheaded on a flight to Honolulu. The following day I met my line crew in the hotel lobby and at the airport briefing we were told that the Honolulu to Guam leg would be an eight-hour flight with a four-hour time change. We were to expect a full load of passengers.

We boarded the plane and were busy all the way, from take off to landing in Guam. We landed at the NAS (Naval Air Station) Agana and were intrigued to see a small group of Navy pilots waiting for our arrival. They did look very handsome standing there in their pristine white uniforms and one of the older girls told me they were waiting to look over the stewardesses coming off the plane. Captain Borg very curtly told us to ignore them and get into the waiting crew van.

The weather was extremely hot and humid, and the sun was blazing in a cloudless blue sky. We were driven to the Cliff Motel where we picked up our room keys and looked for our room.

My roommate was a fun American girl named Judy. When we opened our door we recoiled in horror. Scurrying across the ceiling and darting around the walls we saw creepy green lizard creatures.

This was the first time either of us had seen a gecko let alone dozens of them and all in one room. They were little ones, thank goodness, and seemed to stick to the ceiling and walls so we braved an entry. We were so exhausted, we tried to ignore them. We quickly changed out of our uniforms, dived into the beds, pulled the sheets over our heads and tried to get some sleep for a few hours.

Creepy cockroaches one visit and now geckos!

I woke up early the next morning and tentatively pulled the sheet down off my face, peeking around the room hoping the geckos had disappeared during the night. That was wishful thinking. I warily pulled aside the short blue-striped curtain hanging alongside the bed. Ugh! I shuddered and shrieked, as there, resting on the windowsill, was a much bigger, fatter, brilliant luminous-green lizard with big black bulging eyes. My roommate woke up and gasped too. When we came to our senses we realized with great relief that the menacing creature was perched on the *outside* of the tiny window. This was the tropics after all and we had to adjust to these strange creatures and larger-than-life bugs.

We breakfasted with the crew and the captain shared the good news that we were invited to the Naval Officers Club for an evening party on base. This sounded exciting and different so after a day of sunbathing and swimming at the pool, we cleaned up, dressed up and were eager to have fun and meet some navy officers.

One of the Pan Am pilots drove us in the crew van to the Navy Base and on to the Officers' Club. We were shown into a large room with a bar at one end and a small wooden dance floor. We were instantly surrounded by young men and soon started drinking, dancing and having a good time.

I sat down with Judy for a break and noticed one of the fellows across the room. He kept looking my way. He smiled at me as he crossed the room, sat down on a chair next to mine and chatted for quite a while. My heart was racing and he told me his name was Jay. I was quite smitten as it was quite flattering to be noticed by this handsome young fellow across a crowded room. At the end of the evening Jay offered to drive me back to our hotel. He dropped me off in front of my door and asked for and wrote down my address in San Francisco. I was ecstatic. He then asked me to give him a call when I came back to Guam.

The next morning we had a five-thirty a.m. pick-up. We were working our way to Manila – a less than four-hour flight. I was in the First Class galley and with six passengers the breakfast service was proceeding smoothly. One-and-a-half hours passed and we were dismayed to hear the captain announce that he was returning the plane to Guam due to a fault in the radar system. He apologized for the delay this would cause but it was the best precaution. We allayed the fears of the passengers and knew this would thoroughly mess up our own schedules too.

Landing back in Guam at Agana Airport, everyone was asked to disembark. The crew was given breakfast in the small cafeteria which helped appease us while the maintenance crew tried to fix the mechanical problem. A long two hours passed before we were told to re-board the plane and work the flight to Manila all over again.

Manila was just a stopover to let off some passengers but the captain allowed us to go into the airport lounge for half-an-hour. We were dismayed to find there was no air conditioning and it was unbearably hot and sticky. Many leering men were lounging around looking us up and down. Feeling most uncomfortable we didn't stay and hurried back to the security of the aircraft.

Airborne again we were flying over war-stricken South Vietnam toward Saigon. Captain Borg announced taking photographs was strictly forbidden, so we peered out the windows and thought the ground below looked flat and marshy.

Landing at Tan Son Nhut airport we saw American armed guards standing along the length of the terminal. We were so surprised when the pursers told us to gather up all our leftover milk and take it down to the soldiers. When we handed it out, they beamed and were so thankful, telling us what a treat it was as they rarely, if ever, had fresh cold milk to drink. That made us feel good and we wished we had a lot more to give away. Our stopover was short and so we boarded the plane to fly on to Singapore.

Singapore means Sea Town. It is a two-hundred-and-twenty-four square mile island and was established in 1819 by Sir Stamford Raffles of the East India trading post as a British Trading Colony. It was 1964 and the year before Singapore had joined the Malaysian Federation and we were flying into race riots between the Chinese and Malay groups.

In the airline terminal we picked up our bags and boarded the waiting crew bus. On the drive to our hotel we were fascinated but disturbed to see many scrawny cows wandering aimlessly along the roads. The driver explained the cows were considered sacred to the community, revered as the source of food and a symbol of life, and may never be killed. All the same, they did look pathetically thin with their bones sticking out at sharp angles.

Our bus pulled into a stunning new high-rise hotel, The Singapura. The rooms were a soothing shade of celadon green and we luxuriated in the plushness of the decor. Except for one thing – when we sank into the beds later that evening our heads hit the pillows and bounced right up again. They were as hard as wood. We had a sumptuous bed but had to toss the uncomfortable pillow blocks aside to get any sleep.

Friends in San Francisco had advised me to visit the famed Raffles Hotel and insisted I go there first knowing I would love its British Colonial style. Judy was my roommate again and she was eager to explore with me. We changed into our best dresses and shoes and took the elevator down to the lobby.

We approached the hotel desk and asked them to call a taxi for us. A uniformed doorman opened the hotel doors and we climbed into the waiting cab for the drive to the Raffles Hotel, known as the grand lady of the Far East. The taxi sped away and soon pulled up in front of this amazing building. We stepped onto the sidewalk and faced the old hotel façade, feeling we had gone back in time to the era of the British Raj (reign in Hindi).

On entering the hotel we noticed the staff members were dressed in uniforms of the colonial era: white pith helmets, white jackets, epaulets, gold braid, and khaki shorts or long white pants. We were ushered into an open tropical verandah lounge with lush greenery and palm trees swaying outside. We sank into huge rattan armchairs and were swallowed up by the plump, soft, ecru-white cushions.

The scene surrounding us was like a movie set. We could feel the refreshing sea breeze stirred by the fans overhead – how much more pleasant and seductive than the icy drafts of air conditioning. A smart young, colonial-clad waiter approached and politely asked, "What would the young ladies like to drink?" I had been advised to order the Singapore Sling, and that's what we requested.

We sat there taking it all in and were imagining the likes of Joseph Conrad, Noel Coward, Rudyard Kipling, and Somerset Maugham having walked the same floors and sitting in the same bars.

The waiter returned and broke our reverie offering us two tall crystal glasses of pink Singapore Slings set on a silver tray. The deliciously cool, refreshing, fruity concoction had been created by a bartender long before called Ngiam Tong Boon while working at the famous Long Bar. Judy and I sipped our drinks, wallowing in the romantic, historical ambiance and imagining ourselves back in the days of the British Empire.

A soft breeze continued blowing in through the open lanai and the huge tropical fans spun lazily overhead. I could feel myself becoming drowsy and no wonder for the Singapore Slings proved to be very potent. We were curious and asked the waiter what was in them and he told us with a grin they were a mix of gin, Cherry Heering, Benedictine and fresh pineapple juice – all shaken.

No wonder we were feeling so relaxed.

It was hard to think about leaving but time was passing and we needed to return to the hotel before the darkness of night. Judy and I tried to lift ourselves out of the deep armchairs, but they felt like huge magnets pulling us back down into their comfort. Struggling to retain our composure, despite our heads spinning, we slowly and carefully stood upright and made our way as elegantly as possible through the vast lobby. One of the young attendants led us to a waiting taxi outside and we were whisked away to our modern highrise and characterless by comparison hotel.

With a seven o'clock pick-up the next morning we retreated to our room, crept into our beds and slept soundly until the wake-up call in the early hours.

A perfect introduction to Singapore!

A few months after this visit, in 1965, Singapore became a sovereign and independent nation.

We were returning to a stopover in Saigon and on to hot, steamy Manila. We said goodbye to our cockpit crew as they continued the flight on to Guam and we wished we were going with them. Instead, we picked up our luggage and staggered outside into the scorching heat to board the waiting crew bus.

Driving to the Manila Hotel we noticed armed guards everywhere, standing in hostile attitudes around the statues in the parks, inside the locked gates of opulent homes, and outside the factories. We were surprised to see the poverty of rickety shacks, covered with grey tarps and rusty corrugated tin roofs giving the aura of depression, squeezed in juxtaposition between the glaring opulence of lavish estate homes. The sight was extremely discomforting. As we sped by in the relative safety of our bus, we were met with many dark sullen looks and fleeting furtive eyes staring back at us.

The Filipino bus driver warned us corruption was running rampant and he advised us to *never* go out alone, especially in the taxis. He told us the policemen go out of their way to stop American drivers hoping to be given money for their 'not' being reported – consequently most of the policemen we saw wore a look of corpulence and shady sleaze. These dire warnings filled us with angst and reminded us of our vulnerability in this hostile land. We were anxious to arrive at the hotel.

We turned a sharp corner into the Manila Bay area and there it was looming before us – The Manila Hotel. A palatial and imposing white palace standing at the end of a wide avenue lined with tall palm trees. It was the oldest première hotel in the Philippines and had opened in 1912.

As we poured out of the crew bus I was attracted to a group of young, good-looking men lined up on the hotel steps. "They are sons of the plantation owners," one of the experienced crew members told me and added, "They are standing there to look over the incoming stewardesses." I was warned that they'd be lounging in the lobby, watching and waiting, ready to approach the unsuspecting girl. And, needless to say, I did meet up with some of them later because two were good friends of Judy's.

We found our way to our room and were disturbed by the onslaught of a typhoon. The windows shook and rattled against the torrents of rain that relentlessly lashed against them. The wind blew with such ferocity the palm trees were bent double, their once-graceful green fronds now twisted and jagged thrashing against the flooded roads.

Judy and I hunkered down but couldn't relax with the nightmarish storm howling outside. We tried to read but that soon became dreary so we migrated down to the lounge area to wait with other nervous crew members for the storm to subside.

The lounge was luxurious with marble flooring and unusual capiz, local flat semi-transparent shell, chandeliers hanging from an exquisitely carved wood ceiling. Sitting in the comfortable armchairs, we picked up and read the English version of the Manila Times newspaper.

Against the fear of the storm, we were now horrified to read that a bomb had exploded in the airport restaurant at the Tan Son Nhut airbase in Saigon, and had caused many civilian deaths and much damage. How could this be? We were just there. That news upset some of our cabin crew members because we received no extra pay for flying in and out of the Vietnam War zone.

With the storm slowly abating, we returned to our room just as the phone rang. Judy rushed over to the small table to answer it and became instantly animated. She told me her friend Malcolm was inviting the two of us to join him and his friend Tony waterskiing on Manila Bay the next afternoon. I had limited experience water skiing but I knew the basics thanks to Mary's friend Norman. I was a little leery at first but fearless Judy said it would be an adventure and not to worry about anything.

We slept in till noon and enjoyed a late breakfast in the hotel restaurant. The storm was over and the sun again shone in a clear sky. Our time was running short as Malcolm was picking us up in one hour. We hurriedly pulled on our swimsuits and dresses, grabbed two large towels, and our swim caps, jamming everything into our Pan Am carry bags, and rushed out the door to meet Malcolm and Tony in the lobby. They were tall, handsome, dark-haired, tanned and dressed in classy navy and white shirts and khaki shorts. They escorted us outside to Malcolm's waiting car and there at the curb was a sleek, shiny, red Porsche convertible. Judy and I climbed into the rear seats as if we did this every day and off we sped, our hair blowing in the warm breeze and mine ever curlier in the steamy humidity.

We raced along the busy winding roads and came to a halt at the entrance of an exclusive-looking marina. The uniform-clad official stepped out of his guard hut and had Malcolm sign the member book. The gates slowly opened wide and the car eased forward. We drove on at a slow pace and Malcolm parked his car alongside one of the long docks. The young men jumped out, opened the doors for us and told us to follow them down the pier to the boat. When we arrived in front of a beautiful yacht our eyes opened wide. It was long, shiny white, sleek and luxurious.

Suddenly the thought crossed my mind of how very trusting we were. These two fellows were total strangers, to me anyway, and here I was in a strange country, taking off on a strange venture and on a strange speed boat no less. It was a good thing my mother had no idea what I was getting into so far from home.

Judy and I were a bit dubious seeing the shallow water which looked muddy brown, noxiously murky and felt unhealthily warm. We were helped aboard and ushered into plush white leather seats in the open cockpit and were offered tall glasses of sparkling cold champagne. The boat eased out of the marina and sped out to sea with the mainland diminishing in the distance.

Looking back toward the shore the scene behind us was mesmerizing. Fishermen were standing up to their necks in the water holding onto gargantuan butterfly-shaped fishing nets. Junk boats bobbed on the gentle waves and children dived under the water spearing fish. Women in the shallows were bent over washing their clothes, while the youngsters splashed and frolicked in the same water.

In the distance we heard the neighing of horses as these magnificent beasts were being ridden hard through the shallow surf. Malcolm told us this exercise is supposed to be good for the horses' legs. I felt the riders showed little concern for the people in the water as they were deluged in spray kicked up by the galloping hooves.

The boat took us further into deeper, clearer water and stopped. All was momentarily quiet and Malcolm and Tony invited us to water ski. Diving into the water, Tony helped Judy put on a pair of skis. As the boat revved up she valiantly took off like a pro. She was on the water for a long time skiing from side to side gliding over the boat wake with a confidence I didn't have. Eventually she yelled at us to slow the boat as she wanted to stop and she let go of the rope and sank gracefully into the cool water. My turn was next. I put on the skis and took a deep breath as the boat lunged forward. I was hanging onto the rope as if my life depended on it. I rose up out of the water and thankfully stayed upright.

I was enjoying a wonderful exhilarating ski, thinking this is quite a feat skiing in Manila Bay in the Philippines, one of the finest natural harbors in the world. I was soon ready to stop and, following Judy's example, I opened my mouth and yelled at them and thankfully the boat slowed. I let go and slowly sank into the cool water. I quickly climbed back onto the rear of the boat with as much dignity as I could muster. Thank goodness for swimming hats as both Judy and I could shake out our dry hair instead of having it plastered to our heads.

Time for the guys to ski and Tony steered the speeding boat through the water while Malcolm showed off his daring abilities. We were dismayed to see his nerve and audacity in skiing so close to the fishermen – he was showering them with water, disturbing the fish and even worse, jumping over them. We held our breath as one helpless fisherman was almost decapitated with the rope. Judy and I were most upset and if they were trying to impress us they failed miserably. There didn't appear to be any respect or consideration from the wealthy toward the struggling poor.

As dusk approached the weather was still comfortably warm. We were tiring from all the fresh air and energy of skiing and headed back to the marina.

We witnessed a magical sight as the fishermen wore lit candles on their heads, the flames flickering in the gentle breeze and reflecting on the water like sparkling beads. The shimmering of burnt oranges, scorching crimson reds and swaths of sunflower yellows were stretching across the bay from the setting sun. Even the Filipino locals were mesmerized by the awesome spectacle and were standing or squatting along the low stone seawall, silhouetted black against the brilliance emanating from the heavens. On each side of this magnificent bay we could see volcanic peaks looming tall like sentries guarding the water. The entire vista was reminiscent of a striking watercolor painting.

Tony and Malcolm drove us back to our hotel. Judy and I felt extraordinarily energized from all the unusual sights, the waterskiing and the spectacular sunset we'd been fortunate to experience – thanks to the generosity of these two young men.

With all the outdoor activity of the day before, Judy and I desperately needed the help of a haircut and set. After breakfast in the hotel restaurant, we found our way to the hotel beauty shop where they obligingly fit us into their busy schedule. The local salon stylists specialized in a great deal of backcombing to achieve the Sixties 'beehive' look so we were subjected to much hair tugging and teasing to give our hair voluminous lift and width – almost too much as now we wondered how our uniform hats would balance on top. Despite our sore scalps we felt sufficiently groomed for the upcoming flight to Guam.

On arrival at the Manila airport and reporting for our Briefing we were told to take care of the Philippine Ambassador and his teenage daughter who were traveling in First Class. With only six passengers in front we were able to give each of them our full attention and service.

In Guam, I phoned Jay from the airport and he had time off to drive over to the motel. He invited a group of crew members to join us for drinks and supper at the Hut, a local bar.

Our pick-up the next morning was at eight a.m. but we were jerked awake at six-thirty by the phone jangling in our ears. Groggy and half asleep I picked up the receiver and heard a male voice telling me that we, the cabin crew, were unexpectedly having to go *back* to Singapore by way of Manila and Saigon – again! We couldn't quite grasp this change of events but had to go along with it. This was proving to be a long, arduous trip and we were getting tired as most of these flights had full passenger loads aft and the jet lag was catching up with us.

On our return to Singapore, and arriving at the Hotel Singapura, the new captain took pity on us and offered to escort those who wished to visit Change Alley. (This area was named after the Change Alley of London where the stockbrokers congregated.) Four of the girls including me decided to join the handsome, younger ex-military captain to see more of this fascinating city. Captain Edwards organized a cab for us and we piled inside. On the drive we were appalled to see small groups of children, looking half-starved and painfully thin. They were wearing ragged shorts and holey T-shirts and yet they were happily playing kick ball in the dusty streets and narrow alleyways.

When we reached the Change Alley we poured out of the stifling hot cab and were instantly accosted by two young boys of about seven and ten who latched onto us, gesticulating wildly, and shepherded us into the congested bazaar.

The arcade was jammed with bodies, mostly men, and we had to squeeze ourselves through the jostling crowd. Once inside we saw myriad rows of tiny cramped shops and stalls covered with makeshift tarpaulin covers to ward off the sun and rain. We instinctively held on tight to our purses as we had been warned about the many pickpockets who lurked among the seething crowds.

Just as I had imagined, it was brilliantly colorful with gold, silver, reds, crimsons, deep blues and greens intricately woven into multi-patterned fabrics, rugs and clothing everywhere. The noise was deafening with all the bartering and chattering from the hordes of people buying and selling. The smell was a bewitching mix of oriental spices and dank bodies.

I tried hard not to stare at the strange sights before us: the pitiful blind beggars holding their tin bowls and sticks, the Indian Muslim money exchangers, and the ubiquitous sellers aggressively enticing us into their shops.

We did notice wrist watches everywhere – lots of imitation Rolex and Omegas. The captain warned us to barter for anything we wanted to buy and even walk away if we didn't think the price was right, but to watch out for the seller who might run after us and offer a much reduced price. He impressed on us that the merchants tend to lie terribly about the carat of gold and to beware the temptation of buying jewelry.

There was a booth for everything in this long, narrow, confined alley – bags, clothes, electrical goods, carvings, cobblers, locksmiths, and special engraving. There were even fresh fruit sellers manning stalls of the most ugly-looking fruits – one was called Durian and had a green/brown melon-like shell covered with huge evil-looking spikes. The opened ones were emitting the most unpleasant, overpowering odor which must have belied the creamy yellow custard-like flesh. How could something that ugly and malodorous be called the King of Fruits?

We passed fabric stalls where women were in the back hunched over frantically sewing at their machines. The captain told us many of the pilots could be measured for a suit in the morning and it would be finished and ready for pick up that evening – perfectly cut and stitched and for an unbelievably low price.

Once we extricated ourselves from the far end of this noisy riot of humanity, we left the bazaar behind us and wandered the busy streets.

Sadly, this arcade with all its character and old oriental charm has now disappeared having been razed in 1989 and replaced with a modern, sterile complex of shops and offices. How thankful we are today that we were traveling in the Sixties and able to visit all these old colorful institutions in their heydays.

Captain Edwards led us across a nearby bridge to Collyer Quay from which we saw a postcard scene of barges, sampans and junks lazily traveling back and forth on the flat calm water. Larger ships and tankers were anchored further out in the bay. We enjoyed the water views but the late afternoon heat was soaring to unbearable temperatures and we all agreed to hail a taxi and return to the hotel.

That evening Captain Edwards generously offered to treat the crew to dinner in the hotel dining room. Everyone attended – all ten of us, the four pilots and six cabin crew members. The captain asked the waiter to recommend some uniquely Singapore dishes, which he did with a happy grin. He disappeared into the kitchen but soon appeared carrying a huge white platter. He explained that this was Teochew-style Bak Chor Mee – flat yellow noodles covered with pork slices, mushrooms, meatballs and beansprouts. This was placed in the center of the table and he retreated again and returned bearing a second dish with Satay Bee Hoon – a chili-based peanut sauce poured over fried fish cakes and kang kong shoots. This unusual vegetable, he told us, is a river spinach or swamp cabbage. That didn't sound too appetizing but actually tasted very sweet and mild.

We bravely sampled a little of each and enjoyed the different tastes and unusual aromas. Then came time for dessert and the waiter was excited to bring us two very unusual but Singapore-style dishes. A large glass bowl arrived full of almond pudding covered with longan fruits – these were called 'dragon eyes' and the flesh was translucent, sweet and juicy, and surprisingly delicious. Another bowl was placed on the table and this one was full of Ice Kacang. This was described to us as red beans wrapped with shaved ice, shaped into balls and topped with colored syrup. We thanked the waiter who bowed and beamed at us as we were so appreciative enjoying his native foods.

After that feast we retired to the hotel lounge to relax and watch the entertainment. We stayed for a short while but wanted to see more of the local nightlife especially as it wasn't late. We excused ourselves and taxied to the nearby Adelphi Hotel but found it deserted and ventured further to the New World, a typical local dance hall. Local girls were sitting along the front row of seats and the music sounded like typical English old-time music hall ballroom. We didn't stay there very long but it was interesting to see. Not quite the nightlife we were expecting, so disappointedly we returned to our hotel.

We were up early as we had to don our uniforms for the return flight to Manila. I was working the aft cabin and the purser assigned me to work the galley. I had to prepare a breakfast of omelets and bacon with fresh fruit, warm breads and lots of coffee. We had many Muslims on board who had pre-requested vegetarian meals so I heated those special meals first to free the time for preparing the omelets.

On landing in Manila we were expecting to continue on to Guam per our newly changed schedule. But we were in for yet another schedule change as a Pan Am representative boarded the plane and told the cabin crew to disembark and layover at the Manila Hotel for two days. Objecting was pointless – we just went along with this renewed schedule change.

There must have been a jet shortage due to engine trouble somewhere and we were the one crew that was caught in the right locations to fill in the rescheduled flights. We were getting pretty worn out at this point and on arrival at the Manila Hotel we ignored the pleas from the 'lobby guys' to go partying.

By this time our uniforms and casual clothes were in dire need of washing and ironing. How convenient to pick up the phone and call the hotel laundry service. Within minutes a laundry person came to our door, picked up all our clothes and returned them a few hours later beautifully cleaned and pressed.

Judy and I decided to unwind and relax by the pool. We took our time changing into our swimsuits and cover-up dresses. With our towels hung over our arms, we ambled down the long dimly lit hall looking for signs directing us to the pool area. The arrows directed us through an elaborate white stone archway. We followed a gravel path leading us through a lush, tropical garden littered with dry, brown-splotched leaves.

We leapt in surprise, startled to see the leaves jumping and darting around our feet. We stopped to examine this unusual phenomenon and gasped to see the leaves were actually hundreds of tiny frogs.

These tropical climates certainly breed jumpy, creepy, crawly creatures. Regaining our composure, we carefully maneuvered our way, hopping around these miniscule creatures to reach the pool.

Not a soul was there. Undeterred, we found a couple of empty lounge chairs under the protective canopy of a lush, green tree and spread our towels, laid back and almost fell asleep. Our lazy spell didn't last for long as we were slowly broiling in the scorching heat and sultry humidity, even in the depth of shade.

No wonder we were the only ones out there. We couldn't stand the oppressive heat any longer and soon retreated into the refreshing cool air conditioning of the hotel.

I realized Jay in Guam had no idea we had been held up for these extra days and there was no way to contact him so I hoped he'd understand.

On the flight to Guam I was working in the rear cabin serving a hot luncheon of steak with tiny potato croquettes and buttered carrots to a full load of passengers. Inside I was feeling drained but I was determined to make our passengers feel special. It had been drummed into us that no matter how 'you' feel we still had to take care of our 'guests' and do everything possible to make them feel comfortable and 'at home.'

The fun male purser Charlie sensed I was slowing down. When the meal service was over and the cabin cleared, he suddenly grabbed my hand, put an arm around my waist and danced me all the way down the aisle, turned and led me all the way back to the aft galley. I was taken by surprise and felt momentarily embarrassed, but the passengers loved the entertainment and clapped heartily. Charlie went out of his way to help and the diversion worked as I felt revived for the duration of the flight.

At Agana, Guam, Judy's boyfriend was waiting for her and he told me that Jay had the Night Duty and wasn't able to get free but the next afternoon he called and drove over to the hotel. He suggested we go to a place called Pirate's Cove for drinks and dinner. It was a fun place but I couldn't stay long as we had to be at the airport by nine o'clock that evening.

Arriving at the airport we half expected to be scheduled back to Singapore but were elated to hear we were finally on our way to Hawaii.

I was working the First Class galley but with only nine passengers the service was handled easily. We did have to make an unexpected stop at Wake Island Airfield for a one-hour refueling.

Wake Island is a coral atoll with a twelve-mile coastline sitting in the North Pacific Ocean between Guam and Honolulu. In 1935 Pan American Airways constructed a small village there which was nicknamed "PAAville" to service flights on its Pacific routes. It remained in operation up to the day of the first Japanese air raid in 1942.

We were so happy to be arriving in Honolulu and on our way home. We had a three-day layover first and I was thrilled to see Tina and Roberta who had flown in on an earlier flight. It was always fun and comforting to meet our roommates and classmates in our different layover cities.

I looked at Roberta in puzzlement and asked her, "What on earth have you done to your hair?" It looked shaggy and uneven.

She grinned and explained, "There was a picky supervisor on my flight to Guam and she told me in no uncertain terms that my hair was touching my jacket collar (the big violation!). She insisted I get it cut shorter or I wouldn't be allowed on the next flight."

Tina butted in with, "Well, on that tiny island of Guam there are NO beauty salons and as Roberta and I were rooming together, I

170

took out my manicure scissors and told her to let me have a go! Roberta didn't have much choice and sat quietly while I snipped away, a little bit at a time, with my tiny nail scissors."

"And," Roberta said, "there she was, that obnoxious supervisor, laying in wait for me when we arrived at the Briefing Office. She ordered me over to check my hair, and turned me around to make sure it was short, regardless of how it looked. Thank goodness she was pleased to see it had been cut so I got on the flight. Now I'm on my way to the beauty shop to have it cut properly."

I joined them later for lunch in the Snack Shop which was a small, cozy café on Kalakaua Avenue not far from the Royal Hawaiian. Roberta did look much improved with her new professional haircut. We all ordered the Chili Omelet. This was my favorite meal on the menu and was the best omelet I'd ever eaten though not exactly slimming as it was full of gooey cheese and lots of spicy chili. I felt so worn out that it was just what I needed for an energy boost. After an afternoon on the beach, the three of us decided to go to the local cinema to see Gregory Peck in 'Behold the Pale Horse.' Tina was enraptured as Gregory Peck was her favorite actor.

We were, finally, after fifteen days on line, on our way home to San Francisco. I was working the First Class cabin and when the meal service was over, a young passenger brought out a ukulele and started singing. The other passengers didn't seem to mind. There weren't any television screens and movies to watch so entertainment of any kind was always welcome.

After all that time together it was quite sad saying goodbye to the girls in our crew, especially Judy. With only four stewardesses not counting the pursers, we had lots of time to get to know one another and form close short-term friendships.

I picked up my suitcase and walked away to find a taxi to Burlingame and home to our apartment.

Mail was waiting on the table and I opened an official-looking envelope with the Pan Am logo on the front. I was thrilled to read I had passed my six-month probation period!

27.

BANGKOK, THAILAND

I was headed to Bangkok, the capital city of Thailand, where we would enjoy a three-day layover. The flight was the 'Round the World flight One.' The passengers on these flights were usually well dressed – the gentlemen in suits and the ladies in smart dresses and sometimes hats. Even the children, few as there were, dressed up in their best outfits.

On the leg from Tokyo to Hong Kong to Bangkok one of the passengers in First Class was Mr. Patterson, a senior executive in the Pan Am hierarchy. Despite the added pressure of his presence, the services went perfectly and the passengers were extremely appreciative. Flying into Hong Kong at night, it looked like a fairytale city of twinkling lights, in contrast to Vietnam where we could see the explosions and flares of battle flashing far below us.

In Bangkok we were staying at the Siam InterContinental Hotel on Rama Road, which in the Sixties was owned by the Pan American InterContinental Group. Architecturally unique and elegant, the hotel sat on twenty-six acres of the Sra Paduma Palace Gardens, and was a breathtaking sight as we approached in our Pan Am mini bus. The oriental pagoda-style roofline was unique and the hotel was surrounded by the most vivid, perfectly manicured landscaping of exotic vines and flowers in a riot of radiant reds and crimsons, deep oranges and brilliant yellows – a garden resort.

Bangkok was the meeting place of the two main Pan Am bases. The New York crews flew the Round-the-World flights half-way, through London, Africa and India, and the San Francisco crews flew west across the Pacific via Japan and Hong Kong, and the crews met in Thailand.

Mr. Patterson appeared in the spacious hotel lobby with its enormous vaulted ceilings, and approached our newly arrived crew. He smiled broadly and told us how pleased he was with the excellent service he'd received during the long flight from Tokyo. As a 'Thank You' he had arranged a special Klong Tour for us the following morning.

We were excited about this unexpected treat as most of us had never been on a klong before. So the following day after breakfast in the sunlit hotel restaurant, we met in the lobby ready for yet another interesting adventure.

The local driver maneuvered us through the mayhem of bustling traffic to the floating market klong. He told us a klong is a canal and Bangkok was known as the 'Venice of the East' because of the many klongs that served as streets through the city. Sadly, in the name of 'progress' many have now been filled in with concrete to make roads for all the cars.

Our small bus stopped alongside a busy canal and the driver helped us out. We had to carefully climb down some narrow wooden steps to a small unstable-looking dock, and then clamber into two flat-bottomed boats with a guide sitting in each. Once settled we floated off down the waterway. We couldn't help notice how murky the water looked. The boat guide told us in broken English it was cleansed of the sewage and waste by the tidal movements of the Chao Phraya River – it didn't look very clean to us!

The klong was a patchwork of color and cluttered chaos as a multitude of boats clogged the narrow waterway – it looked like a Los Angeles freeway in slow motion. The boats were filled to the maximum, struggling to stay afloat under the weight of their wares. They were stacked high with exotic fruits and foods laden in baskets of all shapes and sizes. Even small barbecues were emitting heat and wafting smoke as delicious-smelling foods were being tossed in huge woks and sold from boat to boat. All around

173

us we saw a sea of flat-topped straw hats bobbing up and down on the heads of the many boat peddlers.

We were enthralled. The fragile-looking boats hung so low in the water we were amazed we didn't see any submerge. We held on tightly, hoping we didn't capsize and sink into the sewage-laden water.

As we paddled forward dangerously weaving our way through this tangle of boats, we saw many rickety, low, wooden shacks crammed along the klong banks – hanging precariously on stilts with fragile steps leading down to the water's edge. These were peoples' homes. And the families living in them used the river for *everything*.

Our eyes opened wide as we saw naked children peeing into the water, washing and bathing in this huge communal klong bathtub. Mothers were bent over at the base of the wooden steps scrubbing their dirty laundry in the same water; the 'clean' clothing hanging out for all to see from makeshift lines strung along the canal's edge. Yet, despite the hardships as we saw them, they were all happy, smiling, laughing and having a good time.

What shocked us more was seeing the klong people lowering their well-worn pots and pans into this unsanitary water and hauling them up for use in cooking and probably for drinking as well. We just couldn't believe it.

Maneuvering unsteadily through this circus of klong activity, we noticed many beautiful temples further along the water called 'wats.' They were glittering brilliant gold in the glaring sunshine. The guide told us they are covered with gold gilt decoration and many roof tiles were small green and orange mosaics. Tall needle-like spires rose from each, pointing toward the heavens.

We truly felt we were in another world and were saddened to have such an inspiring, surreal tour come to an end. We reached our destination and had to leave the fascinating klong life to board our waiting bus and return to the international sophistication of our hotel.

The next day the four girls from our crew met for breakfast in the Golden Palms restaurant. We eagerly planned a trip to explore the local temples and squeezed into a small taxi for the short ride. We marveled at the incredible awe-inspiring golden spires, and were fascinated with the groups of monks walking around in their brilliant saffron-colored robes and shaved heads.

There were many stalls outside the temples selling rubbings taken inside the shrines. I riffled through the ornate designs of animal and temple architecture until I found the one that stood out from the rest – a vertical design with three elephants intertwined and beautiful in its simplicity. I purchased it and carried this masterpiece all the way back to San Francisco where I stowed it away until I could get it framed.

Later in the day Elke, a blonde vivacious German girl, was impatient to venture downtown to buy a set of Thai brass cutlery. She'd heard about the shop from a stewardess friend of hers, who had already bought a beautiful set of this cutlery on a previous trip. She asked if I would like to join her and I was only too pleased to go along to check out this 'Bargain of Bangkok.'

We scrambled into a small cab and asked for Silom Road, the address Elke had for the store. The driver cleverly wound his way through and around the congestion and snarls of noisy traffic. No-one stopped for anyone and there were cars, bicycles, carts and scooters all vying for a place on the road. We sat in the back seat hanging on and shut our eyes at many chaotic intersections. Before long the cab braked to a halt and the driver pointed to the street sign, so we happily paid him and jumped out onto the bustling sidewalk.

We jostled along looking for the shop named "Starrys" and soon saw the sign hanging above a wide open doorway inviting us inside. The small interior was dark and warm but looking around we found ourselves surrounded by beautiful sets of wooden-handled brass cutlery. Many intricate, elaborate designs and sizes were set in beautiful satin-lined wooden boxes, and looked very expensive. Elke explained what she was looking for and the charming Thai saleslady was so thrilled to have a customer that she busily opened wooden boxes of sets all across the counter. I was quite taken with the combination of lustrous rosewood handles and rich bronze blades, forks and spoons.

Elke eventually saw the set she was looking for. The saleslady told us, in a serious tone, that this complete set for eight, one-hundred-and-two pieces, including tall iced-tea spoons, and twelve serving pieces, all laid out in a heavy wooden box lined with deep pink satin, would be twenty-four dollars! We simply couldn't believe it. That's all? On hearing that, I started taking a serious interest in buying one for myself. This was an outstanding deal.

We looked at each other and tried not to sound too excited. The saleslady was grinning widely when we ordered a complete set for each of us. I was very pleased with my bargain purchase but now had to figure out how to lug it along with me for the rest of the trip.

The box was very heavy but did survive the flights home tucked in behind the last row of cabin seats. I have enjoyed using that special set of cutlery every year since, especially during holiday celebrations.

Every time I lift the lid to open the box there is an unmistakable scent of the Orient emanating from the depths and transporting me back to those wonderful days of innocent travel and adventure.

28

MILLISECONDS FROM DEATH

Six days off! Karin and I luxuriated in a sauna bath and unwound with exercises at the local gym. I bought many aerograms at the local post office and wrote long-overdue letters home. This form of stationery was far cheaper than using letter paper and envelopes and was sheets of thin blue airmail paper which when folded over and sealed along the edges, negated the use of an envelope – unheard of today. I handed over my photo films to Greig, a good friend also residing in our apartment building. He worked for a photographic company and generously offered to have them developed and did so for most of us.

During this break, Mary came home one early evening from a ten-day trip to Australia. She dragged herself into the bedroom changed out of her uniform and put on something comfortable.

We heard a rap at the door and jumped up wondering who it could be. We opened the door cautiously and there stood Barbara and Karin. Barbara looked ashen and hurriedly explained that she had just been through a terrifying experience. Karin was very concerned and thought it was a good idea for Barbara to come over and share her story.

Mary made some tea, opened a packet of gingersnap cookies, and we sat down around the kitchen table. By now we were anxious and curious to hear what had upset Barbara so much as she sipped some tea and struggled for a deep breath.

"The most frightening thing happened while I was working the aft cabin on the evening flight from Hawaii to Los Angeles."

Barbara drank some more hot sweet tea and continued, "We had an unusually full passenger load and as the flight neared Los Angeles I stepped into the lavatory to replenish the supplies for the passengers, and to freshen myself before our arrival. I was standing there before the mirror putting on the mandatory lipstick and back-combing my hair when I felt the disorienting sensation of my whole body being sucked down toward the floor. I couldn't fight it and found myself cramped in that confined space completely dazed. I felt as if I weighed three-hundred pounds, and, much as I tried, just couldn't lift myself up off the floor. Instinct told me this must be some kind of gravity effect, but I was scared stiff and felt totally helpless trapped on that lavatory floor all alone."

We sat listening with quiet thanks that it hadn't been us in this situation and wondering what we would have done.

Barbara continued, "I was stuck to the floor and the thought struck me that I must look like something out of a horror movie with my hair sticking out in backcombed tufts." It was so typical of our training that Barbara, like most of us, would be concerned about her appearance at such a time.

"I was terrified when I felt the sensation of my eyes glazing over. I became light-headed and felt the dizzy feeling of blacking out. My mind was filling with the awful thought of 'was I going to die?'"

Her voice choked with the memory and we were all listening in disbelief, but she continued, "My whole body went limp with an eerie 'out of body' experience, as I felt myself slowly rising off the floor. I grabbed hold of the sink to steady myself and stood up groggily. I was breathing fast, and my heart was thumping loudly in my chest. I stared into the mirror and was horrified at the sight of my hair. I knew I couldn't appear in the cabin looking like that.

"Hanging on with one hand, I tried to comb my hair and flatten it with the other. At least I looked more presentable. What do I do now? I thought. I hesitated to open the door afraid of what terrible chaos and wreckage I would find in the cabin."

We sat around the table in stunned silence – our tea had become cold and the cookies uneaten. Barbara continued her story.

"I sensed I had been very close to death. I slowly and cautiously opened the lavatory door and peered out. My hand flew to my face as the first thing I saw was the purser laying flat on the floor, and a female passenger slumped over an aisle armrest. The passengers were totally silent and flattened into their seats. I felt myself draining into shock.

"I was sinking into a bizarre dream. In surreal slow motion, the cabin crew rose from the floor and out of their seats.

I was instantly energized on seeing a near semblance of normalcy returning and bravely stepped into the cabin.

"Within seconds, true to the grit of the Pan Am flight service girls, although as equally scared as the passengers, we slowly walked the aisles and tried to offer smiles of reassurance. We knew something very wrong had just happened but somehow were able to restrain our own troubled emotions. The senior purser took charge and pragmatically ordered us to start making coffee in both galleys to keep us busy. With brave faces and shaky legs we handed out cups of steaming hot coffee, trying valiantly to convey the feeling that everything was back to normal.

"Not surprisingly some of the passengers were feeling airsick but amazingly, with ninety-one passengers on board, not a single person had been injured. Amazingly, there was no panic even though no-one knew what had happened – not even the cockpit crew at that point.

"The cockpit door suddenly opened and two of the pilots, the second officer and the student navigator, rushed frantically down the aisle. Their voices choked as they told us their unnerving mission was to check that the engines were still intact, not twisted on the wing pylons, and that the wings were not damaged!

"They stopped in their tracks as they couldn't believe what they were seeing. The stewardesses were calmly handing out cups of coffee. We still had no idea what was happening but kept telling ourselves the pilots must know what they were doing, although we weren't too reassured by their actions. We were thankful at least to hear the engines were still attached to the wings! The pilots were stunned, explaining that it was quite remarkable due to the incredible forces the aircraft had just experienced."

We sat silent.

"I can't believe there wasn't sheer panic in the cabin. It was dark outside and the passengers looking out the windows said they saw the stars whirling in the sky. An alarm bell had been ringing loudly in the cockpit, and the noise level in the cabin had increased dramatically.

"We all prayed fervently and quietly for the rest of the flight until the plane landed safely. We were so relieved to get out of and well away from that aircraft. We had to continue on and board another plane to fly up to San Francisco, as if nothing had happened."

We just looked at her and couldn't believe she was alive and relating this horrifying tale.

Barbara later learned the cause of the incident was never entirely explained, but that the plane had suffered major electrical failures, flipped over onto its back, and gone into a spiral dive for more than two vertical miles. There were some reports of CAT (clear air turbulence) in the area which may have contributed to the loss of control. The plane dropped from an altitude of 37,000 feet, inverted (rolled on its back) at least twice, and attained an indicated airspeed of 433 knots, 498 miles per hour. The pilots miraculously recovered normal flight at an altitude of 16,000 feet. They ultimately climbed back to their assigned cruising altitude and continued on into Los Angeles, landing safely there. The entire event took place in one minute and a half, just milliseconds from total catastrophe!

Flight recording instruments indicated the plane pulled 4.33 positive Gs, which equals the maximum safe G load for a 707. A human in normal conditions pulls one G standing on the surface of the earth. Most people are unconscious at 5 Gs. Thankfully the positive Gs forced passengers back and down into their seats, and prevented them from flying about the cabin and becoming seriously hurt. One pilot reported later that some passengers holding coffee cups during the event did not lose a drop of coffee.

There was no significant damage to the aircraft and no injuries to the passengers or crew – a demonstration of the superb airmanship of Captain Evarts and his first officer and the excellence of Boeing's designs.

Over the next few days in mid-November 1964, all the local and national papers were carrying headlines: CAB Probes Wild Dive of Airliner with 102 aboard (including crew); Airliner's Close Call in Pacific; and Jetliner's Terrifying 2-Mile Dive.

After this disastrous flight and near-death experience, the cabin crew received NO extra time-off between their scheduled flights; not one person from the company or the Transport Workers Union (we were required to join this union) followed up with them to determine their experiences, or state of mind, during or following the incident; and most amazingly, not one of the stewardesses involved elected to stop flying or quit the airline.

How differently this incident would be handled today – fifty years later.

Barbara was haunted by this aircraft. Reporting for her next scheduled flight, after only *four days* at home, she glanced up at the airplane on the runway and almost hyperventilated on seeing the Clipper name, bold and black, above the first class windows.

It was the same plane!

She was a wreck, but had no choice but to board and begin work in the cabin. She kept telling herself that the jet had undergone an extensive inspection. But she was very aware during the entire flight of every unusual noise and motion. Her nerves were frayed at seeing the emergency exit lights flickering throughout the flight and reported it to the cockpit crew but they seemed totally unconcerned. For the second time, she was thankful to land safely and get off this seemingly jinxed airplane.

During her layover in Hawaii she ran into the young pilot/student navigator who was on that ill-fated flight. He confided to her he was on his *very first flight* with Pan American and was thinking throughout those terrible seconds in the cockpit, "Here I am on my very first and very last flight with Pan Am." He honestly felt he was facing the end of his life.

Barbara went on in her career to become an accomplished private pilot and flight safety instructor. She knows only too well that 16,000 feet of altitude is a dangerously thin margin in a 433-knot inverted dive at night over the ocean.

29

HAWAII, GUAM, SINGAPORE

After hearing Barbara's disturbing story, I was quite happy to report for an Emergency Refresher Class at the airport. It was mandatory to take these courses every six months and we did appreciate the opportunity to keep up-to-date on the safety procedures. I also had to report to Medical for another cholera shot; it was imperative to keep vaccinations up-to-date as well.

Arriving in Hawaii on the way to Singapore, I was surprised to run into Gunnel and roommate Mary at the crew hotel. The three of us spent the day on the beach soaking up the sun and swimming in the cool ocean water. Gunnel was bursting with the news that Kate had become engaged only months after our graduation. According to Gunnel, Kate had met her fiancé when she had been re-scheduled to deadhead on a flight from Honolulu to Sydney and arrived in the hotel lobby on her own. She was perusing the postcards on the reception desk counter and no doubt looking ravishing with her blonde hair and her suntan-bronzed skin. A tall, athletic-looking young man also standing in the reception area took notice and was duly impressed. He didn't hesitate to walk up to her and ask her to join him for dinner that evening. She readily accepted. And that was the start of a jet-paced relationship. Gunnel told us he came from a wealthy family and was on a traveling spree before attending Harvard Business School.

Kate was living her dream – and ours too!

We reported at the Briefing Office to pick up a charter flight to Guam. The flight was a Peace Corps group of one-hundred-and-thirty young people. The Peace Corps had begun recruiting just two years earlier in 1962.

The crew became irritated from the start because, for whatever reasons, the 'kids' took forever to board the plane, dawdling and slow to take their seats. This behavior delayed our take-off time.

Once airborne we were disappointed and aggravated to see these hand-picked representatives of American youth crowding the aisles and clambering over the seats, totally lacking in consideration and manners. We had to tolerate their very demanding attitudes, and witness them verbally abusing the purser when he tried to control them for everyone's safety.

During the lunch service I was balancing meal trays in my hands while carrying them to this unappreciative group, who despite being asked repeatedly to stow their bags under their seats, had casually dumped them in the aisle. I was trying my best to dodge these obstacles but my foot hit a bulging bag and I tripped. By some miracle I hung onto the trays and managed to salvage the food. (Food trays were not taken from an aisle cart as they are today).

The entire cabin crew was not impressed, and saddened that these young, ill-mannered people were ambassadors of America. We wondered how could they possibly teach developing countries about cross-cultural understanding?

On landing in Guam we couldn't wait to get off the plane and leave that obnoxious group behind. We felt sorry for the new crew taking over and warned them what to expect.

At the hotel I called Jay but his ship was still out at sea and due back in that afternoon. It was such a glorious hot sunny day the crew decided to drive over to the USO beach to lay on the rafts and watch the fish. It was so relaxing to lay there in the sun while bobbing lazily on the crystal clear water. We were fascinated by the shoals of beautiful, colorful fish darting around beneath us –

constant flashes of brilliant blue, black and white stripes, sunshine yellow and orange.

That evening Jay returned my call and drove over to the hotel. It was good to see him again and we went out for a casual Mexican dinner and later went for a long walk in the moonlight along one of the sandy white beaches.

Two days later we boarded the flight to Singapore. The flight was uneventful with the service running smoothly. We had a well-tuned crew and we worked well together which wasn't always the case.

The four stewardesses, Eva from Germany, Marit from Sweden, Alice an American and me, were eager to see as much as possible during our three-day layover in Singapore. After breakfast the following morning, we decided to find a taxi and take a tour of the area. We approached the young man at the hotel Reception desk and asked him what and where he would recommend visiting. He had many ideas and we hastily made a note of his suggestions.

The weather was very warm and mildly humid so the four of us dressed in cool summer dresses. The hotel bellboy hailed over a taxi for us and we squeezed into the small, cramped vehicle. We tried to explain to the Indian taxi driver where we wanted to go. He told us to call him Rajid and he happily gave us a running commentary in broken English as he drove haphazardly through town. He amazed us by maneuvering through serious traffic congestion, narrowly missing running rickshaws and wobbly bicycles, careening around numerous deep potholes and aimlessly wandering sacred cows, and all on the poorly maintained roads inside and outside the city.

After jouncing around inside the taxi, we sighed with relief when Rajid turned into an extensive driveway and explained that we had arrived at the first destination – the Tiger Balm House of Jade. The four of us poured out of the taxi, gave him a generous tip and asked him to please wait for us. He grinned and replied, "Me wait here." We hoped he would.

Before us was The Jade Museum, an oriental-style building, property of the famous Aw brothers who came from Burma and made their fortune in Singapore. Once inside the darkly lit building we were awed to see this priceless collection of jade and in so many delicate colors – green, pink, blue, grey, and white. I had only ever seen green jade. A short, skinny tour guide introduced himself and escorted us around the showroom. He looked very official in his white uniform. With a permanent grin he explained to us in English with a definite accent, "Jade turn color – pale mean bad luck and if color darken it mean good luck." We learned that the higher the iron content, the greener the color.

He continued to tell us, "Chinese rub jade Buddha stomach every morning and only diamond hard enough to cut jade and should have 'crack' type mark to prove it genuine."

The guide led us to the more precious jade pieces which were displayed in tall glass cabinets and represented every important dynasty of China.

I would have loved a small green jade elephant but the prices were astronomical. We enjoyed the learning experience, thanked the guide profusely for his knowledge and for the tour, and headed for the exit door.

In 1979 this collection was donated to the National Museum of Singapore and sadly, the historical mansion was demolished in the 1980s to make way for a posh condominium complex.

Stepping outside into the bright sunlight, rising heat and damp humidity, I saw before me, along the entire length of the curving stone pathway, a line of Indian-looking men. They wore colorful loose robes with white turbans on their heads and were chanting and playing pipes while slowly lifting lids off tall circular straw baskets. I had definitely not seen them there when we arrived.

To my horror I saw huge curling snakes writhing out of the depths of the woven baskets. My legs seemed suddenly heavy and stuck to the ground, I was frozen in place.

My irrational fear of snakes goes back to my seeing an adventure movie at the age of nine – a school outing to the local cinema. We had no televisions at home and this was my very first visit to a movie house and my first experience of seeing a projection on such an enormous wide screen. The movie was about jungle animals and after seeing all the lions, elephants, and tigers, there suddenly appeared an enormous boa constrictor writhing toward the audience – its menacing ugly head filled the entire screen. For me, so impressionable, young and unfamiliar with these hideous creatures it was a horrific, nightmarish sight which haunts me to this day.

The charmers continued their chanting and played their pipes enticing the snakes to coil further out of the baskets and I was still rooted to the pavement. The other girls ran ahead seemingly oblivious of the spectacle and there I was left behind by my fear. The taxi driver, Rajid, must have realized what was happening. He yelled in some unknown Indian dialect and with flailing arms motioned the charmers to stop and put the snakes back in the baskets.

Amazingly, they did.

Once the lids were securely in place, Rajid approached and gently led me down the path to the waiting taxi. I threw myself in and slammed the door.

Rajid drove on to our next destination and stopped the cab at the Street of the Dead in the Chinese quarter. The entire street was a row of open wooden doorways leading into the Chinese death houses. Those who were near death waited inside for the end of life while watching their coffins being carved. Rajid told us the Buddhists keep their dead in the houses while the family mourns outside. We peered respectfully through the gaping openings into the dark interiors but all we could see were candles glowing around the coffins which were lying on top of old wooden trestle tables.

Not long after our visit, later in the Sixties, this incredible street of death, culture, and history was demolished for the construction of a new highrise development!

Rajid asked us if we minded a detour to the Tiger Balm Gardens. He was a happy soul with a permanent gap-toothed grin who was enjoying our outing as much as we were. He parked his cab along the roadside and reassured us that he would wait for us.

We braved the heat and higher afternoon humidity and entered through an impressive Chinese gateway where we stopped to read the Chinese saying 'Kindness begets kindness and Evil begets evil.'

Further along the path we read a bigger sign that told us the gardens were opened in 1935 to teach traditional Chinese values. The same Burmese brothers who owned the House of Jade, Aw Boon Haw and Aw Boon Par, built the garden to create a theme park of Chinese legends and stories depicting scenes from Chinese mythology.

One scene was particularly gruesome at the Ten Courts of Hell. A reminder for children to behave themselves or they'll end up in one of the pits of Hell – being boiled in a vat of oil!

We wandered along the pathways and noticed many colorful birds, their songs making a happy musical backdrop as we stopped to admire all kinds of statues and many enormous Buddhas. There were beautifully carved concrete animals standing guard outside caves or dotted over the hillside. Our impression was that the park had a look of Disneyland about it. Many families were enjoying afternoon picnics on the lawns under the trees, while children were running free and climbing over the stone animals – from large snakes to horses and crouching tigers. We were fascinated by a huge pavilion which looked like a giant parasol floating in air.

As we meandered around the sprawling gardens, we noticed a thin little Indian boy, about seven years old, following us. He was wearing ragged-looking pants, and a tattered tee shirt. He persisted in tagging along and I couldn't resist taking a picture so I opened my camera and took a photo of him grinning from ear to ear. Marit told me to sit with him while she took yet another photo and again he sat there grinning happily. We continued on with our walk but he kept following us yelling loudly and angrily about something. We couldn't understand what he was upset about and he stubbornly continued the wailing and became quite annoying. He refused to leave us alone.

Marit and Eva finally realized he probably wanted 'payment' for us taking his picture. I delved into my purse and found some coins and without hesitation he stretched out his scrawny little arm. I put the coins in his grubby little hand and he sped off across the dry, brown grass in great haste. Thank goodness. But we learned a lesson.

Rajid was patiently waiting for us when we found our way back to the car and said, "Botanical Garden next." On the way he drove us up a narrow winding road to Mount Faber, the second highest point in Singapore. We enjoyed the feel of a gentle cool breeze as we stood there at the peak and drank in the romantic views of the wide expanse of the Indian Ocean on one side and the South China Sea stretching before us on the other. We could hardly believe we were seeing such breathtaking sights and they seemed more real with the buzz of cicadas and shrieking of exotic birds all around us.

This was becoming a long day but we braved the intense afternoon heat and again squeezed into the tiny hot taxi and Rajid drove off to the Botanical Gardens. The gardens looked like a jungle in some areas with lots of monkeys swinging and jumping free in the trees and bushes. However, our fascination was soon dampened when he explained to us that many of the monkeys are captured and exported for medical research.

After that depressing information, we meandered on through acres of manicured gardens and our spirits lifted on seeing the most exotic, tropical orchids growing everywhere in a profusion of colors.

By this time we were tiring and becoming uncomfortably hot. There was no air conditioning in the taxi and we were ready to return to the hotel. On the way back we were driving along some rough dusty roads, when, with no warning, Rajid slowed to a stop. On the roadside we saw three local women covered from head to foot in loose-fitting, colorful clothing crouched on the ground surrounded by baskets full of a fruit we'd never seen before. With curiosity we climbed out to see what they were selling. Rajid picked out a handful and surprised us by buying some for us to taste. They looked like lichen fruit which is a typical Malaysian fruit with a very bitter kernel. The pinky red skin was rough and prickly but Rajid showed us how to peel it off. The sweet whitish pulp fruit was delicious in a tangy way and helped give us a needed energy boost.

Rajid's generosity left quite an impression on us.

On approaching the hotel, Rajid pulled up to the curb, jumped out and opened the car doors for us to descend. We thanked him profusely and offered him a very generous, well-deserved tip. He gave us a little bow and appeared saddened as we waved goodbye and disappeared through the main doors.

What another unforgettable day in Singapore!

We left early in the morning for our flight to Saigon. When the plane landed at Tan Son Nhut, three unaccompanied American children were boarded – all boys between the ages of seven and ten. They were seated together in First Class and we kept an eye on them as far as the next stop in Manila. It was pouring down heavy tropical rain when we touched down and I had the job of escorting the boys to the transit lounge. We were hopping through puddles on the tarmac huddled under an enormous umbrella, but once inside I was able to leave them in the safe hands of a Pan Am ground representative. Once they were officially signed out of my responsibility, I grabbed another umbrella and braved the relentless rain and dashed out to the plane and climbed aboard.

Our captain came out of the cockpit and regretted having to inform us of a change of plan. We all sighed! Instead of heading for the comforts of the Manila Hotel, we had to disembark, find our luggage, and take a minibus to Clark Air Base. Traveling in that monsoon rain, the air was unbearably muggy hot with clammy humidity. There was no air conditioning on the bus so off flew our jackets, gloves and hats. It was a very quiet ride as we conserved our sagging energy.

The bus stopped at the guarded military gatepost and the driver showed all necessary identifications before we were allowed to continue. On arrival at the small terminal an official informed us we had a two-and-a-half-hour stopover.

We felt wilted from the oppressive heat and humidity until Alice suggested we head for the beauty shop and have our hair done. The girls perked up hearing that. We asked for directions and as we were on a military base we didn't have far to go to the one and only salon. The Filipina ladies were happy to fit the four of us into their schedule and with fans buzzing stirring the heavy air, it felt so good to be pampered that we opted for manicures as well – no nail polish. The charge was $2.50 each!

The girls boarded the plane looking like a crew of Barbie dolls. We all had the identical short, backcombed hair style and felt far too glamorous for a MATS flight to Guam. We felt so refreshed we didn't mind another half-hour delay waiting for a very important military documents briefcase to be delivered on board.

After a routine flight to Guam, I did get to see Jay for a brief visit before he had to report back to his ship.

At the hotel I noticed Mona and Tina were booked into a room together so they must have worked on the same flight. I left a message for them at the front desk and when they checked back in they stopped by my room to say hello. The three of us decided to go to The Office, the new coffee shop, to relax and visit. Mona was looking horribly sunburned and I asked her, "Where have you been to get burnt like that?"

She replied laughing, "Tina and I put on our swimsuits and walked down toward the water. We found a perfect spot with some lush grass under the palm trees, so we spread out our towels and lay down to soak up the sun."

Tina added, "We were chatting away in our Swedish and Norwegian, when all of a sudden this big truck came driving straight toward us, screeched to a halt, and a huge Guamanian man jumped out of the driver's seat. He scratched his balding head and yelled at us, 'What in hell are you doing – you are laying in the middle of the road.'"

We had a good laugh over that story. It didn't look like a road to Mona and Tina but they very quickly covered up, picked up all their belongings and sped back to the hotel.

Next stop was Honolulu and three days to unwind on the beach. I decided to spend an hour or two soaking up the sun in front of the Royal Hawaiian. I was quietly relaxing on the sand and, becoming too hot, went in for a refreshing swim. I came out of the water feeling cooled and invigorated, settled down on my towel and thought I heard a male voice from behind me calling, "Can I join you?"

Was it 'me' being asked? I hoped not as I really wanted to be left alone. My reaction was to ignore whoever it was and lay back on the beach towel. That didn't work as 'he' appeared and sat down next to me. I felt a bit silly when he informed me he was the Navigator, Todd, who had flown in on the same plane from Guam. These pilots look very different in swimming trunks after seeing them in uniform! Todd looked muscular and tanned and I noticed soft brown eyes under his dark crew cut. We talked for a long time and he asked me to join him for supper later on and I readily accepted.

After a fun dinner at a Hawaiian hangout where guests cooked their own steaks over a huge barbecue, Todd suggested we wander over to the Queen's Surf to see the entertainment. He was disappointed as Kim Lee wasn't performing that evening but he wasn't deterred and suggested we enjoy the balmy night air and walk on to see Don Ho at the International Marketplace. Don Ho was a local Hawaiian and becoming quite a star with his popular song "Tiny Bubbles." It had such a catchy tune – *'tiny bubbles in the wine, make me happy, make me feel fine.'* We had a good time and Todd escorted me back to our hotel and left me thinking how very charming and decent he was. Sadly though, our paths never did cross again.

The next day, I flew home to San Francisco.

30

HOLIDAY TIME

During time off between flights I received a phone call from Roberta inviting me to San Francisco to celebrate an American Thanksgiving dinner with her roommate and other friends. Luckily the friends, Dick and Anne, lived down the Peninsula near San Mateo. I was pleasantly surprised when they phoned and offered to pick me up on the way so I could drive into the City with them. I happily accepted.

Thanksgiving was a new American experience for me. Roberta explained it is an annual tradition of giving thanks and celebrating the harvest of the year. Everyone was helping in the small, cozy avocado-green kitchen (in the Sixties avocado green and gold were the 'in' colors). Dick was spooning chunks of savory stuffing into the cavity of a huge turkey, Roberta was busy preparing yams, her roommate Terri was in charge of a corn succotash dish, and Anne was covered in a large white apron preparing a cranberry sauce and lots of gravy.

When the turkey was done and the side dishes cooked, we adjourned to the dining area, just off the kitchen. In the center of the table was a huge cornucopia of fresh fruit. Grace was said before the feast and Dick gallantly carved the golden-skinned turkey at the table. Every dish tasted so good, especially the yams which I'd never eaten before. The dish seemed so decadent mashed with butter and brown sugar with tiny browned marshmallows on top. For dessert Roberta had bought a large Pumpkin Pie, a dessert unknown to me, but with dollops of whipped cream it tasted custardy, spicy and delicious. The meal reminded me of our traditional roast turkey Christmas dinner at home in England.

After it was all over and we couldn't eat any more, we helped clear the table and wash the dishes. Roberta offered to drive me home as she was driving that way anyway on US 101S to visit with old friends in Santa Barbara for the remainder of the holiday weekend.

I was realizing how lucky I was to have had Roberta as an American roommate in New York. She had exposed me to so many experiences I might not have had otherwise.

Next day, I planned a visit to the Scheduling Office to ask Dwayne, our favorite Scheduler, if there was a chance I could fly over the Christmas holiday and possibly through Guam. I hoped to be on line and working as I knew I would miss my family and all our holiday traditions in England. Dwayne was surprised but guessed the reason for Guam. He said he'd do the best he could. Dwayne was bombarded with girls begging for flight routes that enabled them to visit boyfriends and he good-naturedly tried his best to accommodate us all. In the office, I ran into Pam, another English stewardess, and I was so pleased when she offered to drive me home in her boyfriend Bob's sporty red car.

A few days later it was Gunnel's birthday and she had a small Swedish party to celebrate. Two of her Swedish friends Solveig and Lottie, came to join Mona, Tina, Mary and me. The table centerpiece was a very special Swedish Princess cake, a dome-shaped sponge cake layered with raspberry jam, lots of whipped cream and covered with a thin sheet of green marzipan with a pretty pink marzipan rose on top. It was absolutely divine. We tucked into wafer thin Swedish ginger cookies, Swedish Marybou creamy milk chocolate and lots of champagne, followed with cups of very strong Swedish coffee. No wonder we had to endure weight checks every few months.

Tina told us how upset and embarrassed she had been with her weight gain at one of these mandatory weight checks.

194

"To make matters worse," she said, "I received a formal letter telling me I was taken off line for a whole month or until I reduced my weight to the acceptable level. I was so distraught that a few days later I left San Francisco and flew to Sweden to spend the time at home. I felt it would be easier to lose the weight there than in this land of large portions and rich food."

We told her we had been wondering if she would ever come back and how happy we were to see her again and her new svelte shape.

Roberta called deeply upset and sounded subdued and down in spirits as she explained her friend Terri was in the hospital with cancer.

The phone rang again and I rushed to pick it up. My heart beat fast when I heard Dwayne's voice on the other end. I crossed my fingers hoping it was the call I'd wished for. Dwayne kept me in suspense by answering very slowly, "I have a Singapore trip for you, via Guam, leaving in one week."

I was ecstatic and shrieked with delight and Dwayne said, "Just say thank you." And I did, over and over again. What a wonderful man he was – always trying so hard to juggle schedules to fill all our requests. I'd be away for ten days, working over Christmas, with a layover in Guam too, and the possibility of seeing Jay.

In the meantime, Roberta invited me to have dinner with her and her father who was visiting for a few days before the holidays. He was a charming man and a well-reputed architect. Roberta was still torn apart over her parents' divorce and now the added strain of her friend Terri in the hospital. I stayed overnight and the next day I was honored to be invited to join them at the Opera House to see Josef Krips and the San Francisco Orchestra. Josef Krips was an Austrian conductor and violinist and led the San Francisco Symphony from 1963-1970. The Opera House surprised me by rivaling the old theaters in London. It was a stunning white building in the French Renaissance style with colossal arched windows. Inside I was impressed with the huge vaulted and coffered ceilings and golden sweeping balconies. It was quite breathtaking and in such a striking setting the performance was outstanding. I was lucky to enjoy such a special holiday outing and thanked Roberta and her father for including me.

Mary was scheduled to fly over the Christmas holiday as well so we decided to have our own early English Christmas dinner. We invited the girls from our class who were in town – Barbara, Roberta, Tina and Gunnel, making six in all. We only had four chairs but we improvised by using our two suitcases and upended them with a cushion on top.

Mary and I spent the morning stuffing and roasting a turkey and covering it with rolls of bacon. We roasted potatoes, boiled Brussels sprouts, made lots of gravy and apple sauce.

My thoughtful mother had mailed a generous chunk of my favorite rich dark fruit Christmas cake with marzipan and hard royal icing on top. Amazingly it arrived through the postal system intact. Everyone enjoyed a sampling for dessert. We were used to dried fruit cakes and marzipan and I found out later that most Americans were averse to such a combination. We had a very good time but missed our English traditional pull crackers, paper crowns and silly mottos.

Gunnel was in good spirits and told us about meeting her latest boyfriend. "I was sitting on the beach in front of the Royal Hawaiian with three other girls soaking up the sun in our bikinis. Three Air Force pilots strolled by, most likely checking out the girls, and asked us into the bar for drinks. But I didn't want to do that, I wanted to swim. I asked, 'Who'd like to go swimming with me?' One fellow said YES and followed me into the water. His name was Don and I found out that he hated swimming. But we really hit it off and had such a good time." She was looking forward to seeing him again.

I had to excuse myself and finish packing for the long trip to Singapore with a nine forty-five report time that evening. Ed offered me a ride to the airport which I yet again was thankful for. The Floribunda guys were like brothers to us all, but becoming more than brothers to some. By now Tina and Grieg were dating and seeing a lot of each other.

Roberta arrived in Hawaii on a later flight and in the morning she called my room. She was energized with the idea of hiring a car and driving across the island of Oahu. The plan sounded like lots of fun and I had another layover day and readily agreed to go along.

After breakfast we headed to the nearest car rental and Roberta picked out a white Thunderbird convertible. Off we zoomed with the top down, racing along the coast and exploring the less-traveled roads of the island. The lush hills and bays were beautiful with spectacular views of the Pacific Ocean and crashing surf. Toward the north end of the island Roberta veered off onto a rural side road leading inland and we drove through a flat plain of the central valley with not another vehicle in sight.

We were enjoying the warm sunshine and the wind in our hair. I loved exploring all these exotic new places. We had no cares and lost track of time.

But not for long!

Much to our chagrin, away in the distance the sky was rapidly clouding over to a foreboding, gloomy grey. The temperature cooled noticeably and we started shivering. 'Splat' we felt the first big fat raindrop. In no time at all we were caught in a sudden downpour. It was raining in sheets and by the time Roberta had cursed mightily and figured out how to put the roof up we were soaked through. We were only wearing short muumuus and sandals and now we were drenched and cold and trying very hard not to let it bother us. Back in the now damp car but under the roof cover we soon forgot our woes. Despite the noisy windshield wipers swishing back and forth in constant motion, we did see more breathtaking, though blurry, scenery.

The monsoon-like rain wasn't letting up, so we were happy to see signs of civilization ahead. We returned the car which now had a musty wet-upholstery odor, and hailed a taxi back to the hotel.

When we walked through the lobby, we passed by an enormous gilt-edged mirror hanging on the wall behind the reception desk and had to laugh at how sopping wet and bedraggled we looked. Our hair was plastered to our heads and our clothes were stuck to our bodies. We did not resemble the image of the Pan Am stewardess!

One quick glance in that mirror and we knew we had to get our hair done before our next flights. We rushed along to the hotel beauty salon and begged and pleaded with Andre to please fit us in as it was nearing his closing time. Much to our relief, he grinned at our plight and said, "Yes, I can see you do need help – so who's first?" Roberta offered to begin the transformations.

After an hour of washing, drying, primping and backcombing we looked much restored. I had a three forty-five in the morning pick-up time for Guam and Roberta was leaving on a different flight to Tokyo.

At the Briefing I was surprised and happy to see Gunnel had joined our crew. It was always fun to have a fellow classmate on the flight, as it happened so rarely. I was working the aft cabin with a full load of passengers and helped serve a waffle and fresh fruit breakfast before landing at Wake Island. We were on the ground for forty-five minutes to refuel due to head winds. From there we served a snack and arrived in Guam at ten a.m. at the Andersen Air Force base.

We checked into the Cliff Motel and I called Jay but the ship was still out and not due back for an hour. Gunnel, Raiku, Asa, and I went to the USO beach and lazed on the sand. Later in the afternoon I heard from Jay and he drove over to the motel. Gunnel and Mike, one of the pilots, joined us and we went out for a casual dinner and on to the Pirate's Cove for a drink and a game of shuffleboard.

Jay and I wandered down to the beach. It was close to Christmas and I pulled from my purse a little package in which I had a small sliver of English Christmas cake I had carried all the way from San Francisco. It was part of the larger piece my Mother had sent and we had enjoyed at our Christmas dinner in Burlingame. The cake had survived the long voyage by mail all the way from England and again survived being crushed in my suitcase all the way to Guam. How crazy I must have been as I had it all wrapped up to give to Jay – a Christmas present of sorts. I saw it as a piece of my heritage and never gave a thought to the fact that Americans don't care for dark rich English fruit cake, especially covered in marzipan and royal icing. I explained what was in the package and he graciously thanked me – but didn't open it. What his real reaction was I'll never know, but can certainly guess!

The next day Gunnel was on her way back to Hawaii and happy to be seeing her boyfriend Don. Jay was out at sea for a few days so I spent the time relaxing by the pool. I had to get to bed early because our crew had to leave at three-thirty in the morning to get to the airport and board the passengers for the flight to Manila.

From Guam to Manila I worked the First Class galley, busily preparing omelets and chicken livers, warming rolls and making fresh coffee for sixteen passengers. The Purser and Raiku poured champagne and orange juice, and made Bloody Marys for those who requested them.

The seat tables looked festive this time of year as we decorated each place setting with a little wood-carved red Santa placed next to a white Snowman. They had movable heads and adorable, individual hand-painted expressions. The passengers loved them and were thrilled to keep them as mementos of the flight.

The plane had to make a short refueling stop in the Philippines before proceeding on to Saigon. En route we served champagne and finger sandwiches to only two passengers.

Captain Thomas treated this trip leg like a military mission and was quite clear that he didn't want *any* of us leaving the plane in Saigon. Asa was downcast on hearing that and pleaded her case that her husband was serving in the army and had scheduled a stop in Saigon to greet our incoming flight. With that news the captain did relent and let her dash off to see the husband in the terminal for thirty minutes before the flight continued on to Singapore. Under the circumstances, we were happy she was able to have a few minutes with him.

We arrived in Singapore on Christmas Eve and were driven to the Intercontinental Hotel Singapura on Orchard Road. In the hotel lobby Captain Thomas surprised us by inviting us to his room for a crew party.

After drinking Bourbon and 7 UPs the girls decided to leave and go to Change Alley for some shopping. We piled into a taxi and startled the poor driver by singing Christmas carols all the way. To compensate for our exuberance we paid him a dollar each (a very generous tip) and he dutifully returned an hour later and happily picked us up. I was pleased with myself as I bartered for a wood Slazenger tennis racquet for eleven dollars. Probably a knock-off but I didn't care. We also found some streamers and sparklers and took them along to a second crew party in the captain's room before dinner. I don't think he was too pleased when the girls lit the sparklers and tossed streamers all over his room.

Pan Am had organized a special Christmas Eve dinner for the whole crew at the hotel's "Four Lions" restaurant. For this special occasion we dressed up in our best dresses and heels and were ushered into the main dining room. All ten of us, including the captain and pilots, were seated at a long elegant table covered with a deep red and gold cloth. The menu had been pre-selected and the waiters soon arrived with a colorful array of local foods and set them before us.

We were in wonderment with the most unusual dishes presented in delicate china bowls and platters, with exotic smells wafting from each. We all wanted a sampling of everything. The dishes were piled high with flat minced pork dumplings in a delicious sauce, small crabs sitting atop thick tomato chili gravy, big prawns with a peanut sauce and noodles, and a delicate steamed chicken in rice scented with ginger. All the food was delicious and the most unusual, memorable Christmas Eve meal I had ever eaten.

Following this sumptuous feast we retreated to the adjoining lounge where a local five-piece band was playing for entertainment. We relaxed and listened to the strains of Asian music but when we heard a lively Beatle's beat, we found the energy to step onto the dance floor and had fun dancing with the pilots. Exhausted, we sat down and sipped hot coffee and after-dinner drinks. The next program performance was a colorful floor show of local singers followed by a spectacular acrobatics performance. We sat there spellbound by their daring, intricate feats.

After this memorable Christmas Eve, we retired to our rooms and slept soundly.

It was Christmas morning when I awoke – in a strange hotel room in the middle of Singapore, on the southern tip of the Malay Peninsula in Southeast Asia. It felt just like any other morning. No thrill of seeing a Christmas stocking hanging on the end of the bed, no Christmas tree and no holiday breakfast awaiting me with my family.

I was happy to be working and keeping busy on such a special day. We were called early as we had to meet in the hotel lobby at seven for our pick up to the airport. I was assigned to work the aft cabin and I kept thinking of my family back home and how I wished I could be with them while here I was on an airplane half way around the world flying from Singapore to the Philippines. It all seemed rather unreal.

The first leg was a three-and-a-half hour flight and we only had thirty-six passengers. We served many special-request vegetarian meals plus the regular breakfast. I was fascinated by three Buddhist monks traveling with us and was enchanted with their brilliant orange saffron robes and their humble, serene demeanor.

We arrived at the Manila Hotel in the afternoon. We found our rooms and slept till six o'clock that evening when the wake-up call jarred us and we hurried to dress and meet the crew downstairs. The captain invited the crew to Stan's Bar and treated us to a new experience – Chloroform cocktails – a decadent mix of vodka, ice cream and coffee. In the heat they tasted so creamy cool, refreshing and good. Later we enjoyed a light dinner in the restaurant to celebrate Christmas.

The following day we lazed around the pool and I was thankful the holiday was over.

31.

SNOW SKIING WITH MARY

M ary and I were meeting many young men – but it seemed to us that one of the first questions we were asked was, "Do you ski?" and we had to admit that, "NO – we don't." And we had the distinct feeling that our negative, though truthful, response was the damper on any future friendship. We were getting tired of having to say 'No' to these potential boyfriends and/or dates. There are no mountains in England so neither of us had any reason to ski.

It was evident that most of the people living in the San Francisco Bay Area grew up learning to snow ski. No wonder, being so close to the Sierra Nevada mountains, roughly nine-thousand feet high at Lake Tahoe, the largest alpine lake in North America. With the mountains only a three-hour drive away, we thought it was time we learned this new adventurous sport.

We had scheduled time off together and made plans to drive to Lake Tahoe and explore this mountainous area. We rented a car and were advised to go to Squaw Valley which was the site of the winter Olympics just a few years before in 1960. We packed our bags full of layers, warm sweaters, and thick socks. We left in the wee hours of morning with our map at the ready, and took turns driving.

As we climbed higher and neared the lake we saw the towering snow-clad mountains reaching high into the clear blue sky. The brilliant sunshine transformed the scene into a snow-sparkling paradise. All this breathtaking scenery was just a few hours from

San Francisco. Fortunately for us, the roads were clear of snow and ice so we didn't have to deal with the hassle of putting chains on the car tires.

We stopped at a roadside gas station and asked for directions to Squaw Valley. It wasn't far away and we soon saw the impressive mountain resort entrance. We drove into the snow-covered parking lot, left the car and headed to the main area. The morning-cold air nipped at our faces and we ran back for our heavy jackets.

Not knowing the first thing about the procedure we felt like a couple of novices. Fortunately, we found everything well marked and joined the short line at the kiosk to pay for day-long lesson passes. We were directed to the rental chalet where we were fitted with enormous bulky boots and had very long skis clamped onto our feet. We were handed our poles and, outside, we slowly clomped along the snow-laden path feeling strange and awkward.

We found the instructor waiting patiently with a small group of other eager beginners. He introduced himself as Pierre and he presented an incredibly intimidating image equipped with all his fancy equipment and wearing a splashy red outfit. However, we were determined to learn and make some progress.

The struggling line of beginners staggered up a small slope and we were put through exhausting paces practicing the basics of the snow plow, learning to slow and control our speed. After practicing all morning, up and down continually, we graduated to a higher slope to learn snow plow turns. We were tiring from all the strenuous activity but we were learning fast.

As the afternoon wore on, the warm sun grew weak and soon disappeared behind fast-moving, menacing grey clouds. Big fat snowflakes began falling in a blinding white cloud and we shivered in an unwelcome icy-cold wind which penetrated our jackets. GOOD, maybe now we can ski down the hill and head for a warm building to thaw out. But NO, despite the increasing cold and decreased visibility, the resolute instructor kept us out there on that freezing mountainside and continued on with the class.

Our feet were numb and our hands frozen. The wind gained momentum. Snow gusted past us with such force we had a hard time standing upright. The lesson became a torture session.

The class finally rebelled and the instructor reluctantly caved in and stubbornly led us down the mountainside so we could escape the bone-chilling cold.

Mary and I slogged through the slush to the rental building and once inside were so thankful to feel the warmth envelop us. We couldn't wait to get all the snow-clogged gear off our chilled bodies but with our bloodless fingers it took twice as long as it did to put it on. Finally free of all the cumbersome equipment, we checked out and went in search of the lodge café. We ordered steaming hot milky chocolate drinks and ever so slowly began to thaw.

Early the same evening we climbed into the car ready for the drive home. We felt the experience had been incredibly exhilarating but Mary was so cold she declared she didn't care if she ever skied again.

We drove all the way back to Burlingame and felt pleased with ourselves that we'd given snow skiing a try.

32.

TOKYO

Mary and I were surprised to be scheduled on the same plane out of Hawaii for Tokyo. It was fun to be working with my roommate in the aft cabin.

The passenger load included a large group of Japanese men returning home after a business trip to the United States. It was a cartoon picture to see them all carrying cameras. Most were extraordinarily large, and some small, dangling from their necks and bobbing on their chests. During the flight these men were up and down in their seats like yo-yos, obsessed with photographing us – but Mary and the Swedish stewardess, Anna, in particular.

We quickly realized the Japanese were fascinated with the girls' blond hair. When we viewed the cabin we saw a sea of their jet-black heads. After a while it seemed both funny and annoying with camera flashes continuously blinding us as we walked up and down the aisle. For nine hours we put up with this constant blinding light, with the ever pleasant smiles on our faces!

Mary and I arrived at the Palace Hotel in Tokyo. We stepped into the waiting elevator and both gasped in surprise as we saw our classmate Mona staring back at us from a poster on the wall. It was a large framed picture advertising the ground-floor restaurant. There was Mona seated next to a handsome young man at one of the restaurant tables. We couldn't wait to return home and ask her how she ended up on a wall poster in the Palace Hotel elevator!

We decided to venture out for the afternoon and shop the Ginza area surrounding our hotel. Again, Japanese men carrying cameras snapped pictures of us as we walked down the streets. They were filming Mary because of her blond hair, even though to her horror it appeared to have a strange shade of green which she felt could have been a mixture of pool chlorine and the dye. Mary was worrying about how she was going to rectify the color before any Pan Am supervisor caught sight of her. She knew it was severely frowned upon to color our hair.

We turned down a narrow street and before us loomed an impressive oriental theater – the ancient Kabuki-za Theater in Ginza. Climbing the steps we saw huge posters mounted along the exterior walls announcing a Kabuki performance that evening. We pushed open the large front doors but there was no sign of life anywhere – the place was completely deserted. We knew we were intruding but couldn't tear ourselves away. We tiptoed around the building and by chance happened upon an open door. Peering inside we were surprised to see what appeared to be a rehearsal of the Kabuki in progress.

I had experienced the one performance in Hawaii but this was taking place right here in Japan and in their very own theater. We were so intrigued by the eerie voices coming from within we felt compelled to quietly step inside the theater itself. We discreetly sat down in seats against the back wall beside the door, and unobtrusively watched what was unfolding on stage, an extraordinary sight to behold; the unique fanciful costumes, acting unlike any we'd seen before on the London stage, strange voices that echoed out the strains of sorrow and happiness in each scene. We were so enthralled we hoped no-one would ask us to leave, and fortunately no-one did.

We had stumbled upon a rehearsal of classical Japanese dance and drama. The actors wore the elaborate make-up I had seen in Hawaii and on this stage they were making dramatic entrances and exits via a hamamichi or walkway extending into the theater. The actors stood motionless with their eyes wide open at the end of each performance. We were fascinated by the clacking sound of the traditional wood blocks which emphasized the importance of the act.

Not a soul approached us. When the rehearsal was over, we quietly stole away, but with a deepened feeling of reverent understanding for the culture of this nation.

The time had passed and evening was approaching so we forewent our shopping expedition and hailed a taxi back to the hotel.

33.

FAREWELL TEA FOR BARBARA

Mary and I planned a farewell tea for our friend Barbara. We invited those of us who were home and Gunnel, Tina, and Mona were happy to join us.

The sad reason for Barbara's sudden departure was another unusual story. Barbara had told us she had been on a recent flight to London, and on arrival at Heathrow, she was asked to stand at the bottom of the ramp to help the passengers onto the tarmac and into the terminal. She was busily occupied with her task when a Pan Am representative rushed up to her and asked if a 'Barbara' was on the crew.

"That's me," Barbara said at the same time wondering why he wanted to speak with her. With forethought the young man blurted out, "Your mother has died!"

Barbara was in shock on hearing this, as her mother was quite well the last she had seen her and was only fifty-two years old. Was this a sick joke?

She was told a car and driver would to take her to her father's home near Brighton. In a daze, Barbara looked for the captain and senior purser to explain what she had just heard and to be excused from the flight crew. They were as startled at the sudden news as she was.

At our tea, Barbara told us she had decided to return and help her father in England. She planned to take a non-flying position with Pan Am in London.

209

To lighten the mood we soon turned to our most recent adventures. Mary and I bombarded Mona with questions about her picture being in the Tokyo hotel elevator. She laughed and explained, "When our crew checked into the hotel, we were all invited to attend a special dinner in the brand new restaurant that evening. The invitation sounded like one not to be missed so we dressed up and headed downstairs where we were escorted to a long table. I sat next to the handsome first officer.

"To our surprise a photographer appeared and began taking lots of pictures of us, explaining that one would be selected as an advertisement for the restaurant. I never thought another thing about it.

"Pan Am crew members kept approaching me and asking, 'Where do I know you from?' and, guess what, 'They had seen me in the elevator at the Tokyo Palace Hotel.'"

That solved the mystery for us.

Mary and I told them about our harrowing ski excursion at Lake Tahoe. Gunnel was bursting with news of her own ski adventure with her boyfriend Don, the American Air Force flight officer.

"Don too asked me the inevitable question, 'Do you ski?' And being from Sweden, I answered, 'Of course I know how to ski.'"

Evidently, Don got nervous because he knew he didn't ski well, and here was this ravishing Swede who was probably an ace skier and he didn't want to appear unable to keep up with her. Gunnel admitted to us she wasn't that good a skier either but she didn't tell Don. Don invited her to Lake Tahoe for a day of skiing and an overnight at a lodge before driving back the next day. "That sounded like lots of fun," Gunnel told us, and she agreed to go.

"On the drive up to Tahoe I told Don, 'I want separate rooms for us!' Well, when we checked in at the Lodge they told us there was only one room left and on hearing that my heart sank but I insisted, 'It has to have two beds.'"

This wasn't going her way as Don explained there was only one bed in the room and it was a King-size bed.

They skied the mountain all afternoon under a clear blue sky. Don was so happy to find out Gunnel was no better a skier than he was, and she was just as relieved, so they had a lot of fun on the lower slopes. All the while though, Gunnel was dreading the oncoming night in the one-bed room.

With skiing over they entered the lodge and headed for their room. Gunnel took one look at the one and only bed and immediately set her boundaries.

"I insisted that one side of the bed was mine and Don was not to make a move over to my side. And that is what Don did. He acted the perfect gentleman and as ordered, dutifully stayed on his side of the bed."

But Gunnel told us she was thinking, 'Well, what kind of man is this – he could at least have *tried* to make a move toward my side of the bed and I was, in fact, quite disappointed that he didn't.'

We all had a good laugh over that story and the fickle female mind!

Gunnel admitted she told all the American guys she was Italian when she first arrived in California because when they heard she was Swedish they automatically assumed she was into free and open sex – which was all we heard about coming from that country in the Sixties. We wondered how any fellow believed her as she looked classic Scandinavian with very blonde hair and fair skin.

I ran into our bedroom and brought out my elephant brass rubbing from Thailand and proudly showed the girls my treasured purchase. Mona took one look and knew of the perfect frame shop for such a thing in Tokyo of all places. I didn't have a scheduled trip there but Mary did, so she offered to take my precious rubbing on her upcoming Tokyo flight and deliver it to the frame shop for me. Mona gave us the name and address and I could easily pick it up on a future Tokyo trip. That settled my dilemma.

As we were talking about Tokyo, Tina started laughing and told us she had wanted to buy a pair of shoes there. That was the place for stylish, pointy-toed shoes. Tina grinned as she told us, "I was sitting in the shoe store and the sweet little sales girls were giggling a lot with their hands covering their mouths. I looked at my feet and realized they probably had never before seen such big feet. After that I knew there would be NO shoes in Japan for me."

She added with a grimace, "Some of the shops in Japan seemed to have incense burning all the time and I felt sick every time I entered through the doors." It just smelled funny to her but we all agreed it didn't seem to bother us.

Many of us were buying beautiful Thai silk in Bangkok and many of us had Thai-tailored dresses and pantsuits made at unbelievably low prices. I had a straight shirt-dress with long sleeves made in a shimmering teal shade of blue and green.

"I can't even wear the Thai silk as it doesn't agree with me. The fabric gives me bumps all over," wailed Tina.

We chatted on for a while and finally wished Barbara well in her life's new chapter. We all vowed to keep in touch as we were very sad to see her go.

Mary packed for her Tokyo trip the following day. She very kindly took along my brass rubbing rolled up tightly in a long cardboard tube.

Ten days passed and Mary returned from her Japan trip about the same time I came through the door from a Hawaii flight. I could tell something was wrong as she looked so downcast and I asked, "Whatever's upsetting you?" And she blurted out, "I took your Thai rubbing in the taxi to the frame shop Mona had suggested, but when I jumped out of the taxi, it sped away. I watched it disappear in a blur of traffic and realized I had left your rubbing on the back seat, never to be framed or seen again." She felt awful and I did too, but I did realize through my disappointment that it could so easily happen and she was trying to do me a tremendous favor.

I never did find another elephant rubbing to replace it.

34.

ROBERTA

Roberta was sitting in our apartment when I burst through the door after running some errands. As soon as she saw me, she broke down in a flood of tears and sobbed, "What am I going to do, Terri has died."

I gasped in shock as I dropped my shopping bags on the kitchen counter.

"What! When did this happen?" I asked, unbelieving, as Terri, her roommate and good friend, was our age – a young twenty-two year old.

Roberta was grief stricken and was crying openly now she had the sympathy of a friend.

"Why does everyone and anyone I love get taken away from me or leave me all alone?" she wailed.

I felt for her and didn't quite know how to react.

"I can't go back to the apartment with all of Terri's things there, what shall I do?"

I poured her a glass of champagne as I knew she would not appreciate a good cup of hot English tea.

That helped relax her a bit and we sat down at the kitchen table with the warm sun streaming in the window and through her distress she told me, "Terri had cancer symptoms for quite a while. She had lost a lot of weight and I found her passed out on the bathroom floor."

Roberta said she was panic-stricken but managed to call an ambulance. Terri was rushed to the hospital but there was little they could do.

I was finding it difficult to face the fact that someone so young had died. Especially someone I had seen and talked with not so long before.

Mary was out on a London/Paris trip and not due back for a few days so I offered Roberta Mary's bed for one night but told her she had to go back into the city the next day. Terri's parents were flying in from New York and would need to get into the apartment.

Roberta was wracked with grief and begged me to let her move in with us.

"Roberta, I can't possibly make that decision without talking it over with Mary first." I insisted.

We only had one bedroom with two beds so a third roommate would mean moving to another larger apartment – a major move.

"Please, please try hard and persuade her, I can't live on my own after this dreadful thing happening," Roberta pleaded.

Next morning after a fitful night Roberta felt a little better. Bolstered by a mug of strong black coffee, she was able to drive back to her apartment in San Francisco. She looked pale and forlorn but knew she had to help Terri's family through their grief. At the same time she had to deal with her own emotions.

I loved where we were living and knew when Mary came home I had to broach the subject of moving. Mary returned from her trip. After she had time to unwind, change and have a bite to eat, I told her the whole heart-rending story.

"Oh no!" was her reaction.

Mary wasn't keen at all on the idea of having Roberta move in with us, let alone moving to a larger apartment as she was all for saving money, not spending more for rent. Mary knew Roberta was a free spirit, and her common sense foresaw turmoil down the road.

I argued, "Roberta was my roommate and mentor during training and had entertained me royally on many occasions, so I do feel obliged to help her under the circumstances." After a lot of thought, Mary finally agreed to the move. When I called Roberta she was ecstatic and thanked us profusely.

Roberta lost no time in driving down to see us the next day. She was determined to drive around Burlingame looking for a building with a furnished two-bedroom apartment for rent. Needless to say, she quickly found a furnished apartment, not far from our current one, and insisted on driving us over to see it. Mary and I grabbed our purses and climbed into her car.

Just two blocks away, she pulled up in front of an enormous building. Roberta rang the bell and asked the manager if the three of us could take a look at the furnished apartment for rent. The manager was a pleasant, older grey-haired lady and she welcomed us in. The three of us followed her to the elevator, climbed in and rose to the second floor. We walked along the carpeted corridor to the available apartment. The manager unlocked the door, held it wide open to let us in and showed us around.

Mary and I were wide-eyed in wonder as we wandered through a spacious, bright apartment. There were two large bedrooms and two bathrooms, a larger modern kitchen and more furniture than our current one. Also, the building had a swimming pool. Roberta was grinning and told us, "This is the place, don't you just love it? I think it's perfect for us. I can have the larger bedroom with my own bathroom and you two can share the second, smaller one with the twin beds and the second bathroom."

Mary and I were wondering what this was going to cost us. Roberta must have read our minds and quickly added, "I'll pay half the rent and you two can split the other half. It's the least I can offer for having my own bedroom and bathroom. I really don't mind at all." Mary and I thought that sounded very fair and agreed to her terms and much to the apartment manager's delight, we signed the rental agreement. And that quickly it was done.

Roberta possessed intense persuasive powers. She was so relieved and comforted at the prospect of living with roommates and not left on her own.

And the American wild child moved in with the proper English girls.

Roberta, Mary, and I embarked on a whole new chapter starting the New Year 1965. Burlingame Towers on Belleview Avenue became our new home and we were happy to be only a few blocks away from our friends at Floribunda.

Mary and I didn't have much to pack, having lived in a furnished place. Greig, now Tina's boyfriend, happily helped us move our filled-to-bursting suitcases, and the linens, blankets, pots and pans, my stereo and all the records we'd accumulated. The move required a couple of trips but we were thankful to have Greig help with the lifting, carrying and driving.

Roberta had a lot more possessions and managed to store most of them in her room. Amazingly, we'd managed all of this while all three of us were between flights. After a frenzy of unpacking and organizing we were physically exhausted. None of us felt like cooking dinner so Roberta offered, "Let's go out and eat – all on me, as a big thank you."

We cleaned up and squeezed into Roberta's Corvette and headed for the Skyline Boulevard to the Bella Vista restaurant. We curved up and around the winding roads and finally found it perched on top of the Boulevard surrounded by towering redwood trees. We enjoyed a good pasta dinner in a relaxed atmosphere with spectacular views of sparkling nighttime lights across to the San Francisco Bay.

Roberta ordered glasses of champagne and we celebrated the move to our new home.

35.

VIETNAM

*"It is only those who have neither fired a shot
nor heard the shrieks and groans of the wounded
who cry aloud for blood, more vengeance, more desolation.
War is hell."*
William Tecumseh Sherman

One of my flights into Saigon left a particularly distressing memory. I was on a crew boarding a military charter in Guam which had flown in from Hawaii with a full passenger load of young military personnel destined for Tan Son Nhut airport.

As they boarded the plane we could see the young men were more or less the same age as us. We immediately noticed and commented on how abnormally quiet and withdrawn they appeared. The atmosphere in the cabin became heavy with despair, and as we walked up and down the aisle, we heard many heart-rending comments. The anguish, 'I'll never see the US again,' the despondency, 'I'll be coming home in a body bag,' and the forlorn, 'Please write to me.'

Keeping a happy face became exceedingly difficult in this sea of hopelessness. These young men were about to face the horrors of war and I had the fleeting thought that I was glad to be female and not among them.

For the dinner service we prepared and served the best all-American meal of top-grade grilled steaks with cheesy scalloped potatoes, a green Caesar salad, fudgy chocolate Brownie dessert and lots of cold milk. We tried to make the atmosphere as light-hearted as possible but their thoughts were drawn elsewhere. They had no appetites and at the end of the meal service, we were appalled at scraping plates still full of good food straight into the garbage bags, especially many untouched whole steaks.

The captain announced our approach into South Vietnam, and a sinister quiet seeped through the cabin. We felt it with them – a desolate sense of doom. The cabin became weighted down with an eerie tense silence.

The plane touched down and not a sound could be heard throughout the cabin. We hurried to get on our uniform hats, white gloves, and heeled shoes to bid goodbye to these stricken young men. They moved slowly out of their seats and with great effort shuffled off the plane. We stood at the door with tears streaming down our cheeks as one by one the 'boys' thanked us and said goodbye. Many were fighting back the tears welling in their own eyes.

This flight was the most deeply moving, emotional experience I ever had during my Pan Am career.

There was a war-time curfew hour at the airport and we had to be off the runway and in the air before nightfall at seven p.m. The captain asked us to stay on the plane for our own safety and to prepare for the next load of military passengers to board.

The Vietnamese airport ground crew came aboard and unloaded our bursting-full galley garbage containers. We were standing in the open doorway trying to get a breath of fresh air, and were watching our galley garbage being lugged over and tossed into huge grey dumpsters sitting on the hot tarmac alongside the airport building.

Seemingly from nowhere, we noticed emaciated looking Vietnamese men dart warily across the airfield, stealthily approach the searing hot bins and plunge their bare hands deep into the mess of garbage. We gasped with revulsion as they quickly pulled out the discarded food: the beef steaks, half-eaten bread rolls, and anything edible they could find. They crammed these scraps into sacks they had carried with them and disappeared as quickly as they had come.

This grim sight brought us the sickening realization that these people were so destitute they were forced to rely on our garbage for their survival. I later learned that some of these men were probably not eating the food themselves but were more than likely selling it for money!

Time passed, the plane received a thorough cleaning ready for departure, and the new group of military men embarked.

What an emotional difference!

These young men were the survivors. They were thrilled to be leaving and so happy to be done with the terrors of war. The cabin atmosphere became light and joyous.

The engines roared and the plane sped forward. The instant we were airborne the plane filled with deafening cheers and loud upbeat clapping. What a night and day difference from the silent flight we had brought into the hell of war and the boisterous departure of the lucky survivors. They were jubilant to be leaving the agonies and death behind them.

The first thing these young men asked for was MILK. They were desperate for milk and when we served them, they kept saying, "Oh my God, is this real milk?" Every drop of that precious substance had been drunk by the time the flight was over and they still yearned for more.

Unexpectedly, as we walked the cabin and talked with many of the men, it became sadly apparent that not all of them were joyous about their return home. We patiently listened to stories of heartache from those who received news from wives who had strayed and girlfriends who had broken off relationships. Others were left wondering if their wives or girlfriends would even show up when they arrived. Some appeared shattered and we struggled to bolster their feelings as best we could.

These were very sobering experiences for us young and naïve stewardesses.

I was lamenting about these tragic stories to Mona, Bonnie, and Tina over a pizza lunch in Burlingame not long after that trip.

Tina (who had been Kate's roommate) told us of Kate's unforgettable experience on a plane at Tan Son Nhut airport. "A ground person approached and requested Kate to stand at the top of the First Class ramp by the open doorway as they were expecting a VIP passenger to board. She was instructed to greet him and be absolutely sure *not* to touch him. Evidently there were hordes of children and people waving palm branches and flags. As she was standing there on high, surveying the vast airport area before her, Kate noticed an unusual number of armed guards standing at attention around the perimeter of the airfield.

"All of a sudden, the VIP passenger emerged from the terminal surrounded by even more guards. Kate was informed that this was the top Buddhist Monk in South Vietnam. He was dressed in flowing, glittering golden robes. Kate watched his slow approach to the airplane and was standing right next to him as he reached the top of the ramp. Tina said Kate had told her, 'Here I am a sitting duck for a target for any wild man down there trying to shoot this fellow.'" As it turned out, Kate was quite unharmed and survived to tell the tale.

Mona had a different and more traumatic experience when her plane landed at Da Nang, a military stronghold to the north. As the crew disembarked some military officers approached and asked the crew members if they wanted to go with them to the military hospital closeby and visit some of the American soldiers. The whole crew of pilots and stewardesses willingly agreed. Some of the girls wanted to take something with them to give away and with the captain's permission, they climbed back aboard the plane and picked up all the discarded magazines, newspapers, playing cards, and anything else they could find. They took all of it with them to hand out.

Mona told us, "We were asked to climb into a military jeep and on the way to the hospital one soldier said, 'Look up the hill there – you see the smoke? That's the Viet Cong shooting.' Hearing that statement scared me to death. We eventually arrived at a small white building which was the hospital. We were led inside and I will never forget seeing rows upon rows of beds and all the badly injured men laying there covered in blood-soaked bandages. Their haunted eyes followed us and they were all so thankful to see us and to have visitors. We were there for only half-an-hour making small talk and we left feeling so small, helpless and sad. All of us were subdued, wrapped up in our own sobering thoughts, as we walked back to the plane."

Tina finished her pizza and told us a different story. She had been surprised when, on arrival in Saigon, the military guys on the ground came up to the plane and asked for all the unopened milk cartons they had left. Second to milk, a lot of them asked for cans of hairspray. With no hesitation the girls raided their bags and parted with their precious hairspray wondering whatever they wanted it for. When they asked they found out embarrassingly that they were contributing to the local sex trade!

"We couldn't figure that out and asked the Pan Am pilots what it meant, and they readily explained to us that the hairspray could get a guy some relief at night, or whenever, with a 'not for free' girl, as the girls were only too happy to get their hands on some good American hairspray. We were even more embarrassed hearing that.

"We flew into Da Nang too," Tina added, "The crew was allowed off the airplane and it was unbearably hot, muggy and very dirty. There were soldiers all around us and one fellow took me into the trenches. They were telling me they practiced target shooting on the Pan Am blue ball logo on the tail of the plane. I often thought of that afterwards during take-off and landing, and it wasn't a comforting thought. It was quite exciting and surreal at the same time, and I took lots of pictures. I knew this was against the rules, but found out later that I had no film in my camera anyway."

Bonnie became very quiet as she recalled a very sad sight at Tan Son Nhut. "There were dozens of metal caskets lined up on the tarmac awaiting loading into the C130s to be returned home. Some, I was told, would have very little of the soldier in them."

Many flight crew members had thought we should receive hazard pay for flying in and out of the war zone. Then we learned that Pan Am got a new Union contract. The pilots received hazardous duty pay, and flight service staff got a promise that our bodies would be shipped home for free!

JET CLIPPERS MEAN NEW SPEED, NEW COMFORT
A NEW CONCEPT OF THE WORLD YOU LIVE IN

Come with us to meet a new miracle. A miracle with graceful swept-back wings. A great and powerful sky giant — a new kind of air transport that can make all your most wonderful worldly dreams, and many you never thought of, all come true.

It's Pan Am's magnificent new *Intercontinental* Jet Clipper — fastest, largest, longest-range Boeing 707 on the Pacific — introduced by the world leader in air transportation, Pan American.

The above picture and text are from a **Fly Pan Am** handout brochure of the early 1960s.

The front cover of a First Class menu.
One in a series of four clipper ships.

223

Graduation morning.
Waiting for the bus to transport us to the airport. Reidun facing the camera.

Lesley waiting for the graduation-bound bus.

224

Roommates in New York - Louise and Lesley.

Barbara, Louise and Roberta. Note the identical hairstyles.

Graduation Day
Friday, April 17th, 1964.

The Graduation Certificate.

Roommates in Burlingame - Mary and Lesley.

Lesley, Karin and Tina on the steps of 1415 Floribunda.

Lesley, Karin, Gunnel and Barbara in Golden Gate Park, San Francisco.

Karin, Lesley, Mary and Mona enjoying 'tea' and stories.

The Floribunda pool. Lesley on far right wearing the frilly white swimming cap.

Left: Kate demonstrating the Hawaiian hula by the pool.
Right: Mary and Karin in the apartment kitchen.
Note the fancy hats we wore to cover our hair rollers.

229

Above: Lesley amid ruins of Anchorage, Alaska earthquake.

Right: Feeding a kangaroo in Sydney Zoo. See the baby's legs poking out of the mother's pouch.

Below: In the Philippines before entering the gold mine.

Mary and Lesley off to a party.

Roberta, Mary, Lesley, Gunnel, Mona and Tina.

Karin, Greig and Lesley.

Lesley with her pride and joy – the Austin Healy Sprite.

Mary and Lesley on Norman's ski boat in the San Joaquin.

Left: Lesley, a crewmate, and Gunnel enjoying the waters in Guam.
Right: On the beach in Guam – extracting milk from a coconut.

Dan and Lesley's first meeting –
the evening before Dan left for a year's tour of duty in Vietnam.

The Pan Am building in New York with the rooftop helipad.

Five cabin crew members, Purser Lesley second from left, on the tarmac in the Philippines. Our jackets were left aboard the aircraft due to the heat and humidity.

Lt. JG Dan Robson aboard a Vietnamese Navy junk off Phu Quoc Island.

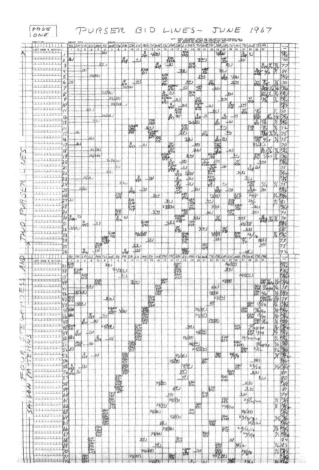

Purser Bid Lines.

Lesley wearing the new uniform.

The Girls in Blue

Almost fifty years later – nine of us together
Mary, Bonnie, Gunnel, Mona, Lesley, Kate, Tina, Edith and Barbara.
(Karin and Reidun were unable to join us from Sweden)

36.

INDONESIA

After six days at home, it was time to pack for our next flights. I was embarking on my first trip to Djakarta, Indonesia. Mary was flying off to Australia and Roberta was packing for Bangkok. They were all long, hard-working trips. I had to pack clothes for ten days away to cover layovers in Honolulu, Guam, Manila, and Djakarta. This wasn't difficult as the climate at all the stopovers was hot and humid.

In the midst of all this commotion, Tina and Mona surprised us by walking over and stopping by for a visit to see our new apartment. Greig had told Tina all about our new home and she was curious to see it.

I was telling them how excited I was about flying to Djakarta for the first time. Tina gave me a grim look and said, "I just returned from there and, believe me, it was a frightening experience and I don't ever want to go back."

I wasn't happy to hear that so we put off packing until later. I gave Tina and Mona a short tour around the apartment while Mary made a pot of tea. Roberta joined us as we sat at our kitchen table and Tina told us her harrowing story about Indonesia the month before.

"The flight was progressing with no problems until our plane landed at the Djakarta airport in the early evening. I eagerly looked out the airplane windows and was shocked to see an angry mob of men crowded on the tarmac. There were so many of them and they were all jostling and shouting loudly. Of course, we couldn't understand a word of what they were yelling. And, worse than the uproar, they were brandishing signs, sticks and poles, and to our horror started hurling big rocks and stones toward our plane. One of the young pilots stepped out of the cockpit, looked at me, grinned, and said, 'Well, Tina, you have a Swedish passport so you're safe, you can open the door.'

"You have to be kidding, I told him, as the noisy, angry crowd advanced toward the plane. It was very frightening to us as well as the passengers. They were up out of their seats and craning their necks to see out the small windows wondering what all the commotion was about. The cockpit door opened again, and we were relieved to see the captain stride into the cabin.

"He took one look at the wild mob about to attack his airplane and loudly ordered everyone to return to their seats and fasten their seat belts. He dived into the cockpit and immediately started up the engines. The plane roared down the runway at high speed and soared off at such a steep angle we were sucked back into our seats. We were so thankful to have made it out of there safely and even the few passengers who were debating the safety of disembarking were cheering even though they were now headed for Singapore."

Tina learned that Indonesia was experiencing a series of uprisings against the strict communist regime.

After hearing that disturbing story I now had mixed feelings about my upcoming trip and my initial enthusiasm drained. We finished our tea, said goodbye to our visitors, and returned to our suitcases and the chore of packing.

Mary and I called a taxi to deliver us to the airport, where we headed to our separate briefings.

I checked in just before the report time and met the new crew. Captain Charles introduced himself, as did the two male pursers, Dennis and Chet. I hadn't met any of the girls before – Carol and Sharon were American, and Helga was from Germany. The senior Purser Dennis asked me to work the First Class cabin with him and asked Sharon to handle the galley. This segment of the Djakarta trip was from San Francisco to Honolulu. Once all the passengers were on board and belted in their seats, Dennis asked me to make the French announcement and Helga followed with the German version.

Sharon, in the galley, had to prepare a multi-course dinner service. There were only eight passengers so we could take our time and really get to know them.

We had Lance Reventlow on board. He was the wealthy playboy, Formula One racing driver, and only son of the Woolworth heiress, Barbara Hutton. She was one of the wealthiest women in the world at that time. Her handsome son was only twenty-eight but stayed subdued in his seat for entire flight. We also had a Congressman from Ohio among our guests.

I handed out the dinner menus and took drink orders. A couple of businessmen sitting together ordered "Bullshots" – a cocktail I'd never heard of. "Whatever is that?" I asked Dennis. Thank goodness he knew what it was and took the time to show me how to make two of them – a mix of vodka, consommé, Tabasco, salt, pepper and lemon. What a concoction! After that lesson the entire drink and meal service went calmly and smoothly.

Three nights later in Honolulu we were picked up at eleven-fifteen for the next leg heading for Guam. In First Class we had five members of The Champs on board. They were a rock and roll instrumental quintet from Los Angeles, and were most famous for their hit "Tequila" sung by Danny Flores, the saxophonist, who also wrote the words. Tequila was a number one hit on both the pop and R&B charts.

Helga, who was helping in the aft cabin, clutched her stomach and started complaining about pains. With seventy-six passengers to feed and take care of, the purser politely told her, "Forget about the pain and get on with the service!"

When we arrived in Guam at five-thirty in the morning and opened the doors, we were greeted with sheets of monsoon rain. Umbrellas were brought up the ramp to protect the disembarking passengers.

During our layover Helga continued moaning about her pains. Sharon and I were becoming concerned and looked for our captain to ask him what we should do. He eyed us warily and said, "Take her to the Naval Hospital to find out what's going on as she can't continue the trip with a medical problem. Get the hotel driver to take you." So Helga, Sharon and I, piled into the Pan Am crew van and were driven to the Naval Base Hospital.

Sharon and I were not amused at spending the afternoon stuck in a hot hospital Emergency waiting room while Helga was being examined by one of the doctors. On looking around we did notice the doctors were really cute young navy officers; maybe that's why Helga wanted to be there.

We sat patiently in hard plastic chairs in the stark, small waiting area. The monotony was suddenly broken when we heard a lot of loud voices and commotion rushing through the glass swing doors of the main entrance.

A large raucous group of locals burst into the waiting room and filled up what little space was left. They were hovering around a huge middle-aged Guamanian woman. She was sobbing and wailing hysterically, flailing her arms wildly and refusing to settle down. She was a mountain of flabby flesh thankfully hidden under an enormous orange muu muu dress. We couldn't help but overhear that her husband had just died unexpectedly but through all the uproar we couldn't understand what had caused his death. Three nurses materialized and tried unsuccessfully to calm this hysterical wife as her theatrics became more disturbing with increased grief-stricken hysteria and louder bawling.

We were so absorbed in the scene before us we hardly noticed Helga re-appear. She was smiling happily and told us, "The doctor gave me some pain medication and told me not to worry." Probably not showing the compassion we should, we hoped that would put an end to her complaints and the driver hurriedly drove back to the hotel and let us out of the van.

That evening the First Officer, James, invited the crew to his room for drinks and two pilots and Sharon began planning a scuba diving trip the next day. I didn't want to be left behind and out of curiosity agreed to join them.

We set out on a beautiful hot sunny morning. We parked the car under some palm trees by the beach and then clambered over a long line of boulders leading into the deeper ocean water. I followed behind and watched them struggling into their scuba gear, and very quickly realized this wasn't an activity for me. I begged off and told them reluctantly, "I don't think I should dive as I've never done it before but I'm quite happy to wait up here and sunbathe on the rocks."

The small group of divers disappeared into the dark depths of the ocean and much as I would have loved to join them, I felt I'd made the right decision. I enjoyed some peaceful time alone for a change and was quite happy to be above the water. I found a flat rock and stretched out on my towel and was mesmerized by all the colorful fish darting in and out of the rock crevices below.

A couple of Guam-related stories come to mind. Gunnel has fun memories of joining a Pan Am crew that planned a driving trip to a small pond in the middle of the island. They spent the day swimming and swinging from a strong rope that was tied to a huge tree limb hanging over the water. Gunnel said hanging on to that rope and dropping into the cold clear water below was so much fun and so exhilarating. I never did discover that secluded spot. Most of our experiences depended on whichever crews we were with and the plans they made.

Gunnel also remembers the horror of seeing a horrifying shark frenzy. On a specific day of the week, the garbage trucks drove to the cliffs, reversed up to the edge and tipped the contents of their overflowing bins straight down into the pristine Pacific Ocean below. Gunnel said she was watching with other crew members from the cliff top and saw hundreds of shark fins racing ominously through the water. She felt very uneasy seeing these massive beasts thrashing and splashing furiously in the broiling waters. It was a scary sight to see their vicious jaws gaping wide as they fought ferociously for the flood tide of good food that suddenly appeared in their midst – as if thrown from the heavens.

On a lighter side, Tina tells the story of surviving a bumpy flight into Guam flying through a typhoon. When the plane landed, thankfully safely, the crew was informed that because of the rough weather conditions, the one and only hotel on the island was not considered safe. The only option was to send them to the BOQ (Bachelor Officers Quarters) on the military base for the night. The girls didn't mind that diversion at all.

The following day we left Guam for Djakarta via Manila, Saigon and Singapore. Pick up was at four in the morning so we were wakened at three and sleepily headed for the shower. In the heat and humidity it was always an unpleasant performance squeezing into the mandatory tight girdles and pulling on nylon stockings.

At the short briefing I was assigned to the First Class cabin and was surprised to see fifteen passengers on the seat chart, all businessmen. We settled them into their seats and before takeoff handed out glasses of ice cold orange juice which was greatly appreciated in the hot cabin at that early hour of the morning.
After take-off we offered flutes of cool sparkling champagne and served a hot breakfast.

At the Manila airport the cabin crew, wearing our white gloves and hats, but thankfully allowed to leave our jackets on the airplane, waited in the newly air-conditioned transit lounge. We could stay refreshingly cool while the ground crew boarded the plane to clean and re-supply the cabins and galleys for the rest of the trip.

The next stopover was Saigon, and as soon as we landed at Tan Son Nhut Helga started complaining again, but this time she was experiencing severe back pains. The captain rather brusquely told her to get off the plane and go to the Naval Hospital. By this time we were convinced she was faking the aches and pains. The captain refused to wait for her and explained that we would pick her up on our return and, much to my surprise, we left without her.

The captain knew we could manage quite well with one less crew member, especially one with her ailments.

We picked up one new First Class passenger, the British Ambassador to Vietnam, who was headed for Singapore. He was the only passenger to disembark when we landed there.

Next stop was Djakarta, the capital of Indonesia, on the north-west coast of Java. I was so excited to be seeing this remote country for the first time. I was relieved not to see any angry mobs on the airfield and the passengers safely disembarked with no incident.

The first officer, in front of the whole crew waiting to deplane, announced in his American drawl, "Well, Lesley, you are the only one among us with a British passport and it's too dangerous to let you into the country. The Indonesian representative here tells me they are stoning the British Embassy!" I was mortified, imagining myself camping overnight all alone in the empty airplane. I must have looked horrified because the pilots all chorused in, "Not really, you'll be coming with us."

They did love to tease and I was far too gullible.

However, we found out just a couple of weeks before our arrival, a group of angry protesters had attacked and burned the United States Information Agency office.

I was so relieved to be with the crew 'family,' especially in this strange, unwelcoming country. Even the weather was depressing with heavy rain pouring down from low bleak clouds.

We faced a long drive to the hotel and our route was lined with enormous threatening billboards. We were looking out of the bus windows seeing hideous depictions of huge gnarly hands in evil-looking chains and jagged lettering underneath that we couldn't translate; others were showing lines of half-starved, peasant-looking men bent over under the weight of chains hanging from scrawny necks. This appeared to be a propaganda campaign inflaming the imaginations of the people. I was reminded of a statement I had read in a book by Jean Jacques Rousseau, 'Man is born free and everywhere he is in irons.'

The atmosphere in the crew bus became hushed and quiet. We were experiencing the uncomfortable feeling that our safety could be in jeopardy even though we were in an official Pan Am crew bus. We continued along the main city roads and the local driver advised us to look straight ahead and *not* at any of the unruly mobs of men shouting and shaking fists at us along the roadway.

We had arrived in the beginning stages of a purge of the Communists, the PKI (Indonesian Communist Party), and mounting pressure to oust then President Sukarno. I was reminded of Tina's story and thought how lucky she was to have avoided landing here.

Adding to the unease was the constant torrent of rain beating against the windows and the flooded roads we were driving through. The water in places came half way up the bus tires and was spraying wildly. We feared breaking down and finding ourselves stranded in this hostile environment.

We finally arrived at the Hotel Indonesia which appeared as an austere rectangular concrete block. We checked in at the reception desk but were disappointed to be informed NOT to venture out of the hotel grounds. It was considered far too dangerous and we were put on *curfew* for the entire stay. There went my plans to explore Djakarta!

My roommate Sharon and I found our room and resigned ourselves to remaining in the hotel. We craned our necks to see what was going on outside. The small double windows limited our view of the flooded river Citarum. Emaciated looking men with fishing nets were surrounded by half-naked children shuffling barefoot through the muddy-brown floodwater sloshing over their ankles.

Even though we didn't feel hungry under the circumstances, we ordered a Room Service meal of Indonesian rice and bean curry for dinner. We ate at a small table on chairs that were straight-backed and hard, chatting away and trying to enjoy the local food.

We choked in shock when the room was suddenly engulfed in total blackness.

We sat there in momentary silence wondering what had happened and whispered our fears to each other sitting there in the eerie darkness. Outside we could hear a massive thunderstorm raging with heavy monsoon rains pounding against the side of the building.

A loud siren blaring throughout the hotel startled us. "Hotel have power problem – STAY IN ROOM!"

Was this an attack on the hotel? Our imaginations were running wild. Slowly our eyes adjusted to the darkness and there were no further warning messages. We calmed down and decided to go to bed as we had an early pick-up at four forty-five. So, per instructions, we stayed in our room and tried to sleep.

The first hints of daylight peeked through the window as the alarm clock buzzed. We were hungry and happy to have the room phone working again and called Room Service. We ordered the American breakfast of orange juice, fried eggs and bacon, toast and coffee. We finished our meal, dressed and made our way down to the hotel lobby to meet the rest of our crew.

The crew bus drove at a painfully slow pace through the rising flood waters. But at that early hour of the morning we didn't see any angry mobs of men threatening us. Thick muddy water was splashing over the windows and again, we were hoping the engine wouldn't drown out and cause the bus to break down.

At the airport briefing our captain looked glum as he was advised the airfield was under water. Not surprising with all the heavy rain still pelting down. We all dreaded being trapped in this hostile place and Captain Charles wasn't about to risk that predicament either, and made the decision to proceed – with caution.

There was a long delay in getting the passengers on board. It was an arduous process in the pouring rain as the plane was sitting way out on the flooded runway. The passengers didn't mind the conditions as they were as pleased as we were to be leaving.

The crews felt a deep confidence in our captains and pilots which was a good thing under these conditions. The majority were ex-navy pilots with the best military training and experience.

The plane doors closed, the passengers and the cabin crew were belted in, and we heard the welcome roar of engines as we slowly taxied down the waterlogged runway, gathered speed and took off. We were elated to be out of that unsettled, angry, troubled country and headed for the safety of Singapore.

Later that year there was an abortive coup attempt and six top generals were killed. This precipitated a violent anti-communist purge in which thousands of people died.

We stayed on the plane at Singapore for the refueling stop before continuing on our way to Vietnam. Arriving in Saigon we saw Helga waving frantically in the terminal. The cabin crew had become fed up with her antics as there didn't seem to be a thing wrong with her. She offered to help us in the aft galley preparing a hot lunch for sixty-five passengers, plus several pre-requested Kosher meals. We did thank her for the effort.

Our flights were with crew members from many different cultural backgrounds, and despite this the stewardesses worked remarkably well together. Once in a rare while there was a definite clash of personalities and it seemed to always affect the entire cabin crew and their service. One instance comes to mind of a flight with a domineering German purser. She set a strident tone by putting us through a full half-hour briefing. We were ordered or commanded to do this and do that. This fostered resentment among the crew so we were all on edge. Unfortunately, this negative mood trickled down and was inevitably felt by the passengers.

In Manila we said sad goodbyes to Captain Charles and the cockpit crew as they were continuing on to Guam while we, the cabin crew, were driven to the Manila Hotel for a three-day layover.

During check-in at the hotel, we were pulled aside by crew members waiting in the lobby to leave who warned us with disturbing stories.

The hotel 'help' had been caught climbing up and peering at crew members through the high windows in the rooms. These were wide narrow windows that were just below the ceiling and opened to the hall outside, and there were no shades or curtains to close them off.

They told us of a Pan Am pilot who was found unconscious in a narrow side alley with his head beaten and his wallet and watch stolen. Fortunately he survived.

A captain had been called in the middle of the night and a mysterious voice asked for the names and room numbers of his crew members which, of course, he didn't divulge.

We had left one alarming situation and had now landed in the middle of another!

Sharon and I were rooming together again and, after hearing these disturbing tales, we lugged a big heavy armchair across our room and shoved it up against the door – just in case someone tried to open the door in the middle of the night and enter our room unannounced. Despite this precaution, we didn't sleep well as the slightest sound woke us.

We survived the night without incident and in the morning ventured down to the hotel dining room for breakfast. A couple of pilots joined us. One, James, told us he'd had his room ransacked while he was asleep and all his money and cigarette lighter were gone. Bob, the other one, was sure someone had turned his door handle but he woke up and shooed them off. They warned us to be extremely careful.

When we were finished with breakfast and the pilots had left, some 'lobby' men wandered over. I knew Tony from a previous visit and he introduced his friend Jose. As before, they looked well dressed and suave. Sharon instantly asked them to join us. I wasn't pleased, but after casual chitchatting they invited us to spend the day with them and arranged to pick us up in the lobby in one hour.

They were there waiting and offered to take us for a drive. How naïve we were, or was it the lure of adventure, taking off with two young men who we hardly knew, in a sleek sports car to who knows where? Tony was showing off his brand new bright red Porsche. Sharon and I were squeezed in the back and Jose followed in his shiny black car. The roof was down and off we sped. The weather was hot but pleasantly breezy.

Tony told us we were headed for the Manila Golf and Country Club. We raced along curving, tree-lined country roads and then slowed in front of massive iron gates. The entry was manned by an armed guard smartly dressed in a white uniform with lots of gold braid. On recognizing Tony he opened the gates and ushered us in.

Sharon and I were enthralled. What a magnificent, opulent setting. Tony took pleasure in telling us we were entering the most exclusive, pre-eminent golf club in the Philippines.

Tony left the car with a valet and we were escorted through the spacious sunlit lobby. The walls sported huge pictures of prominent golf club members throughout the years. We walked along a plush green-carpeted hallway leading to a veranda in which stood a heavily polished, thick wooden bar. Without asking, Tony ordered rum manhattans. We sat at a table from where we could enjoy superb views of the golf course through enormous wide open windows. Heavy brown plantation shutters framed the opening on each side. The course looked extraordinarily lush and green; the grass appeared too perfect, as if cut by hand and the sand traps were filled with snow-white sand. Huge, many-trunked old trees formed umbrellas of welcome shade over the manicured greens.

While we sat there in awe, another of their friends entered the bar and introduced himself as Martin. These young men were dressed impeccably and we were told that Martin's father was the coconut king of the islands. After a while, Martin invited us all to his house. Sharon and I finished our drinks and reluctantly left the plush comfort of the club.

We climbed into Tony's Porsche and zoomed off. Martin led the way in his sporty car with Jose following. We raced along more lush country roads and eventually stopped in front of high ornate-iron gates, this time set into a heavy stone wall. An armed guard approached and on seeing Martin he saluted and opened the gates and the three cars wound their way up a long curving driveway. Acres of luxuriant green lawns stretched on either side and palm trees swayed everywhere. The entire scene seemed surreal, as if we had stumbled upon a Hollywood movie set.

Before us stretched an enormous mansion in the midst of this expansive estate. Sharon and I exchanged glances and raised our eyebrows, speechless.

Martin welcomed us into his lavish home. I had the feeling they were enjoying showing off their wealth and opulent way of living. The spacious marble entry hall was filled with masses of colorful fresh flowers arranged to perfection in huge exotic urns and ornate vases. Delicate sparkling-crystal chandeliers hung high above us. Many rooms led off in all directions. Filipino maids were everywhere dressed in black with crisp white aprons. We entered the 'blue room' where all the furnishings were in beautiful shades of blue which were striking against the polished dark wood floor.

Martin ordered drinks. The atmosphere was very formal and Sharon and I were taking it all in; I felt I was in a dream world. Our drinks arrived, carried in by one of the meticulous maids. They were offered from a huge ornate silver tray in exquisite crystal glassware and we sank back into the plush chairs and tried to relax and converse in this rather strained scenario.

Jose approached and invited me to join him for a visit to a casino in town. I couldn't resist the temptation to see what that would be like – never having been to a casino in my life. I did have flashes of being entirely stupid in taking off with this relative stranger but it was all so exciting with the lure of more adventure. I left Sharon with Martin and Tony but she seemed quite happy and didn't mind my leaving.

Driving toward Manila Jose turned to me and announced, "Gambling is illegal in the Philippines!" This statement prompted dreaded visions of being thrown in jail and losing my 'glamorous' job. But I was powerless at that point to change the plan.

We sped into the city, where Jose jerked to a stop and in one swift motion parked the car. He helped me out and took my arm as we walked down a quiet side street. He guided me down a flight of narrow stone steps through at least three heavy metal doors, the last one having an iron grille over a slit window. Jose seemed to know what he was doing and rapped sharply on the door. Was this a code signal? A pock-marked face appeared through the grille and I could hear metal bolts and bars being scraped back as the heavy door creaked open to let us in. We entered the gambling room. I heard the locks bolted securely behind us. Now I did feel cut off and wondered if I'd ever get out in one piece.

We were soon enshrouded by thick clouds of swirling cigar and cigarette smoke and, through the haze, I could see a lot of well-dressed people huddled around the gambling tables. There was a long wooden bar alongside one wall where many men were seated on stools and drinking heavily. I felt very out of place.

Jose wanted to try the roulette wheel and he was gentleman enough to explain how it was played and let me participate. I had beginner's luck as a couple of my numbers, twenty-one and twenty-six, came up. Black Jack was even more fun. I felt such a novice but we were extremely lucky as Jose had a big win.

Despite my initial fears, my illegal gambling experience turned out to be fun. Jose seemed happy and asked, "Would you mind if we leave now?" I was so relieved to hear the words and replied, "No, not at all."

It felt wonderful to be above ground and in the daylight again.

On the way to his car Jose turned to me and said, "I'm famished and would love to have you join me for dinner." We had a fantastic meal at a cozy little restaurant called Pappagayo's. The wait staff knew Jose well and we were treated with flair. Jose was a real charmer all evening and I reveled in all the attention.

I had the feeling these wealthy young men had nothing to do all day long but amuse themselves by showering stewardesses with their generosity.

How naïve we were and how different back then with no thoughts of rape or kidnapping. Would anyone today venture off with strangers like that?

The following day started out just as hot and even more humid. Sharon and I walked down to the lobby and wound our way to the hotel beauty shop to have our hair trimmed and set. On the way back, feeling uplifted with our new hairdos, we met another of the 'lobby' young men named Joe. He invited us to the bar for a drink and we chatted when suddenly he produced a credit card from his wallet and told us we were welcome to buy whatever we wanted in the hotel gift shop. We couldn't believe what he'd said, and responded, "No way, we can't possibly do that."

Joe was persistent and kept urging us, "Please, have fun and treat yourselves to something special." He practically forced the card in Sharon's hand and told us to go. So, off we went with a twinge of guilt, but he insisted it was supposed to be a gift. We couldn't decide what to buy and spent a long time looking at the many beautiful wood-carved objects, inspired by the culture of the people. A salad bowl set, made from the ubiquitous Acacia wood, seemed the most practical and least extravagant. The set included a large round salad bowl, salad servers, and eight round wooden bowls, all for the very low price of eight US dollars.

Joe was grinning from ear to ear when we returned his card with a shower of gratitude and thank-you kisses. We did later surmise that he or his family probably owned the store.

At noon we met a trio of new 'lobby' guys – Enrico, another Jose, and Santi. They invited Sharon, me, and Helga for lunch at a local restaurant. Sharon and Helga appeared to know them and were eager to go and encouraged me to join them. I did so reluctantly.

At the restaurant they ordered rum manhattans for us all, their favorite drink it seemed. We enjoyed the ice cold drinks and the delicious fresh seafood that followed. When the meal was over, the men wanted to move to a side room. We joined them and sat around in comfortable brown leather armchairs while they began a dice game. Much to our annoyance, they became totally absorbed in their playing and it was becoming very loud and competitive.

Helga was fussing over Enrico, and I was becoming thoroughly bored. When the clock on the wall turned to five o'clock, I had had enough and wanted to leave. I knew I was foolish to walk out alone but I couldn't stand the monotony or the obvious rudeness of the guys any longer. They were still engrossed in their intense game and didn't even see me go.

My first instinct was to hail a taxi, but then I remembered that was strictly forbidden for our own safety. With that option gone, I took a deep breath and started walking. I did know we were only about four blocks from the hotel and once I turned the corner onto the main road I could see the enormous white hotel at the end of the boulevard.

I marched straight down the street as fast as I could and felt the stares and leers from the Filipino men as I hurried past. I hung on tightly to my purse and kept my eyes fixed on the hotel ahead. I soon reached the steps and with a surge of relief ran into the welcoming safety of the lobby. Walking the street alone wasn't the wisest thing to do but I was lucky.

I enjoyed a long cool shower and looked forward to reading a good book before settling in for the night. I put on my black and white striped nightdress, sank into the soft bed, propped up on the pillows, and started reading. Peace didn't last long.

Sharon burst into the room and I was highly embarrassed as she was followed by Enrico, Santi and two strange guys! They squeezed into our small space and I was sitting up in bed with my nightdress on, my hair still curly wet from the shower and feeling very uncomfortable with this unwelcome intrusion.

Sharon apologized and the two new young men introduced themselves. They didn't stay long as I politely refused an offer to get dressed and go out for a late dinner. The lunch experience was enough for one day and thankfully they all left.

The following morning I was very ready to leave for the airport and board our next flight back to Guam. I was assigned to the First Class cabin but we had few passengers.

Two days later we flew back to Hawaii. Helga, after all her aches and pains, had now come down with a bad cold and I didn't feel great either – the price I was paying for having too much fun in Manila. We were both working the aft cabin and despite our maladies managed to struggle through a long lunch service between downing aspirin and cold remedies. How thankful we were when the last passenger disembarked and we could leave the plane.

At the Honolulu hotel I slept fitfully. In the morning I decided to keep going despite fighting waves of nausea in the crew bus on the way to the airport. My system was obviously not used to such a constant barrage of partying and its resultant cocktails and rich food.

I was working in the First Class cabin and fighting off a debilitating lethargy. I had myself to blame. There were only seven passengers so I was able to make it through the next five hours to San Francisco. There were few passengers aft and I must have looked poorly as one of the girls came forward, took one look at me, and offered to take over so I could sit down and rest.

Everyone looked out for one another and helped support each other under *most* circumstances which added to the feeling of 'family.'

After we disembarked and found our baggage, Sharon offered me a ride home as she also lived on the Peninsula. What a relief not facing a long bus ride or the bother of finding a taxi when feeling ill.

In the apartment I found a scribbled note on the dining table that told me both Mary and Roberta were away on trips. Relieved to be on my own, I dropped by bags, collapsed into bed and slept soundly until morning.

Mary came home around noon and coming through the door she looked pale and exhausted. "Whatever happened to you?" I couldn't help asking as she stumbled into the apartment. She dropped her suitcase and bags inside the door, plopped down on the sofa and took off her shoes. I made her a cup of tea while she told me about the long traumatic flight she'd just endured all the way from London.

"I was working in the First Class cabin handing out the grey-zippered Pan Am pouches (each contained an eye mask, travel toothbrush, mini toothpaste and mouthwash) and despite some mild turbulence I walked down the aisle handing out the dinner menus. We finished the drink orders and were just beginning the meal service when the plane hit a severe down draught, dropped and lurched. We were caught unawares and before we could secure the galley, the china went flying around the cabin.

"The noise from all the breakage was deafening. The meals and trays were tossed all over the passengers and the floor. The drinks spilled and the glasses shattered so we had broken glass everywhere. The passengers were seated which was a blessing and there were no serious injuries considering the amount of china and glass flying about."

She drank some tea and continued, "What a mess. I actually levitated and hit the ceiling and bonked my head hard, but amazingly didn't fall to the floor. My head was throbbing but we had to concentrate on cleaning up as best we could. Because of this chaos, the captain had to announce an emergency landing in Winnipeg.

"Everyone was asked to disembark on landing. The passengers weren't happy because it was bitterly cold, and they were holding their jackets and coats tightly to their bodies finding themselves enveloped by an unwelcome arctic freeze. They were led into the airport cafeteria, which thankfully, was cozy and warm. A hot meal was served to compensate for the fact we weren't able to finish the dinner service on the airplane.

"The ground crew took an extra hour to clean up the plane as they had the added task of removing all the glass and china fragments scattered throughout of the cabin. Then they had to re-equip us for the rest of the journey. Passengers and crew were frazzled by the long wait for re-boarding time. Once everyone was back on the plane, the flight continued and we finally arrived safely in San Francisco, well over two hours beyond our scheduled time.

"It was a long day and I've still got a pounding headache."

The phone rang and Mona and Gunnel invited us over to have supper with them. The two of us were not in the mood for cooking so we happily accepted and decided to walk over to enjoy some needed fresh air.

We exchanged our harrowing stories while we ate. Gunnel said she'd also experienced a frightening flight between Manila and Honolulu. She told us, "The turbulence was so strong, tossing the plane up, down, and sideways. It felt as if the plane would break apart under such pounding. I belted myself tightly in the jump seat feeling absolutely scared stiff and seriously thinking, if we ever make it to Honolulu, I'm taking the next BOAT home." We laughed at that, and, of course, she did make it to Hawaii but soon forgot about sailing home to Sweden.

Mona was sure she had just survived the longest flight ever. "We were in Tokyo and had to fly an empty plane to South Korea for a chartered flight back to the United States. After a short flight to South Korea we were surprised to be picking up members of the Philadelphia Symphony Orchestra.

"What a nightmare from the very start. The orchestra members were carrying all sizes of instruments in huge bulky cases and smaller odd-shaped ones. Can you believe they adamantly refused to check any of it as baggage and insisted on taking the instruments onto the aircraft. The captain reluctantly allowed the instruments onto the plane. There were instrument cases everywhere in the cabin. Some passengers held them on their laps – but not many. The larger ones had to be strapped into available seats and that took up lots of extra time and space. After the exasperating delay we finally took off and were happily headed for Anchorage.

"We were only three or four hours out when we heard the captain's voice over the intercom. He was apologizing profusely because he had made the decision to turn back because of unusually strong head winds.

"No-one was happy to hear that. Amid moans and groans from the passengers, we ended up having to make an unscheduled landing at a United States Air Force base in Japan and had to stay there for hours waiting for the gale force winds to die down.

Neither the crew nor the passengers were allowed off the plane because it was a military base.

"To make matters worse, we only had beverages to serve during this long wait. We were all exasperated, the passengers especially, but not one of them was understanding. Someone from the military base did fill up our water tanks but that was all. After what seemed an eternity, we did take off and a long eight hours later landed in Anchorage."

"The *good* news was that, back in South Korea, the captain had taken orders from any of the crew who wanted a box of Alaskan King Crab delivered in Anchorage, and had called ahead with the orders.

"Once on the tarmac the ground staff came aboard and regretfully told us the *bad* news. Because of all the long delays, there was no new crew to take our place, so, instead of having a much-needed layover, we had to keep going and take the plane and orchestra members on down to San Francisco.

"What a nightmare!

"To soften the disappointment, the airport cafeteria had at least made us some ham and cheese sandwiches and lots of hot fresh coffee. After a couple more hours on the ground, huddled in the small terminal, we boarded the plane yet again and started our final flight to San Francisco – another four-plus hours.

"When I staggered home, I could hardly stand on my feet. My one highlight was the big box of King Crab I had brought with me all the way from Alaska. I figured out we had been on duty for thirty-six hours!"

How would the Unions today react to that?

And guess who enjoyed fresh Alaskan King Crab hand-carried all the way from Anchorage for supper that evening?

37.

THE DRIVING TEST

Mary was becoming enamored of an affable Pan Am pilot, Jerry. They had met on one of her flights and we all liked him. They became good friends and he encouraged her to buy a car so she could enjoy some independence.

Jerry drove her to a nearby VW dealership and helped her make a selection. She proudly drove home in a cream colored VW Beetle – very practical and very Mary.

To the other extreme, Roberta owned her shiny, navy blue Corvette convertible sports car. She was so proud of it and was always eager to drive anywhere at any time and I was only too happy to go along for the adventure, always with the top down, giving an exhilarating feeling of California freedom.

As the months passed it became clear I couldn't always be dependent on others, especially my roommates, for transportation to and from the airport. It didn't take long before Roberta cajoled and prodded me to buy a car of my own. It was a huge step to take but I figured out all the finances and it did seem doable.

Before I could own and drive a car I needed a valid driving license. Roberta soon overcame that hurdle. We were both home from flying and she called her friend Butch and asked to borrow his VW Beetle for my driving test. There was no way I was about to take the test in her precious Corvette sports car, or Mary's brand new VW for that matter.

Butch was only too pleased to help and dropped off his well-worn car that afternoon. A bit soon for my liking as that gave me no time to obtain or read through a Highway Code booklet.

But that was Roberta. She didn't hesitate for a moment.

She ordered me to sit in Butch's car and drove straight to the driving license bureau. I was feeling apprehensive as I had *never* driven the car I was about to take the test in but Roberta kept reassuring me, "It's okay, it's not difficult, and you'll pass both tests easily." And, "Remember, you're a Pan Am stewardess and you can handle anything!"

I was having dire memories of the difficult driving test I had endured in England. There was no easy multiple choice written test and, worse, I had to sit in the car and orally answer questions fired at me by a humorless examiner.

We entered the quaint brown stucco, ivy-covered building. What luck as the place was devoid of people! (Not like today's DMV experience.) An official-looking middle-aged lady wearing heavily framed glasses handed me a long sheet of test questions. She directed me to the large wooden table in the middle of the room and instructed me to fill in the answers with directions to complete both sides.

Standing over the high table poring over the multiple-answer choices, I looked up and Roberta materialized on the other side. I was nervous as she proceeded to read the questions upside down and pointed to the answers. I didn't want to be accused of cheating.

The clerk looked up, saw what was happening, and tersely ordered Roberta, "Young lady, you are not taking the test so please sit down on the other side of the room."

I wanted to do this myself and could now focus on the questions and figure out the most logical answers. At least we were allowed a fair number of errors. I slowly worked my way down the list and agonized over some of the answers. I guessed a couple of them and hoped for the best. When completed, the lady took my paper and while I waited, she tallied the number of incorrect answers. "Only three wrong, so you've passed," she said. I couldn't believe it and let out a big sigh, "Thank you."

But now the hardest part was coming. I had to sit in the driver's seat of the VW parked outside to take the driving test. And, not only drive, but reverse and parallel park, all in a car I'd never driven before. Roberta stayed put and said she'd wait for me inside.

Before long, a fairly decent-looking fellow appeared and introduced himself as Mr. Goodwin, the test instructor. He was casually dressed in tan slacks and a yellow open-neck shirt. My heartbeats slowed a trickle as I led him over to Butch's VW.

The examiner squeezed into the passenger seat. There were no seat belts in those days and the car was a stick shift. Luckily that is all I had ever driven in England. But, unlike England where I was used to driving on the left-hand side of the road, I now had to concentrate very hard on driving on the right-hand side.

I slowly pulled out into what little traffic there was in this quiet town, and off we motored. I was instructed to turn right, left, left again and around a few blocks we drove. We turned into a shady, elm-tree-lined street and the next thing I heard was, "Pull over to the right and stop the car." I veered over and stopped, pulling on the hand brake. I wondered what was coming next.

Mr. Goodwin settled in his seat, turned toward me and proceeded to ask lots of questions, but not about driving conditions, rules and regulations. He was curious about England, about my experiences flying with Pan Am as a stewardess, and he seemed genuinely interested in my story.

This is easy I thought as we were chatting for at least ten minutes or more. Then he calmly told me to start the engine and drive up the street. I was aware that I still hadn't been asked to parallel park.

"Pull left into the parking lot and into one of the parking spaces and shut off the engine." I dutifully did as asked.

"That's all, Miss Peters – you've passed!"

Just like that.

I hadn't done a thing – I couldn't believe it. How different from the experience in England with a severe test examiner making sure I went through every road condition imaginable.

Of course, I wasn't a young Pan Am stewardess then either.

One week later I was the proud owner of a California driving license and could now seriously think about buying a car. At the same time Roberta surprised us by trading in her Corvette for a brand new Jaguar XKE convertible. She was proudly driving us around town and enjoying all the attention she was garnering in her beautiful sleek new car.

A week more passed with short flights to Hawaii and back via Los Angeles. Roberta and I were home at the same time. Roberta suggested she drive me to the local British Motors dealer in San Mateo just to take a peek at the cars they had available. This was a giant step for me but I couldn't see the harm in looking.

Once there, Roberta grabbed my arm and led me into the salesroom where a young salesman approached and introduced himself as 'Oppie'. He was only too happy to steer us around the extensive showroom.

Being used to driving with Roberta in her exciting sports cars, I felt myself drawn to the sports cars on the showroom floor. I fell in love with the smallest car they had – an Austin Healey Sprite. Roberta was goading me into making a decision then and there so I made an offer. Oppie wrote down all the details and then asked, "Which color would you like?" That was the hardest decision of all as I was shown a multitude of different shades to choose from. Hearing my English accent the salesman made the obvious suggestion, "British Racing Green – that's the color you should have."

And that is the color I chose. Roberta insisted I opt for the convertible top which I agreed to add. The total cost came to two thousand dollars which was a fortune in those days. This was a major purchase, a necessity, and the little car would be brand new and all mine.

What a huge decision and purchase – and responsibility.

I looked forward to driving myself to the airport instead of relying on offered rides, taxis or worst of all – busses. The car was ordered and I had to wait patiently for the big arrival day.

Meanwhile, I had a call from the Medical Office asking me to report for more vaccinations. Maybe it was the stress of buying a car and the wet weather but I was suffering through a cold. The Doctor could tell I was in no shape to be flying and wrote the order to take me 'off line,' meaning no flying, which allowed me a few days off to recover. The negative side was I had to give up my scheduled line of flights and go on 'reserve' for the rest of the month not knowing when, or where, I could be sent.

Roberta came home exhausted from a London trip during which she'd made up her mind to own a brand new camera that had just been released – a Polaroid. The next morning she headed to the local photography store and came home with this large ungainly looking camera that she said actually printed the photos as you took them. Mary and I were eager to see this phenomenon and Roberta spent the day taking snapshots. We watched in amazement as they developed in front of our eyes. Instant photographs!

Every month Roberta received letters from her mother and father and usually there was a check enclosed. Mary and I felt her divorced parents were vying for her affection with money, and lots of it from our perspective, hence her ability to buy all these expensive toys. But she was always very generous and offered to treat us to dinner to share the proceeds with us. And yet, despite all this easy money, she seemed at a loss. She desperately needed love and attention and was constantly battling internal conflicts. She was looking for attention in the wrong places and going out with the wrong type of guys. Mary and I thought of her as our 'poor little rich girl.'

I was excited to receive a letter from Jay in Guam telling me he was flying to San Francisco the following week and he would like to stay in Burlingame for a couple of days before driving on to his home in southern California. This was a major development in the relationship, I thought, and just my luck, here I was stuck on 'reserve' with a head cold. I had an appointment at the medical office three days later and by then, fortunately, I was feeling back to normal and was taken off medical leave. Or was it so fortunate?

Within minutes of returning home, the Pan Am Scheduling Office called and told me to report for a flight to Honolulu the next day. It was a five-day trip that entailed flying to Hawaii then to Los Angeles, back to Hawaii before flying home to San Francisco. We called this a 'W' trip. I rushed to look at my calendar and as soon as I checked the dates I felt my enthusiasm sag. I wouldn't be back until two days *after* Jay arrived.

I grabbed the phone and called Scheduling begging them to change the trip, but not this time.

Mary and Roberta were home witnessing my frustration and both of them said they'd be home the day Jay arrived. I had no choice but to ask them to take care of him until I returned.

In Hawaii I made a point to call Roberta to see if Jay had arrived – but the phone rang and rang with no reply. When we landed in Los Angeles I called the apartment again and, same as before, the phone rang forever with no response. I was wondering what was going on.

Mary answered the third time I called and said Jay had arrived and was in San Francisco with Roberta. I didn't like the sound of that and called again when we flew back to Hawaii. I asked Mary to put Jay on the phone. I was so let down to hear he was planning to leave that afternoon. He said he couldn't wait for my return and was continuing on as he had to get home. That sounded reasonable but I urged him to at least wait one more day until I arrived, which he grudgingly agreed to do.

My last leg of the trip went without a hitch and as soon as I found my bags and bade farewell to the crew, I hailed a taxi to get to the apartment as fast as possible. On entering our front door, I was overjoyed to see Jay but he responded with a noticeable lack of enthusiasm and was adamant about leaving. I urged him to stay for an early supper but what on earth was I going to prepare! I had just come in the door.

Roberta had left on a Sydney trip early that morning and Mary was still home. We looked in the fridge and all we saw were bare shelves.

I made a crazy decision to cook liver and onions with bacon, mashed potatoes, and gravy. It was a favorite dish in England and not difficult to prepare. I was totally oblivious of the fact that most Americans don't relish it in quite the same way we English do!

Mary was only too pleased to have an excuse to get out of the apartment and leave Jay and me alone. She offered to run out to the supermarket and buy the supplies. For some unknown reason a hint of tension was lurking in the air. Mary walked to the store to add more time away but soon returned with the groceries. Between the two of us we broiled, boiled, mashed and eventually got the meal on the table.

During all this 'busyness' I had the intuitive feeling that something was not right – even *before* we dined on the liver and onions. Jay had little to say and choked back the meal and Mary was unusually subdued. He abruptly got up from the table and announced he was leaving, saying he had a long drive ahead of him. I was left with a nagging feeling that something was very 'wrong.'

After badgering Mary for days with this distressing concern, she broke down and told me Roberta had sworn her to secrecy. She reluctantly explained that during my absence Roberta had been wining and dining Jay in San Francisco. She even entertained him at Ruth's Chris Steakhouse which had to be the best steakhouse in the city. She had toured him all over town in her brand new sporty convertible XKE – no wonder he had had a good time. I could see why he was so quiet when I arrived and especially at the thought of staying to eat home-cooked 'liver and onions'!

I felt despondent hearing all of this and could understand the tension that had hung heavy in the air. Worst of all, I felt deeply hurt by Roberta's deception. I had asked her and Mary to take care of Jay never thinking that Roberta would throw herself at him.

It was a good thing Roberta was away for another eight days.

38

FAMILY IN AUSTRALIA

I didn't have time to fret about the situation with Jay as I was approaching my vacation month. Many stewardesses spent their holiday traveling, but that was our job, and Mary and I opted to fly home to spend time with family instead.

I was excited about a special trip I had arranged for my mother. One of the great benefits of flying was the ability to fly anywhere in the world on Pan Am for only ten per cent of the regular fare and this applied to one companion. For some time I had planned to fly to England, stay for a few days and then take my mother all the way, via Los Angeles and Hawaii, to Australia. The purpose was for her to visit her long absent older brother and his family.

After the devastation of World War I my mother's oldest brother Sam and his new wife Mabel emigrated to Australia hoping for a better life. They settled in the outback of New South Wales and founded the family farm and raised their children.

Sadly, not long before our trip, my mother received the news that her brother had died suddenly from a heart attack. I was so disappointed but decided I would take her anyway. At least she could visit Mabel and the family.

Mary and I were booked on the same London flight and eager to get home. At the airport we were thrilled to be upgraded to First Class and enjoyed an uneventful flight. When we stopped in Winnipeg for refueling we were told it was twenty degrees below zero outside and we were happy not to be disembarking.

At Heathrow the ground was covered with a blanket of thick white snow. Coming from California I noticed the frosty chill in the air and was thankful I'd packed a warm scarf and gloves in my bag. I said goodbye to Mary and climbed on a bus to Victoria Station to catch the train to Chichester.

It was a good feeling to be home and my parents were happy to see me. I visited friends and was invited to 'tea' with aunts and uncles.

My eighteen-year-old sister Sue asked me to visit her at her College, north of Liverpool in Ormskirk, Lancashire, as she couldn't get time away to visit at home. I took two days off and caught a train to London and crossed over from Victoria Station to Euston Station via the tube, where I was thrilled to be boarding the magnificent old Red Rose steam train – the 'express' London to Liverpool train.

My sister showed me around the extensive campus grounds and after the bracing walk she led me inside a red brick building to see her dorm room. Her close friends Pat and Pam had been patiently waiting to meet me and made mugs of hot coffee as we sat around the small, one-bed room.

I surprised them all by producing the menu signed by Ringo Starr and gave it to my sister. The girls were ecstatic and couldn't believe their eyes. They made me feel like a celebrity myself just because I had actually talked with one of the Beatles, as well as living the life of a real Pan Am stewardess.

The day passed far too quickly. I had to say goodbye and find a taxi to head back to the hotel. I left early the following morning to catch the Red Rose train back to London.

The days at home passed rapidly as my mother and I prepared for our Australian adventure. The departure day arrived and my father drove us to Heathrow airport and was quite happy *not* to be coming with us. He didn't care for the hustle and bustle of travel. I obviously hadn't inherited his genes.

We boarded the Round the World Flight One to Los Angeles, and for the month of March it was unusually full so, to my disappointment, we settled in our seats in the back. Mother was by the window and took out her knitting needles and yarn, and sat there in true English style – knitting.

We had one hour in Los Angeles to change planes for the next leg to Hawaii. On boarding the new plane we were greeted by the senior purser who welcomed us warmly. I was surprised when he took me aside and explained that he was happy to have us sit in First Class seats as there were so few other passengers. This was totally unexpected and another benefit of being a crew member. I was happy for my mother as she could now experience the luxury of the Pan Am service and in the best of comfort for this long leg of the flight. The purser went out of his way to make us feel special and comfortable as he understood we had already endured the long eleven-hour flight from London. When we landed in Hawaii he was leaving us for a layover and a new crew was taking the plane on to Sydney.

We had a refueling stop in Honolulu for one hour and were allowed to de-plane. The ongoing passengers were directed to an outdoor area and I took advantage of this opportunity for my mother to experience just a little of the Hawaiian environment. She was enthralled with the sultry balmy air and the tropical scent of the plumeria flowers.

No new passengers boarded the plane so we were thankful to keep our First Class seats. The new purser and crew were equally attentive and kept filling our glasses with champagne.

The purser handed out the President Special menus and we sat back and enjoyed being treated to the excellent multi-course dinner.

After all the rich food we tried to sleep, which should have been easy after all the champagne we had been offered. But sleep evaded us and we could only doze during the six-and-a-half hours to the next refueling stop in Fiji. We were requested to stay in our seats for the short stopover and from there our plane continued on to Sydney.

I was so used to jetting all over the globe that I really hadn't given any thought to my mother having to fly all the way from

London to Australia – non-stop without a break. Quite a marathon trip for her but she didn't complain. Adding it all up, including stopovers, it totaled close to thirty hours!

But our long journey wasn't over yet.

My cousin Reg met us at the airport. This was the first time I had met him and he was a rugged-looking young man in his early forties. Twenty years had passed since mother had seen him in England during the Second World War.

He explained we had a good TEN hours of driving ahead of us westward to Young in the outback, where he and the family lived. I had no idea it was so far from Sydney. In England that would take us from the south coast all the way to the northern tip of Scotland. What a daunting thought!

We stayed overnight with friends of his in Sydney and left after breakfast. Reg surprised me by asking if I minded driving part of the way. I took a deep breath as I hadn't even stopped to consider such a request. I was taken aback by the suggestion, but realized it was too far to expect him to drive that distance all by himself.

For the first two hours Reg drove us through and out of the Sydney traffic and for that I was thankful because Australia, like Britain, drives on the left side of the road. He stopped the car along the Great Western Highway and jumped out telling me it was my turn. I was just becoming used to driving in America on the right side of the roads. Now I had to switch, in this old car which I'd had no experience driving, to shifting gears with my left hand again. It was going to take a lot of concentration. Mum sat quietly in the backseat. Luckily for me there was hardly any traffic.

The views were spectacular as we neared the Blue Mountains but the weather was getting HOT – up to one hundred degrees. Everything around us looked brown and dry and I was so thankful when Reg suggested we stop at a town called Katoomba for lunch. At that time we were about 110 kilometers (roughly 70 miles) from Sydney. We found a small café and ordered lemonades right away. We gulped down the tall cool drinks while enjoying fresh ham and cheese sandwiches. With a restroom stop we felt renewed to set off again. Reg offered to drive from there so I was happy to be able to sit back and see this endless wild country stretching forever before us.

The road led us through extensive bush country. This was rural undeveloped land covered with dried out grass, bare soil, and sparse spindly bushes. Dust whirls spun haphazardly across the road and off in the distance small wallabies jumped and ran through tall, drooping eucalyptus trees.

The car had no air conditioning! Mother was unusually quiet in the back seat and I sensed she was very uncomfortable. Mercifully, Reg pulled into another town called Bathurst where we found a small café. Mum was so happy to get out of that hot car and sit down in front of a cooling fan. We ordered and devoured refreshing vanilla ice cream cones and drank lots of water. We were now 200 kilometers (125 miles) from Sydney on the banks of the Macquarie River in the Central Tablelands. Our rest stop didn't last long and poor mother had to squeeze back into the searing rear seat of the now dust-covered car.

My turn to drive again and now we were on the Olympic Highway headed for Young and hopefully the end of our journey. Mother was probably wondering why she'd ever agreed to come to this forsaken land. She had never in her life experienced such blistering dry heat.

Later in the afternoon Reg took over the driving and thank goodness he did as we soon noticed huge billowing clouds of thick brown dust far off in the distance rapidly advancing toward us.

The menacing clouds completely blocked our route. Reg inched forward slowly and we were aghast to see herds of wild cattle emerging through the whirling dust. The beasts were bellowing unearthly sounds as they lumbered all over the road. Tough-looking drovers on horseback materialized from the chaos and were yelling harshly and prodding the terrified animals off the road.

Despite the risk, it was an awesome sight.

Reg bravely maneuvered the car around this frenzied chaos. Mother was in the back seat ashen and clinging on for dear life.

I'm sure she was wishing she'd stayed home in her cool, quiet England.

On and on we drove and it was nearing eight o'clock at night, the skies became dark, but the air remained stifling hot. Eventually we arrived at the town of Young and our destination – the family home and farm.

Mother and I scrambled out of that car with an adrenaline rush of energy. The car was covered in a thick brown layer of dust and we felt as if we were too. Our limbs were stiff and our throats were dry.

Mother was meeting Mabel for the first time in thirty-odd years and I wished her brother had been alive to see her. Mabel was sweetly old-fashioned, short and plump, and was genuinely ecstatic to have family visiting all the way from her beloved England which she missed terribly. Mabel had been a reluctant new bride who followed her husband out to these backwoods of Australia years ago. Now her husband was gone and she had her grown boys, Reg and Ray, to take care of.

Mabel set out a welcome 'tea' in the darkly-lit Victorian dining room and, after a short visit, we soon retired to get some much-needed sleep.

Cocks were crowing at daybreak and we were soon wide awake.

Ray seemed the quiet stoic type. He was very proud to show us their extensive orchards of cherry, prune and almond trees, telling us that Young is the Cherry Capital of Australia. We met one large ornery-looking bull, a few cows, two fat pigs, two friendly Australian shepherd dogs and a mangy-looking tabby cat.

Mabel told us to sit under the shade trees in the garden and we were only too happy to rest. Mum was hoping for another reviving cup of good strong black tea, despite the heat.

In the early evening we cleaned up and sat down to a wonderful country meal of thick, juicy local pork chops, mounds of creamy mashed potatoes, thick gravy and a fresh-picked cherry tart for dessert. Mabel brought out all the old photo albums and was delighted to have someone in the family to share them with.

We enjoyed a day trip to Canberra which seemed so remote but learned that Melbourne and Sydney had a long history of rivalry between them so neither could become the national capital. Ray led us on more walks around the farm seeing their new prune shed where prunes were laid out to dry, and Mabel took us on visits to downtown Young.

Our morning to leave came around much too soon – especially for Mabel, Reg, and Ray. It was an emotional goodbye with Mabel in tears and Ray struggling bravely to hold his in check.

Reg drove us to the nearby Cowra airport as we were flying on a small prop plane back to Sydney. I don't think Mum, or I, could possibly have handled the long ten-hour return drive in that hot, dusty car back to Sydney. Reg told me I was very welcome to stay with them in Young whenever I flew into Australia, just to let him know and he'd fly to Sydney to pick me up. And I did just that a few times.

Mother and I landed safely in Sydney and, with our bags in hand, headed for the International Terminal. We found the Pan Am desk to check in for our flight to San Francisco.

I looked around in puzzlement as the terminal was totally empty and an eerie quiet surrounded us. I wondered what was going on? I spied movement in the distance and we hurried up to the lone person and asked, "Where is everybody?" We had been out of touch in the outback for a few days and I was shocked to find out, during that short space of time, Pan American World Airways had gone 'on strike.'

I was stunned. Mother was anxious to be home in England and I wondered how long we would be stranded in Sydney. My funds were running low. There were no credit cards in those days as we used travelers' checks for currency and we were near the end of those because I had reckoned on being in San Francisco the next day.

Seeing our stricken faces the airline representative did offer that Pan Am would cover the expense of a room, as an employee with companion, at the Gala Hotel – wherever that was. At least we would have a roof over our heads. So we lugged our baggage back outside and with the address in hand, found a taxi to take us to the hotel.

My poor mother had just endured an exhausting trip and was now anxious to call my father to let him know she was stuck halfway around the world – in Australia. But there was no way to do that as any long distance telephone call was going to cost far more than the money we had left.

At least we had a clean room in a small hotel with twin beds and a bathroom. All we could do was patiently bide our time until we could get on a plane to San Francisco.

To unwind we went for a walk around nearby Hyde Park. Not much was sinking in as my thoughts were all on getting out of Australia as soon as possible.

My vacation month had now officially come to an end. And I was trapped in Sydney.

I checked in daily with the airport and each day was told Pan Am was still not flying. I was becoming very tense with the situation and my mother was helpless to do anything. A few anxious days passed and then on my daily SOS call, I was told they had been able to reserve seats for us on a flight to San Francisco on Australia's Quantas Airline.

We were both jubilant to be leaving and getting back to our normal lives. After the long flight, via Fiji and Hawaii, we finally arrived in California.

On entering the apartment I was surprised to see Roberta and Mary leisurely lounging around the living room listening to Beatles records. They explained with long faces that the Pan Am pilots had now joined the strike. With that news we knew none of us would be flying or working for a while. We had no idea whatsoever how long this strike would last, it was a brand new experience for us. On joining the airline, we had been required to join the Transport Workers Union but gave little thought of what that would entail.

Mother was now captive in San Francisco, wondering if she was ever going to set foot in England again. I imagined my dear father in England fretting and worrying as to how much longer it would be before she arrived home.

Eight long days passed and thank goodness Mum had her knitting. She had almost finished a sweater with all the waiting. She put on a stoic front and quietly put up with all the inconvenience.

With no end to the strike looming, Pan Am called to tell me they were able to offer a seat for mother on a Lufthansa flight the next day. BUT, she had to fly to *Frankfurt*, in Germany, all on her own, and then find her continuing flight to Heathrow/London from there. Mum was just thankful to finally have a definite date for departure.

With that news our spirits lifted and we enjoyed a walk to the telegraph office in town. We sent a telegram home to inform my father of the flight details and that mother was on her way albeit via Germany. I was hoping and praying nothing else would happen to delay her further.

We had a flurry of packing and finally mum's suitcase was locked and ready by the door for departure. At the airport I left her in the hands of a Lufthansa ground staff person, but I had a heavy heart and didn't feel happy leaving her on her own bound for Germany and not England.

Four days later I received an airmail letter telling me she'd enjoyed a good flight on Lufthansa and had received lots of help in Frankfurt. She arrived at Heathrow with no delays fifteen hours later.

Three days after mother's long-delayed departure, the Pan Am strike was called off.

39

PAN AM HELIPAD

Roberta burst through the door after a long trip to Bangkok. She was elated to have seven days off and decided to use the time to go home.

"Why don't you come with me?" she said.

Our friendship had continued with resentment over her dalliance with Jay diminishing.

I also had time off, and was tempted by her offer. Without much thought I replied, "What a super idea. I have three days free and I'd love to see New Jersey and meet your mother."

We made a quick decision and spent the rest of the day buying airline tickets and packing for the visit.

We flew together and her mother picked us up at the New Jersey airport. Their home was a lavish modern one-story ranch house and I was shown to the guest room wing which was spacious and comfortable. We spent the next days driving all over town where I noticed many buildings in red brick which is rarely used in California construction.

All too soon I had to return to San Francisco. Roberta drove me into New York in her mother's car and I thought she was very brave to be driving in all the hectic, erratic, big-city traffic. We turned onto Park Avenue and, without warning, the car screeched to a halt. I looked upward at the massive Pan Am skyscraper which towered over Manhattan. Roberta told me to grab my case and get out fast. She was double parked!

"Go into the building, find the elevator to the rooftop, it's fifty-nine floors up, and get on a helicopter to the airport!"

"What! I've never been on a helicopter in my life – let alone from the top of a New York skyscraper!"

Roberta waved goodbye and stranded me there as she sped off and disappeared amidst the throng of traffic.

Clutching my overnight case I ventured inside the enormous building. A huge plaque announced that it had only just opened in 1963, and was the largest office building in *the world*.

I found myself in a cavernous vestibule and felt dwarfed by the banks of elevators lined up along a side wall. I examined them one by one looking for the Rooftop/Helipad sign, but they only went up to floor fifty-five.

How was I going to reach the rooftop? Then I turned a corner and there it was – an elevator to the Rooftop Helipad. I didn't hesitate and jumped inside. I was the sole occupant and tentatively hit the UP button. Whoosh! The elevator car flew at tremendous speed, non-stop up all fifty-nine floors, and then hissed to a smooth standstill. The doors opened wide and I stepped out.

There I was on top of the world. It was a stupendous feeling looking out over the rooftops of the New York skyline. I was surrounded by smart-clad businessmen standing around with briefcases in hand waiting to board the helicopter.

I purchased my ticket and was told the helicopter flew directly to Pan Am's terminal at the international airport. I followed the other passengers who were already boarding and sat down in a window seat. We didn't wait long before the engines whirred, the blades spun round and we took off, veering through and high over the concrete forest of city skyscrapers. It was a short ten-minute flight but a wild experience.

The helicopter landed and we all disembarked. I found a bus to the domestic airlines terminal and headed for the departure gate and climbed on the plane to San Francisco.

I had to thank Roberta for pushing me into yet another extraordinary adventure.

40

THE SPRITE

I was summoned to attend another refresher Emergency Class at the airport. Our small group was taken to a 707 jet clipper where the instructor had us open the emergency cabin doors and climb out onto the airplane wings, a challenge as the wings aren't flat but we all clambered out with no problem. We were instructed to release the door slides, inflate them and jump in shoeless, sliding down to the tarmac below. Our confidence and readiness were boosted by having the emergency basics drilled into us every few months.

Returning to the apartment, I found my day's mail stacked on the kitchen table. One envelope contained a notice from the British Motors Company telling me my Sprite was in the showroom and ready for pick up. I was jubilant and ran into the living room excitedly telling Roberta and Mary who were relaxing on the sofa intently reading their own mail.

Although it was late afternoon and pouring with rain, Roberta jumped up and offered to drive me to the dealership. We grabbed our bags and rain jackets, ran down the stairs, leaped into her XKE and took off down the El Camino Real.

After more paperwork signing, I received the keys to my brand new British Racing Green Sprite. I was a proud car owner and couldn't believe it.

Now I had to trust myself to drive all the way back to the apartment. The weather wasn't helping as it was still raining heavily. Roberta said she'd follow me and I drove very slowly at first until I felt comfortable with the manual gear shifting and operating the window wipers.

What a wonderful feeling of independence – no more begging for rides to and from the airport or waiting for taxis and busses. The apartment manager was happy to assign me a parking place in the garage under the building.

After a few weeks of flying, I felt the need to drive somewhere and explore the countryside in my new car. I asked Mary, "Would you like to drive down the coast to Los Angeles and visit Disneyland with me?" She thought I was crazy but agreed to go.

We both had days off so we packed our overnight bags and mapped out our route along the coast. I was so excited to be planning a drive down one of the most breathtaking coastal roads in California and on to the all-American Disneyland. We left early the next morning in the Sprite.

The roof was down and there was a cool breeze. We zipped south along Highway One and waved at the truckers when they tooted their horns as we drove by. The countryside was so vast and rugged and stretched on for miles and miles. The Pacific Ocean pounded the rocks way below us and exposed many little beaches in protected sandy coves. We covered many miles marveling at the extent of these incredible views.

We stopped for lunch in Carmel and enjoyed a huge BLT (bacon, lettuce and tomato) sandwich in a bustling main street café. We wandered down to the famous white sandy beach and gazed out at the ocean enthralled with the crashing waves and beautiful views. We visited the Carmel Mission further down the road and were awed by the historic Spanish-style buildings which were so different from the ancient yet stoic grey-stone churches and cathedrals in England. The desert-like gardens were stark yet peaceful. With many more miles to cover we didn't stay long and set off on the next leg of our journey.

We hadn't realized seven hours was a lot of driving. But we were having fun and enjoying more stunning vistas along the Big Sur coastline winding forever ahead of us.

Evening rolled in and the sky became dark as we approached the City of Angels, Los Angeles. We felt intimidated by the speeding traffic surrounding us and weren't sure where we were but opted to stay on the freeway.

As we cautiously drove along, the time was nearing ten-thirty at night and we began noticing, with surprise and distress, the motels and hotels all had huge NO VACANCY signs hanging outside. We hadn't thought it necessary to book ahead in such an enormous city. When flying, all our hotel accommodations were planned for us and we walked into top-rated hotels and straight to pre-booked rooms. How spoiled we were!

Time was approaching eleven and we were still in the car exhausted, stiff and ready to turn in for the night. At this point we didn't know where we were but considered the desperate move of parking somewhere and sleeping in the car. But there wasn't enough room, unless we slept sitting up and that option wasn't very appealing.

We motored on slowly scanning the motel signs and becoming more and more demoralized as *every* place was fully booked. It was time to stop and ask for help.

We turned into the next motel, maybe not the best of places, but at this point we didn't care. It was one story, rectangular-shaped, with a big red neon sign flashing the too familiar ominous words NO VACANCY. We found a parking space and approached the entry door. The sleepy young receptionist sat up straighter as we entered.

"It's nearing midnight and we're desperate to find a room for the night. Do you have any idea where we could find one?"

She shook her curly dyed-blonde head and told us, "We have nothing available here and at this time of night, I don't hold out any hope for you."

We must have looked despondent because she suddenly perked up and, with a flicker of thought, did offer a suggestion.

"There is *one* possibility – we could move a couple of spare beds into the adjoining beauty salon, The Purple Pussycat. We can set you up for the night in there, if you don't mind the inconvenience!"

"Do we mind? We'll be happy to spend the night in there, and thank you so much for the suggestion."

Anything sounded good at that point of our desperation – even a bed in the Purple Pussycat Beauty Salon.

This was another example of Californian hospitality. Late as it was, the young receptionist took the trouble to arrange for a couple of beds, with fresh clean linens, to be wheeled into the salon. We would be sleeping among the wash basins and hairdryers but that didn't matter to us at all. We had a room for the night even though it looked like a scene from a science fiction movie.

The neon sign flashed its 'No Vacancy' message right outside the window and spotlighted the huge bulbous hair dryers, their shadows standing motionless and on guard. The cords and hoses trailed all over the floor like sea serpents, but, never mind, we could get some sleep and in a bed too. The wash basins were adequate with running water and a ladies room adjoined the salon. What more could we have wished for?

We were soon in dreamland.

Awaking refreshed we couldn't believe our good luck. The Purple Pussycat Hair Salon had been a welcome refuge.

With directions from the new 'day' receptionist, we easily found our way to Disneyland which had opened in 1955 just ten years before our visit.

Parking and buying our tickets posed no problem and we stopped at the massive entryway to admire the enormous Mickey Mouse face of colorful flowers.

What a fantastic playground. We whirled around in huge cups and saucers in the Mad Tea Party enclosure, rode through the Jungle River Adventureland awed by the huge lifelike animals, and shook hands with Mickey Mouse, Minnie and Goofy. We spent time in Storybookland and watched live mermaids sitting on rocks in Tomorrowland. Nowhere did we encounter jostling crowds and had no long waits for any of the rides, which added to our total enjoyment.

Reluctantly we left the fairytale world of Disneyland in the late afternoon and drove home on the faster more direct route of Highway 101N and arrived home in the wee hours of the next morning.

How fortunate to have so many days off between our flights to enjoy these adventures.

41

BLIND DATE

I arrived home exhausted and near collapse after a long Polar flight from London. Adding up the extra on-duty hours before the actual flight from the briefing to takeoff, and an hour or more after landing waiting to help all the passengers off the plane, we had worked sixteen-plus hours.

Before crashing into bed, I had the novel experience of playing back the phone messages on Roberta's newly purchased phone message machine. I heard an urgent plea from a stewardess friend I'd met on one of my flights, "My boyfriend is here on his way to Vietnam and he arrived with a fellow navy officer and you have to meet him. He's just your type – I know it. Call me – you must come over."

Depleted of energy I wasn't in the mood for socializing that evening. I didn't even return the call and went straight to bed and slept soundly for twelve hours.

After a late leisurely breakfast, the phone jangled and broke the quiet serenity of the morning. I grudgingly picked up the receiver and Lynn was berating me for not returning her call. She was frantic because she hadn't heard from me and was urging me to come and meet this friend of her boyfriend. They were leaving that evening for Treasure Island, then to Travis Air Force Base the next morning before boarding the plane to Vietnam.

I was thinking 'why bother' if this fellow's off to fight a war for the next year. And, sadly, from what I'd seen, it was quite likely that he'd not return. Lynn was begging at this point and said I had to come to make a foursome for dinner. So I relented and said, "Okay." This would be my first blind date and that alone made me rather wary and uneasy.

It was a lovely warm California evening so I put on a new sleeveless peachy-colored dress and strappy sandals. I took my time, left the apartment and drove over to Lynn's. I parked the car and slowly walked up the steps to her shiny white front door and hesitantly pressed the doorbell. I stood on the doorstep waiting for my friend to appear. I heard footsteps in the hall and the door opened.

Standing in the doorway was this handsome, young officer and he wasn't even in uniform. Wow, if he was my blind date this was a pleasant surprise! All kinds of bells and whistles were going off in my head. I tried to act calm and nonchalant thinking Lynn was right about persuading me to meet this fellow.

Dan introduced himself and led me into the apartment. He then excused himself as he was in the middle of a 'goodbye' phone call with his parents. This gave me needed time to collect myself.

After ending his call, Dan joined me on the couch while Lynn prepared Whisky Sour drinks. This young stranger had soft brown eyes which belied a fun sense of humor, and the typical military crew cut which I loved. He was telling me he had volunteered to go to Vietnam and I thought that sounded like a crazy thing to do.

Lynn eventually broke up our cozy interlude as we had to leave for the restaurant. We were having too good a time getting to know each other over more drinks and dinner, but experiencing these intense feelings was not making any sense. After all, this young man was leaving tomorrow morning for a whole year and into the dangers of a war zone.

After dinner we stayed for dancing and then drove back to the apartment. The evening was drawing to a close and I wasn't ready for it to end. In a moment of madness, I offered to drive this young fellow to Treasure Island (a man-made island owned by the US Navy at that time), where he was bunking at the BOQ before leaving for Travis. Dan readily agreed with my suggestion.

By this time it was already eleven o'clock and I didn't trust myself driving, even my own car, and asked him to drive. He didn't have much choice but was happy to have the opportunity to drive the Sprite. It was at least an hour to Treasure Island and Dan talked most of the way. He was very relaxed and had a warm, easy-going demeanor and the more he talked, the more I liked him.

We finally arrived at the Island and I thought, 'This is it, will I ever see him again?' I really wanted to, and in an impulsive moment offered to drive over in the morning and take him to Travis Air Force Base.

What great advantages to having one's own car.

Around one in the morning I started the long drive from Treasure Island to Burlingame all the while thinking, 'Whatever had possessed me to offer turning around and driving back the next morning?'

I had so much on my mind about how absurd this all was – having feelings about a total stranger who was about to leave for a war zone for an entire year.

With my concentration elsewhere, I must have taken a wrong turn and missed the freeway on-ramp. I had somehow lost my way and didn't recognize the road or anything around me. It was a very dark night with just the barest sliver of a moon and I was aware of strange, menacing shapes of trees and black undergrowth lining an unknown road. I was battling a growing concern wondering, 'Where am I?' and 'Where am I headed?'

To make matters worse, I was alarmed to see the gas gauge registering less than a quarter of a tank and inching too close to the dreaded red line of 'Empty.' It was now about one-thirty in the morning and I was increasingly worried. What would happen if I ran out of gas in the middle of heaven knows where? This was in the days before cell phones to call for help and GPS for instant directions. I had no way of contacting anyone and I was feeling extremely vulnerable being alone on this deserted and unnervingly quiet road.

Driving for what seemed miles and miles, I was too anxious to fall asleep. My eyes were getting used to the blackness, and when I veered around a bend in the road my hopes raised as I strained my eyes toward a faint glow of light far off in the distance.

As I neared the dim light I could make out the welcome sign of a gas station. I felt a surge of relief and my tension relaxed. Would it be 'open?' My optimism was building with thoughts of my tank filled with gas and directions to Burlingame.

My tires crunched on loose gravel as I cautiously pulled in and my heart dropped as the place looked rusty and ramshackle. A blurry low light was visible in a small building set a long way back from the two lone pumps at the roadside. I turned off the engine and wondered what to do. In that moment of indecision three big, burly guys emerged from the far shack, ambling toward my car. I didn't like the look of them and felt a growing unease as they approached, but I was desperate for help. I opened my window, just a few inches, and asked, "Can you give me directions to Burlingame?" I wasn't going to wait around for gas.

They mumbled together and told me they'd never heard of it. When they suggested I walk back with them to the station house so they could find a map and figure out where it was, I instinctively sensed no good would come from getting *out* of my car.

With sudden clarity of this menacing situation, I grabbed the window handle and wound it tight, started the car and took off – wheels skidding on the stones with no added gas in my tank.

I had no idea where I was but kept driving on this road to nowhere. It was still very dark and no other cars appeared, adding to my growing panic.

This route had to end somewhere. The miles slipped by and then in the distance I discerned a roadside sign. I dreaded seeing what it would say. How far had I strayed?

Through the night mist I read the hazy words – San Mateo Bridge. A tremendous surge of relief ran through me for I knew on the other side of the bridge was San Mateo and I was almost home. I was at least headed in the right direction albeit a long way around the Bay. I now happily drove over the bridge and on through San Mateo to Burlingame with just enough gas fumes to get me to my apartment building.

I parked the car in the parking garage, ran up to the apartment and unlocked the door hoping I wouldn't wake any roommates. I threw off my clothes, set the alarm, dived in bed and fell sound asleep.

The alarm buzzed much too soon. I again questioned my sanity at offering to drive all the way back and take this practically unknown navy officer to Travis. I showered, dressed and forced myself to eat a hasty breakfast of tea and toast before setting off for Treasure Island. Knowing I had just a dribble of gas in my tank, I had to take the extra time to stop at a gas station to fill up.

What a relief to drive into the station in broad daylight and have a friendly young man cheerfully welcome me, eagerly fill the tank, and wash both the front windscreen and side mirrors. Oh how I miss the Full Service of those days.

In bright sunshine and with a trusty map beside me, I headed out onto the roads and freeway toward Treasure Island. I was ushered through the military gates, and on I drove looking for the BOQ area. Dan was waiting for me and this time in full uniform.

I asked him to drive and off we went toward Travis Air Force Base. On arrival, Dan had to call his Commander as he had been invited to lunch before leaving. We said our farewells and I was elated when he said he'd love to write and asked for my address which I readily gave him.

Ecstatic, and sad with the thought of him leaving for Vietnam for an entire year, I concentrated on finding the right road for my return route back home.

When I entered the apartment, Roberta and Mary were eager to know the outcome of the fond farewell. I told them we had exchanged addresses and they both laughed and said "You'll be lucky if you ever hear from him again."

Every day thereafter I watched the mail box and there, four days later, was a letter with Dan's military return address. Roberta and Mary were surprised.

Many letters followed, beautifully written with extraordinary accounts of his life in Vietnam. He was an Advisor to the Vietnamese Navy Coastal Forces based on Phu Quoc Island off the west coast of the country, and was living aboard junk boats while on patrol in Vietnamese and Cambodian waters. The missions were to interdict Communist infiltrations and smuggling of contraband weapons.

42

FLIGHT DELAYS

Another 'W' trip was scheduled to San Francisco, Hawaii, Los Angeles, Hawaii, San Francisco.

Mary gave me a lift to the airport as check-in time was four-thirty in the afternoon. She would be home to pick me up if needed on my return date. We did this at times to preserve the security of our cars sitting out at the airport for days at a time.

At the Briefing I met Captain Knight, the pursers Jim and Patricia, the stewardesses Pat an English girl, Helen Chiu a Chinese American, and Rene from Berlin. The short flight to Los Angeles was routine with a service of champagne, an assortment of sandwiches and coffee.

In Los Angeles we stayed at the airport and had a snack in the staff canteen with orders to board the plane within the hour. We were enjoying our freshly grilled cheese sandwiches when Captain Knight came in with a grim expression and announced, "Girls, I'm sorry to tell you our flight to Honolulu has been delayed due to engine trouble. I have no idea how long this will take so try to relax and wait patiently."

We weren't happy with that announcement and hung around the canteen for another hour. We received no update on the flight situation and the delay dragged on toward a second hour. With all the waiting and not knowing what the situation was, restlessness set in. Eventually, an airline representative appeared and told us to board a crew bus that was waiting for us outside. He added, "You aren't boarding the plane, you are being driven to a hotel to wait there on standby."

We were frustrated at being held up for so long and it gave us some insight as to how the passengers must be feeling to be so long delayed. At the hotel we sat in our assigned rooms for two more hours – and still in uniform. We only had our carry-on bags with us as our suitcases were still on the plane at the airport.

Finally, we were called at nine forty-five and told our pick up was in half-an-hour. We cleaned up, straightened our uniforms, put on our hats and gloves, grabbed our bags and met up with the rest of the crew in the lobby. We climbed aboard the crew bus and returned to the airport optimistic that we could finally get on the plane and start work.

Our optimism was short-lived.

A Pan Am ground representative approached us and hesitantly told us of a further delay. We now had to endure another hour's wait till midnight while the cockpit crew was relieved of duty due to the accumulated extra hours. A new crew of pilots was called in to take over the flight. But we, now tired with draining enthusiasm having checked in eight hours earlier, had to continue on and eventually work the five hour flight – whenever that time was announced.

The new Captain Gerry introduced himself and explained there were expected cancellations. That was little consolation and we were eventually cleared to board the plane.

The few passengers on board wanted to be left alone to get some sleep. In the aft section there were plenty of empty seats available so most passengers lifted the armrests and slept comfortably on all three seats, complete with pillows and blankets. We didn't disturb them until it was time for the breakfast service. We arrived in Honolulu in the early hours of the morning and it was pouring down buckets of tropical rain.

On the way to the hotel the crew bus began spluttering and decided to quit running. The driver scratched his head and apologized guessing the engine was probably flooded from going through too many deep puddles. He made an emergency call for another bus and we sat in our seats feeling numb. The rain was pinging and splattering over our heads and gushing down the windows while we were trying hard *not* to fall asleep.

The replacement bus finally arrived. We dragged ourselves out of one bus and into the other squelching through the deep water and getting drenched. We slumped into the seats without a murmur.

We arrived at the hotel when everyone else was getting up and starting their day. We were worn out and soaked as well. We entered our rooms, dropped onto the beds and slept soundly into the afternoon.

A long and far from glamorous day in the life of a stewardess.

Late in the afternoon I was thrilled to see Karin and Edith who had flown in from Tahiti. The rain had abated so we went shopping at the International Marketplace on Kalakaua Avenue, just walking distance across the street from the hotel. It was a wonderful open-air setting with stalls selling all kinds of Hawaiian souvenirs under a magnificent huge Banyan tree. We ended the day leisurely sunbathing and swimming on Waikiki beach – and, for me, that made up for all the earlier delays.

The next day I lazed on the beach and enjoyed a relaxing time doing nothing. As I waded out of the water after a cooling swim I heard a male voice call my name. I wondered who it could be. I saw a man walking toward me and vaguely recognized him. It was James Doolittle, the Theater Producer. He seemed delighted to see me and I quickly grabbed a towel to dry off. After a catch-up chat sitting on the beach, he invited me to join him to yet another theater performance. This time to see the great prima ballerina Maria Tallchief dancing as a guest performer with the American Ballet Company. I had nothing planned and he told me he remembered how much I enjoyed ballet so I replied, "I'd love to join you."

I had a few hours before our meeting time, so I ran down to the hotel beauty salon. Fortunately they had an immediate opening for an appointment to have my hair set. In my room, I rummaged through my suitcase and luckily, this time, I had packed a presentable blue-green Thai silk dress.

As before, Mr. Doolittle picked me up in the hotel lobby at six o'clock and off we went chauffeured in the comfortable limousine. En route to the theater James told me about Maria Tallchief, a name I'd not heard before. She was the first native-American to break into ballet and had been married to the choreographer George Ballenchine. Rudolf Nureyev even requested her as a dancing partner. I couldn't believe how lucky I was to have the chance to see such a leading performer. And what a fairy tale performance it was. Maria's dancing looked effortless and I was completely captivated.

After the show James invited me to join him for a drink. We were driven to the Princess Kaiulani Hotel where he led me to comfortable seats in the tropical bar. He ordered two Princess K drinks. The waiter brought over two beautiful glasses filled with a Pacific Ocean blue liquid. Pale pink orchid flowers were floating on top with spears of fresh sweet pineapple. I was royally impressed. The drinks were a mix of light rum and blue Curacao. How exotic they looked and how delicious they tasted. James ordered two more!

James graciously escorted me back to the hotel and bid adieu as he knew I had an early morning flight.

After these chance encounters, we never crossed paths again!

On the flight to Los Angeles I was working the First Class cabin with an unusually large number of twenty-one passengers. Pat had to prepare a full breakfast service and we had an offering of Guava juice, Papaya fruit salad, Eggs Benedict or eggs cooked to order, ham and plenty of fresh bread rolls with tropical Pineapple jam – plus lots of beautiful purple Plumeria flowers to decorate all the plates as a garnish.

Two male passengers sat in the lounge the whole way obsessively playing cards and smoking for five hours, only taking time out to drink and eat. Smoking was still allowed and nobody thought anything of it – and the lounge area was adjacent to the galley where all the food preparation was going on!

On arrival in Los Angeles we were feeling jinxed as we were told of yet another delay. This time we were waiting for the Polar flight to come in from London. It was at least five hours late so we were sent to the hotel to wait.

I had my own room but I was becoming anxious as the hours passed. By law, we had to have thirty-six hours between flights, and these delays were cutting into that cushion. If I didn't have the full thirty-six hours, I would lose my next scheduled flight and drop back to stand-by status for the rest of the month.

The phone on the bedside table rang and a female voice told me the pick-up time was in one hour. I freshened up yet again. Jacket on, hat on head, and gloves at the ready, I joined the rest of the crew in the lobby and we boarded the bus back to the Los Angeles International Airport.

The Polar flight had finally arrived and the exhausted London crew and most of the passengers disembarked. Not as fresh as we should have been, we boarded the plane to take the remaining few passengers on to San Francisco. We offered assorted sandwiches and coffee or tea for such a short flight. The weary passengers were as relieved as we were to finally reach their destination.

Chatting with the girls close to the baggage claim area waiting for our bags to arrive, I spotted a young pilot I had enjoyed a fun layover with in Hawaii. I was debating whether to approach him to say 'hello,' when I noticed another stewardess running toward him. I vaguely recognized her. I stood there and watched as she threw her arms around his neck and planted a big kiss on his cheek and together they walked off arm in arm.

It just wasn't worth getting involved with pilots!

I did make it home in time to log in the required hours before my next trip and thankfully avoided being on standby.

43.

VANDALISM

One night Mary, Roberta and I were sleeping soundly in the apartment. Our dreamy reveries were rudely broken by the high-pitched jangle coming from our own front doorbell. The irritating noise refused to stop.

I opened one eye and glanced at the bedside clock. This must be a mistake as it was only five-thirty in the morning. By now all three of us were stirring and wondering what was causing such a disturbance. We groggily rolled out of our beds, dragged on robes and Roberta made it to the front door first and warily opened it a crack to peer outside. She stood there speechless.

The doorway was blocked by two official-looking policemen.

Whatever was this about? We were further shocked when one of the policemen asked which of us owned an Austin Healy Sprite. My heart sank and my roommates stood back relief on their faces they weren't involved in whatever was coming. I stepped forward and one of the policemen bluntly told me, "I'm sorry to tell you, Miss, but someone tried to set fire to your car. We found a smoldering packet of matchboxes stuffed under the driver's seat."

I stood before him with a sickened feeling as he continued in his monotone voice, "The seat suffocated the flame so there was only singeing damage on the underside of the seat and to the carpet."

My car, my pride and joy, and I hear this news so early in the morning. The next question really unnerved me, as the policeman asked, "Do you have any enemies?" What an awful thing to think about when only half-awake.

"No, I'm not aware of having any enemies," I blurted out.

I was totally numb imagining my precious car a heap of scorched ashes.

The policeman proceeded to tell us, "There is one other sports car, a Porsche, in the parking garage which did burn badly. Does that belong to any of you?"

And that was supposed to make me feel better?

I gave a statement, signed some papers and they left. That was the end of it for them but not for me. I threw on some clothes and ran down to the garage to see for myself what damage had been done.

It was a devastating feeling to think someone had maliciously tried to burn my car. Not only that, I found the roof had been slashed as their way of getting in. There, under the passenger seat, was burnt leather and singed carpeting and an awful odor coming from both. The police had removed the long packet of matches that had been stuffed under the seat.

I didn't know what to do feeling very much the lone stranger in a strange country. I couldn't call my parents. We just didn't make phone calls in those days, only at Christmas and birthdays. And what could they do anyway.

Roberta came to the rescue and explained to me about notifying the insurance company and getting estimates for repairing the damage. Fortunately, I was home with a few days off and Roberta kindly drove me around town to get repair estimates. I did make an appointment with one company to restore the damaged parts, and was now without a car for a whole week!

To my knowledge there was no investigation and no suspects.

44.

PURSER TRAINING

Mary told me she'd heard about a Purser Training Class and wanted to give it a try. The main advantages of being a purser, the senior stewardess, were having your own room in the hotels, and higher pay. The position entailed a lot more responsibility such as being in charge of the cabin procedures, the timing of meal services, keeping accounts of all the liquor and monies collected and directing the cabin crews. This job would be quite an undertaking after so short a time of flying. Mary was adamant and I thought it would be worth the extra responsibility to garner the advantages. We'd heard rumors that Pan Am was ordering more jets and the older male pursers were retiring so I committed myself to joining her and taking the challenge together.

We had to attend classes on our days off and take more tests but fortunately the schooling wasn't difficult. The final written test lasted two-and-a-half hours but the most daunting task lay ahead. We had to take check rides acting as purser during an actual flight and be assessed by a senior purser at the same time.

The Scheduling Office mailed my check ride notice. I was to take one test the following week on a flight to Anchorage, and a second test on the return flight from Tokyo to San Francisco. Mary's check rides were on flights to and from London a few days before mine.

I checked in and was extremely fortunate to have two very easy-going, yet well-seasoned male pursers, Billy and Bert, for my check flights. I was told that I had to act as the purser and treat the real purser as a steward and had to tell him what to do and when. The purser, at the same time, was watching and testing my performance. I was working the aft cabin with Bert and there were only twenty-eight passengers, a lucky break. I assigned the galley to the stewardess, Missy, and told Bert to help me run the cabin service. I somehow kept my wits about me and maneuvered through the drink service, mixing the drinks and collecting the cash. The meal service proceeded smoothly, serving Chicken Bordelaise, with no problems.

With so few passengers, we took a break and I heard Bert lamenting he had a couple of buttons loose on his jacket and so I offered to sew them more securely for him. He seemed genuinely thrilled and found the sewing kit from one of our emergency boxes and I went to work.

Arrival in Anchorage signaled the end of the first test. I could relax and continue on the next leg to Tokyo as a stewardess. We had three days to unwind in Tokyo before I faced part two of my check ride test back to San Francisco.

Our pick-up was at ten p.m. and we had two new stewardesses join us, Helen Cho from Hawaii and Anne from England. This time I worked the First Class cabin with Purser Bill and Helen. There were thirteen passengers. As acting purser I made all the take-off announcements but in my enthusiasm I somehow skipped the life jacket demonstration and had to tack it on at the end – but at least I remembered it.

I asked Helen to work the galley and had Bill help me in the cabin. The late night supper service went smoothly and I opted not to use the carts at such a late hour.

Preparing for the hot breakfast before landing, Helen was fretting as she had received many egg orders to prepare from scratch. I was taken by surprise and mightily peeved when she just gave up half way through the service saying she couldn't handle it. I had never known a stewardess to react this way before. What terrible timing!

I was momentarily perplexed but soon recovered and asked Bill to please step into the galley and take over. He handled the rest of the cooking with ease and calm. Meanwhile Helen was relieved to be free of the overwhelming egg preparations in the galley and helped me run the cabin. Of course, with Senior Purser Bill in the galley, our breakfast service continued effortlessly and flawlessly. I was so glad when we landed in San Francisco to have that ordeal over with.

Now I had to wait for the check flight results.

At the time I was so trusting, but looking back I do wonder if Bill, the check-ride purser, had primed Helen to overreact and refuse to continue with the galley breakfast orders – putting my reaction to the test.

I will never know.

Just one week later, Mary and I were ecstatic to receive notification we had passed the Purser Examination and Flight Service tests.

We were now officially Pan Am Pursers.

The Scheduling Office requested us to pick up our new name tags and large Purser briefcases. In that big blue Purser bag we carried, and were responsible for, all the silver serving utensils for the First Class meal services, the intercom message books, travel reference books, and the bottle openers for the bar services.

This was one bag we had to keep with us at all times and didn't dare risk losing.

45

HURRICANE

My first flight as a purser was to Tokyo. I had my purser bag equipped with all the necessary supplies and was wearing my brand new purser pin and drove to the airport in my newly-fixed car. I planned to arrive early and headed for the Flight Briefing Office. There I signed in and received the detailed schedule of our flights and layovers for the duration of the trip. We were flying to Alaska, on to Tokyo and returning from Tokyo to Hawaii then back to San Francisco.

I met and introduced myself to the cabin crew and the senior purser. The decision was his to decide who would work where and with whom. I was assigned the Economy section to Anchorage and Tokyo, and the First Class cabin on the return flights.

The flight to Alaska was routine and I was fortunate to have the service run smoothly and efficiently.

En route to our hotel we were dismayed to see heavy rain falling from an ominously dark sky. By the time we checked in at the hotel, the rain had turned into swirls of blinding snow with strong winds gusting and howling.

Despite the miserable weather which continued into the following morning, the cockpit crew wanted to tour the Portage Glacier area which was only an hour's drive south-east of Anchorage. We all decided to go except the captain who stayed behind. The hotel clerk warned us that the town of Portage was in ruins as it had been badly flooded and vacated following the devastating earthquake the year before.

Undeterred, we dressed in our warm woollies and heavy coats. First Officer Gerry offered to do the driving. On the way, we ran into a devilish snow storm, visibility was passing from poor to nil and we were slipping and sliding on the treacherous roads. Gerry was having a tough time handling the steering and a couple of the girls moaned as they were tossed about.

The front end of the car suddenly skidded sharply and sank into a huge pothole. The thump shook us and we were sure we must have a flat tire. Despite the freezing cold we climbed out of the vehicle; amazingly, on close inspection the car seemed intact and the hole not so deep. Gerry had the task of maneuvering the vehicle and after some tense moments he had it up on the road.

With that dire mishap and the weather showing no sign of abating, we decided it was foolish to continue and told Gerry to turn back to the hotel.

The crew was growing anxious about flying with the weather becoming increasingly fierce. Our captain informed us he was in constant contact with the airport flight office.

That evening we met in the cafeteria for some refreshment and in the corner was a cockpit crew from Japan Air Lines headed to Tokyo the next day – same as us. The Pan Am pilots joined them and they were having quite an animated discussion. We could understand some of the conversation and the Japanese pilots were adamant they were NOT going to fly in such severe stormy weather. On the other hand, our own Pan Am captain was equally adamant he was NOT going to let a storm prevent him from keeping his plane on schedule. At this the cabin crew became rather uneasy.

Wouldn't the Japanese pilots know better than the Americans what the weather conditions would be like landing in their own country?

Our captain had the final say and we were told to be ready for departure the following morning. The snow had turned to sleet and rain and was belting down, the winds were still raging and it was bitterly cold. But we dutifully did as told and in the morning reported for the airport bus. The hotel personnel looked at us as if we were crazy, making us even more ill at ease.

We boarded the airplane dodging the deepest puddles and braving the gale force winds. As soon as all the passengers were seated and belted in, the senior purser asked me to make the boarding and emergency announcements.

The captain revved up the engines and the plane sloshed down the saturated runway and slowly lifted off the ground. We braced ourselves to face the expected turbulence and tried as best we could to deliver a meal service while the plane was jerking up and down. There were times when we felt the strange sensation of levitating off the floor and, when it got really bad, the captain ordered us to take our seats and fasten our own seatbelts.

Starting and stopping made the meal service very difficult to handle. The passengers hung on tightly to their meal trays and managed to eat. Drinking was another challenge but I suggested filling the cups with just a little coffee at a time. After this prolonged service, I helped the stewardesses, Missy and Alicia, stow everything away and made sure anything loose was battened down ready for a rough landing.

The turbulence grew worse and we were very concerned as we approached the Tokyo airport. We belted ourselves in tight, again remembering what our safety instructor had told us in training. We held our breath as the captain flew the plane down for landing.

The passengers were unusually quiet and tense.

The plane was buffeted on all sides as we slammed down onto the runway. The hurricane force winds were so strong they forced the plane to skid down the runway sideways. For the first time ever I was unnerved and said a quiet prayer – despite all my faith in the captain and pilots.

It took a long time for the sliding plane to come to a stop, and thankfully it was still in one piece.

We were some distance from the terminal but could see the airport personnel trying to push their way out through the terminal doors. Their huge umbrellas just blew inside out, not surprising in the teeth of such vicious winds and they hurriedly withdrew into the safety of the building.

Inside the plane our pilots were flexing their muscles trying in vain to push open the aircraft door. They were no match for the force of wind power blowing against the side of the plane,and the door refused to budge. We had landed close to schedule but how long would it be before we could get off?

Eventually, a small group of ground crew gave up using umbrellas and bravely attempted to push the disembarking ramp across the tarmac to the plane. The wind was trying hard to blow them all, and the ramp, off the ground and into the air. The rain was sheeting down and the men were soaked through, but with grit and determination, they managed against the odds to secure the ramp to the First Class cabin door. In those conditions they weren't about to tempt fate by trying to get the rear door open as well. The pilots were still struggling to force the door open against the lashing rain and wind. They had a break when the storm momentarily stilled and they were finally successful. We immediately felt the full force of the wind bursting in through the open doorway.

The passengers had to face the prospect of becoming very wet climbing down the gangway to the terminal as umbrellas were useless. But, they were OFF the plane and in Tokyo more or less on scheduled arrival time.

The captain had made a point but this was small satisfaction for the cabin crew, thinking of the JAL crew relaxing back in Anchorage.

46

FILM STARS

The torrential rain eventually subsided. During the dry spell Missy and I walked to the Ginza for a stroll through the shops. We rounded a corner and were surprised to see a large Japanese department store. We were curious to see how different it would be from an American store and pushed our way through the entry doors. Neatly uniformed attendants stood at the top and bottom of each escalator and bowed like robots to each person as they stepped on or off. They appeared to be doing this all day long, bowing and saying "Arigato" (thank you). We hadn't seen anything like that before.

The twang of Japanese music played in the background and after wandering many floors we soon felt the need for a break.

After lunch at a sidewalk café, we dodged a short shower and walked to Fuji Torii where I couldn't resist buying four small framed Geisha pictures showing the unique make-up and traditional Geisha wigs and adornments.

At the end of the layover we prepared for the next leg of the trip to Hawaii. The crew bus picked us up at the hotel and delivered us to the Briefing Office at the airport. The Pan Am ground staff informed me, as the purser in charge of the First Class cabin, that the celebrity film star Cary Grant would be traveling with us and I exclaimed, "Oh, my gosh, the famous film star – Cary Grant!"

The Pan Am representatives soon burst that bubble. They proceeded to tell me very seriously that Mr. Grant was one of the worst passengers to deal with as he owned a great deal of Pan Am stock and was therefore extremely critical of the service he received. They certainly knew how to unnerve a brand new purser.

As I boarded the plane I was determined to do the best I could. I made extra sure the First Class cabin and lounge areas were neat and orderly. Fortunately, we only had nine passengers boarding in this section.

Amidst the hustle and bustle a Pan Am Ground Attendant appeared in the doorway with his official clipboard and passenger list in hand. He announced with forewarning that Mr. Cary Grant was coming up the ramp. So soon! I straightened up and asked the girls to hurry over and stand in the welcoming line.

Mr. Cary Grant, in person, appeared in the doorway. He was smiling warmly and approached me with such casual grace, offering his hand in welcome, that all my fears instantly melted away. In that initial instant, he came across as a gracious, gentle man who was full of charm.

I realized 'I'd been had.' The ground crew were teasing me and making me believe the worst, knowing full well that Mr. Grant would give us no trouble at all. I was new and gullible, and they knew it.

I showed Mr.Grant to his seat and made sure he was very comfortable.

After take-off I made all the intercom announcements. It was early morning and we prepared for a full hot breakfast service. I poured Dom Perignon, a prestigious vintage champagne. Laila, the Norwegian stewardess, walked the aisle greeting each passenger while handing out the menus. I followed her and noted each breakfast order before Missy, in the galley, could prepare the dishes. In First Class eggs could be scrambled, fried, poached and the dreaded 'boiled.' When I approached Cary Grant he calmly ordered 'boiled' eggs and stressed that he would prefer them 'soft' boiled. A twinge of dismay shuddered through my body.

Boiled eggs were one of the hardest things to cook and get right at altitude. I remember learning in class that at high altitudes water boils at a lower temperature so it takes longer for the eggs to cook. Trial and error is the only way, so I told Missy to boil *four* eggs and crack the extras one at a time until the yolks looked right. Despite the extra time and trouble, we got the job done. Mr. Grant was served his two perfect soft-boiled eggs, along with more champagne, fresh fruit, warm sweet rolls – and plenty of hot coffee.

With the service almost over Mr. Grant asked me to join him so I sat down in the seat next to his and was so surprised when he complimented me on how well my voice carried over the intercom. I'm sure I glowed crimson on hearing that from such a well-known celebrity.

Mr. Grant told me he had been in Tokyo filming 'Walk don't Run,' with red-headed co-star Samantha Egger. He explained that it was a comedy set in Tokyo during the 1964 Olympic Games. We chatted about the baby he was expecting with his wife Dyan Cannon. He didn't mind if it was a boy or a girl and I was babbling on about some day wishing for one of each. We were chatting away like old friends – me and Cary Grant.

I was left with another good feeling that celebrities are human too!

Mr. Callahan, a senior Pan Am chief executive, was also sitting in First Class and he was the one who was all eyes critically watching everything. As the First Class purser I managed the breakfast courses without a hitch but I was lucky to have a good crew helping me. At the end of the flight Mr. Callahan took me aside and praised me on an excellent service.

One flight like this made the whole experience worthwhile and boosted my morale about tackling the added purser responsibilities.

On arrival home in Burlingame I was bubbling with excitement over my conversation with the famous film star Cary Grant. Mary and I were both home and invited those of our group who were not flying to come for supper. Karin, Tina, Edith and Gunnel were happy to join us and Tina asked if Greig could come over too and we didn't mind at all. Gunnel was now happily engaged to her Air Force pilot Don and planning a Hawaiian wedding.

We sat around the living room, some of us on the floor and others on the sofa and armchair. We were enjoying tumblers of chilled white wine and soon the subject of flying with celebrities came up.

I told them my story about meeting and chatting with Cary Grant and added another experience with the film star Jack Lemmon on one of my earlier flights. Mr. Lemmon was travelling from Los Angeles to Hawaii with his wife, Felicia Farr, and their two children. Young children were usually a source of concern as so many of them were bundles of unrestrained energy but their two, a girl and a boy about ten and twelve years of age, were the best behaved children I'd ever encountered. They always thanked me with a 'Yes, Ma'am' or a 'No, Ma'am' with no prompting and I was very impressed.

Another celebrity encounter I enjoyed was on a Round the World flight from London to Los Angeles. I was working in the First Class cabin and we had a small group of celebrities with us. The beautiful Ursula Andress was on board sitting alone by the window in the front row. She was the sex symbol of the Sixties, a film actress from Switzerland who was the first ever 007 Bond girl, Honey Ryder, in the movie Dr. No.

The English movie director and producer Tony Richardson was traveling with us too. The year before Mr. Richardson had won two Academy Awards, one for Best Director, and the other for the Best Picture 'Tom Jones.' He was loads of fun and spent most of the long flight relaxing in the lounge with the British singer, Matt Monro, who was one of the most popular entertainers of the day. He was best known for singing the James Bond movie song, 'From Russia with Love,' and for the Oscar-winning title song for the film 'Born Free.'

The two of them were joking and laughing together and, knowing Ursula Andress was on board, they were trying to place a bet on how old she was, to the point of trying to persuade ME to somehow ask her. I got caught up in their antics and approached the beautiful Ms. Andress and asked to see her passport. Amazingly, she handed it to me and I did a quick perusal for the birth date and gave it back to her. Pan Am would not have approved. Tony and Matt grinned from ear to ear when I told them but I never learned who won the bet!

Tina was bursting with the news that she had met her idol, Gregory Peck. "I was working First Class on a flight to London and Gregory Peck appeared in the doorway with his second wife and their two children following behind. I was standing there swooning to be so close to my idol," she told us.

He was one of the world's most popular film stars at the time and we had recently seen him acting Atticus Finch in the powerful movie 'To Kill a Mockingbird.'

"He was so handsome," she said, "And very charming and appreciative of everything we did for him and his family. On the same flight and traveling in First Class was an unaccompanied minor of about twelve, and the Peck children, roughly the same age, invited him to join them. The three children moved up to the lounge and happily played cards and games to pass the time.

"But this pleasant scene didn't last long.

"The captain's voice boomed over the intercom announcing an unexpected route change. We wondered what had happened and he explained that the plane had developed some kind of engine problem. A diversion to Chicago caused a commotion throughout the cabin but we quickly allayed any fears and consoled those with concerns that all would be taken care of.

"On landing in Chicago everyone was asked to deplane and the Peck family took the unaccompanied minor with them, with Pan Am approval, and hurried off to find another flight to London.

"Imagine that child's parents getting an unexpected phone call from Gregory Peck, such a famous film star, telling them their son was in his care and he would deliver him to them at Heathrow Airport!"

Edith was hesitant to tell us her story but we insisted and she said, "Okay, I was in Hawaii and sunning on the Waikiki beach with my roommate Elsa. She was excited about a date she had for the evening. He was bringing a friend along and she suggested I join them to make up a foursome. I thought that would be fun as I had no other plans and agreed."

Edith was laughing and said, "That evening, when we all met in the hotel lobby, I was introduced to my blind date. It was none other than Clint Eastwood – but I have to say, it was a pretty boring date!" That was in the Sixties when his name didn't register the impact it does today.

Karin added her story that she had met the master of suspense, Alfred Hitchcock, on one of her recent flights. She told us, "I was handing out the menus and said to Mr. Hitchcock, 'This is your menu, sir!' and he acted frightened and said to me in a hushed voice, 'You scared me!'" Karin said she was unprepared for such a response but added, "I was very pleased I had alarmed the great Alfred Hitchcock!" Just the year before his successful film "The Birds" was recognized as being among the best of his movies.

Gunnel burst in with, "I had Eddie Fisher traveling in First Class just after his divorce from Elizabeth Taylor and I was dying to ask him what it was like being married to her. But, of course, I never did."

After our supper of pizzas and salad, Greig offered to drive to the local Baskin & Robbins Ice Cream Parlor and buy some ice cream and fudge sauce. How could we say *No* to that and off he went. We cleared the supper dishes, left them in the sink and set out some bowls and spoons in readiness for dessert. It wasn't long before Greig returned with some rich, golden yellow vanilla ice cream and a container of thick, warm fudge sauce.

We all agreed it was the very best combination we had ever tasted and a fitting end to our evening of celebrity tales.

A week later I received a written notice from a supervisor asking me to go in for an interview. What was this all about, I was wondering? Having no idea, I arrived at the appointed hour and entered the office of the indomitable Miss Gottschall. I sat down in a chair across from her desk and waited. She smiled and started right in with, "How would you feel about accompanying the Archbishop of Canterbury on a flight to London?"

I was not expecting that question at all and was quite speechless. She asked me what I knew about the archbishop and other related questions. On the one hand it was quite an honor and on the other it posed a major challenge. A multitude of thoughts were racing through my brain. What would we talk about for eleven hours? I also wondered why he wasn't flying on British Overseas Airways.

Of course, I responded, "Yes, I would be honored to escort the Archbishop to London." Miss Gottschall must have detected a certain minute lack of total enthusiasm as I didn't hear any more about it after I left her office. I was flattered to have been considered but relieved not to be chosen for the task.

A few days later I was called in again for a day-long class on how to work the brand new TV and audio equipment that Pan Am was installing on their 707 aircraft. It was a cumbersome control box placed near the First Class lounge area and into this we inserted the taped movie and timed the programming. This was a new 'first' having big boxy television-like screens above every other row for passengers to watch a movie. They were quite the novelty and the passengers seemed happy to have the distraction on our long flights.

A week after this class, Bonnie and Edith stopped by to visit. Over a cup of coffee and chocolate chip cookies (we'd discovered another American favorite), our conversation eventually led to a discussion of the pros and cons of these new television screens on the planes.

Bonnie took a deep breath and began to tell us a tragic story that happened on one of her flights shortly after the installations. She looked glum as she told us, "The saddest thing that has ever happened to me on a flight so far was having a Pan Am couple, employees, travelling to Hawaii for a vacation with their long-awaited baby. They were sitting in the Economy section and the baby girl had been quite restless so the parents devotedly took turns holding her until she fell asleep. After the meal service, the First Class purser came back and invited them to sit up front and watch the movie to give them a break. It was quite a novelty then and he thought he was doing them a favor. They left their sleeping baby secured on their seats with a pillow and fastened seat belt. During the movie we experienced some light turbulence, but nothing to worry about.

"When the movie was over, the parents immediately returned aft to their seats. We heard this loud hysterical wail echo throughout the cabin and everyone became alarmed. The distraught parents had discovered their precious baby girl with her lower body hanging down from the seat and her lips turned blue. They were inconsolable. Despite being securely strapped down, the baby had somehow shifted or turned.

"The purser immediately requested a doctor over the PA system and, without hesitation, one of the stewardesses started mouth to mouth resuscitation. Fortunately there was a doctor on board and he came forward to offer help. He took the baby's vital signs, and then took turns with the stewardess assisting her with the resuscitation for the rest of the flight. They kept it up all through the landing and taxiing on the runway, not stopping once. The captain had radioed ahead for an ambulance and it was there waiting for us. The moment we opened the cabin doors the nurses quickly came aboard and took over. They rushed the baby, and the hysterical parents, to the hospital.

"We learned later the baby was pronounced dead on the plane. No amount of the resuscitation could bring her back. The whole crew was heartbroken on hearing the sad news and we all felt very subdued throughout our three-day layover in Hawaii. Those poor parents had waited so long for the baby only to have it taken from them so soon."

Today it would not be allowed to leave an infant unattended, nor the parents allowed into the First Class seating section.

47.

THE LETTER

One rare evening when the three of us were at the apartment, Roberta was busy with her paperwork, correspondence, and bid sheets spread out in confusion all over the small kitchen table. Mary and I joined her and sat down for a chat.

We were having a good time swapping stories when I happened to look down at the disheveled mess of paperwork on the table. I stared at the pile because I noticed the corner of an envelope sticking out. I was squinting hard at the handwriting because it looked very familiar and then, in a sickening flash, I recognized it as Jay's writing. I wondered what it was doing there stuck in the middle of Roberta's mail. My eyes were glued to it. I was getting uncomfortably hot and resisted the urge to just leave it be. I couldn't contain myself any longer and my burning curiosity got the better of me. Quietly, without a word, I leaned forward, stretched my arm and slowly pulled the envelope out of the stack.

My heart stopped.

It was Jay's name and military address in the top-left-hand corner BUT it was addressed to my dear friend and roommate Roberta. What dismayed me to the core was seeing it addressed to her at a local post office box number. I sat there motionless and speechless. I didn't know what to think. I held it in my hand feeling very hurt and on the point of fury asked Roberta, "What on earth are you doing writing to Jay – and why are you using a post office box number?" I dropped the letter on the table.

Roberta stared at it in silence and Mary sat frozen to her chair.

I didn't open it – I didn't need to – the address spoke volumes. I asked Roberta to please give me an explanation. She was such a good friend and I didn't want to lose that friendship but at the same time I was furious and felt totally betrayed. I was feeling worse about the betrayal from her than from him. I ran off to our bedroom feeling a huge loss. It was a matter of principle that your best friend did not encourage such a liaison.

The story went back to when Jay arrived at our apartment while I was still out flying and Roberta was there. She drove Jay around San Francisco in her brand new XKE and what guy wouldn't be thrilled by that? She treated him to meals at expensive restaurants with all the trimmings, drinks, and champagne. They had obviously had a good time.

I felt such a fool remembering I had prepared him the home-cooked meal of liver and onions, now hearing of the lavish dining experiences he'd had with Roberta.

I asked her, "Why, oh why, did you need to go to the trouble of getting a post office box?" That was the underhanded stab at our friendship. She didn't want me to see the mail coming in from Jay as we had one mailbox for the three of us. I couldn't believe a friend could stoop to such deception.

However, Roberta had been a good friend and had done so much for me, despite her conflicts, I couldn't see letting this incident destroy that relationship.

As for Jay – I didn't care. He wasn't worth the anguish.

48.

MOVING AGAIN

It felt so good to be home alone and have the apartment to myself. I was awoken early in the morning by the phone ringing by the bed and was surprised to hear Mary's voice calling all the way from Seattle. She'd flown up there to visit her boyfriend Ralph who had driven down from Vancouver, Canada. She sounded so excited and burst out with the news she was 'engaged' and I sat up in bed in shock. So soon!

My stomach churned as I had lost the edge of my friendship with Roberta and now Mary would soon be gone. I was saddened as our comfortable 'family' existence was crumbling with the first one of our trio leaving the nest. I had met her friend Ralph and they were well-suited. Mary was telling me she was going to ask for a transfer to the small Seattle base to be closer to him.

When I told Roberta the news she was devastated too. We realized we would lose Mary's share of the rent and the current space would be too much for the two of us. I couldn't bear the thought of moving again but it did make sense.

Mary flew back from Seattle and with mixed feelings she started the transfer process to another base, packing her belongings in preparation for her move to the state of Washington. It was quite disturbing seeing her cases lining up against the wall signaling her impending departure.

Roberta and I drove to San Mateo to look for a smaller apartment. We looked through a few but none were as big, bright and modern as the one we were in. However, we persisted with our

311

search and decided on a place off the El Camino Real. The building was older and smaller but looked well-kept and clean. We opted for a two-bedroom, one-bath apartment which would be adequate for the two of us. After all, we kept telling ourselves, we were only there half of every month, and rarely at the same time.

The apartment was a ground floor unit with a big bay window facing the front where there was parking for our cars, as well as more permanent parking under a carport in the rear. We reluctantly gave in our notice to the manager of our current apartment.

When the day came for Mary to leave for Seattle we wished her well and I knew I would miss her as the solid, down to earth, common sense one of our friendship trio.

Roberta and I packed our belongings and moved. We settled in and adapted to the cozy, smaller space. I enjoyed the ease of parking my little Sprite in front of the big window where I could keep an eye on it. Or, so I thought.

One morning I was clad in my uniform and preparing to drive to the airport. I tossed my bags into the trunk, climbed in the car, started the engine, and grabbed the gearshift knob. Something was amiss – it felt cold and strange. The knob wasn't there! I looked around but it was nowhere in sight. My hand was grasping a sharp metal stick.

How could someone move so fast, unscrew the knob and take off with it and me only feet away in the apartment? I was peeved but what could I do. It wasn't easy grabbing at the slick bare metal to change gears but I had no choice – I had to get to the airport.

Returning from a short Hawaii and Los Angeles run, I bought a replacement knob. Thinking this was a random act I went ahead and bought another fancy wooden one. Needless to say, a few days later, this time headed out for a shopping trip, I was so annoyed to find that one missing too. I couldn't believe it. Roberta and I were in and out of the apartment all the time. Again, I had to drive off without a knob. It wasn't easy changing gears.

This became irritating – and expensive!

I decided to go back to the plain, black plastic knob and see if that would deter any would-be thieves, thinking it didn't have the lure of the fancier wooden ones. What was it with sports cars in this area?

The cheap black one disappeared too. I was so mad and had no idea how the thefts could keep happening. For a while I just drove the car without a knob at all. I wasn't going to spend money on another one just to have that taken too.

There was something about my little car that courted trouble.

Shortly after these mishaps I left for a long flight to London and Paris. Roberta drove me to the airport so I could leave my car in the safety of the carport in the back of the building. After seven days away Roberta picked me up and drove me home. I was exhausted and not really concentrating on her news that something awful had happened in my absence.

When we arrived at the apartment, she immediately led me to the carport in the back. I took one look at my car and couldn't believe what I was seeing.

Close to tears I stood there in disbelief as, not only the gearshift knob was gone, but someone had ripped the roof open and had gutted the interior. It was a ghastly sight of wanton destruction of something I treasured. I was numb with shock and fuming at the same time.

The police had to be called and later the insurance company. I also needed to find someone to come and haul it off to a repair shop. Was it worth all the trouble and expense? I loved that car and I needed a vehicle to get to the airport and back.

I was carless again but Roberta had time off and offered to help. I only had a few days before my next flight but managed to call a repair shop. I was hopeful it would be fixed and ready for pick up when I returned from my trip.

49

GOLD MINE IN THE PHILLIPINES

My next bid line scheduled a Manila trip via Hawaii and Guam to Clark Air Base in the Philippines. We were given a three-day layover in Honolulu which was lots of time to enjoy the beach, swim in the ocean and get an even darker suntan – and forget about all the trials and tribulations surrounding my car.

On the plane from Honolulu, I worked the First Class cabin, a flight of seven hours and thirty minutes. We served a light dinner after take-off and a hot breakfast into Guam. We arrived slightly ahead of schedule, so we had to wait for the new crew taking over the flight. We were dropped off at our hotel at seven and I slept till eleven.

After a late breakfast, I sunbathed by the pool and was deeply engrossed in a good book, "Leap Over the Wall" by Monica Baldwin. It told of her life as a British nun for twenty-eight years before returning to the secular world. I didn't get far with my reading as a young, good-looking pilot sat down on the chaise next to me and introduced himself as Andy. We talked for awhile and he asked if I would like to join him on a drive to explore Tarague Beach. This sounded like a good chance to get away from the hotel so I said, "Yes."

Andy drove us around the island and down a lush green hillside on a narrow winding road to the United States Air Force Base, where the beach was located. We had to pass through the military gates but being Pan Am crew members security posed no problem. And there through the palm trees I saw one of the most beautiful beaches I had seen anywhere. The sand was pearly white and the palm trees were growing out of the sand, swaying in the breeze and bending toward the water.

Andy and I went for a long walk along the soft sandy beach and swam in the clear blue water, enjoying such a good time being carefree and relaxed. We found a secluded spot under a huge volcanic rock and sat down on the talcum powder soft sand to enjoy this beautiful pristine setting. Or so we hoped.

Our blissful serenity was soon shattered by an almighty blast of noise that momentarily deafened us. We clamped our hands over our ears to block out an ear-shattering roar of engines as enormous planes blackened the once-clear sky overhead.

We were witnessing B-52s taking off from the base runway and heading for war in Vietnam. They just kept coming, waves of them flying right over us casting ominous dark shadows across the beach. Andy knew what they were and told me they were long-range strategic bombers, commonly known as BUFFs – Big Ugly Fat F.......s! With disturbing thoughts of the mission they were on, and the constant shattering noise of the engines, we decided it was time to leave.

Sadly, there ended a romantic interlude.

We were constantly reminded during these years that we were flying very close to a war in which the United States was very much involved. The war had escalated to a full force commitment in 1965.

At one a.m. the following morning the crew drove to Anderson Air Base where we had a full load of passengers boarding the plane. The flight left at three-fifteen. I worked aft and we served a hot breakfast to all the military passengers. That entailed hectic organization in the galley and a lot of walking up and down the aisle carrying the food trays two at a time, one in each hand.

At Clark Air Base the passengers disembarked and we had a two-hour layover in their terminal before flying on to Saigon.

We had another two-hour layover at Tan Son Nhut so we sat in the airport café and sipped ice cold Cokes, bought postcards and some of us perused a stall showcasing heavy cast bronze Vietnamese women's heads. They were beautifully sculpted and some of us couldn't resist the temptation to buy one.

New passengers boarded the plane including General Richard Stillwell who was the Chief of Staff to General Westmoreland. We were flying back to Clark which had become an important logistics hub during the War.

On arrival at Clark, it was stifling hot (as always) near one hundred degrees. We had to wait for our bags to be unloaded and tried to find whatever shade we could. Stripping down as much as we dared, we removed our jackets, hats, and gloves but had to endure the uncomfortably tight girdles, our hose, and high heels.

In that sticky heat the crew climbed into a battered and worn waiting bus. The young Filipino driver informed us there was NO air conditioning. We sighed but the worst news was we had to put up with this discomfort and stay on this hot rickety bus all the way back to Manila; Clark was about forty miles north-west of the city, so we were in for a long hour's bumpy drive on slow roads. There were few expressways to speed us along.

There was no use complaining, this was all part of the job.

By now the pilots were also peeling off their jackets and ties, and unbuttoning their shirts. The humidity in that bus must have been inhumanely high and we were all drained and damp by the time we reached the Manila Hotel.

What a bedraggled group we must have looked. We were not exactly upholding the Pan Am image. As soon as the driver opened the doors, we made a dash for the lobby to luxuriate in the icy cold air conditioning.

Upon checking in at the reception desk Captain Gilbert asked if anyone would like to join him the next day to tour a gold mine not too far from Manila. He knew someone affiliated with the mine and was able to take a small group along with him. What a unique opportunity; I signed on along with two pilots and two stewardesses. We were to leave early the following morning and the captain advised us to wear sturdy shoes and be prepared for a good two-hour drive.

I was exhausted from the long hot bus ride and went straight to my hotel room. I enjoyed a long relaxing shower and changed into a cool dress. After a light supper with the crew in the dining room, I excused myself and went straight up to bed and hopefully to a good night's sleep. Always mindful of 'intruders' I pushed and shoved a heavy armchair in front of the door!

In the morning our small group met in the lobby and the captain led us outside where we climbed into a van to be driven to the gold mine. The morning air felt pleasantly cool.

Leaving the crowded city streets behind us, we drove through long stretches parched-brown, dusty, barren country. Eventually we arrived at the small-scale mining operation, a rough grey rock wall with a large gaping hole of an entrance hewn into the front.

An older mine manager met us and told us he would be our guide. 'Fernando' led the girls to a dilapidated changing room, opened a creaky wooden door and handed each of us a set of well-worn, but washed clean, khaki and grey overalls. This was a shock as we weren't expecting to disrobe. But we changed into the baggy outfits and placed our clothes in neat piles on a shelf. We stepped outside and were handed a heavy helmet with a miner's lamp attached and were instructed to put them on. So much for our hairdos!

Looking like a work gang in our overalls and helmets, we were led to the gaping mine entrance where we were told to climb into an open rusty trolley. We held on tight as it jerked and rumbled down a narrow track – suddenly facing a very steep descent. The light faded and the air felt heavier and hotter; finally, the creaky vehicle slowed and ground to a jolting halt. We clambered out into the opening of a rough-hewn cave leading into a black tunnel with huge rope nets hung across the roofline, and immediately felt the suffocating heat.

To show us how blistering hot the rock surface was, our leader took a raw egg, broke it into a mug and threw the contents onto the vertical side of the rock wall – the egg instantly sizzled, cooked hard and stuck to the rock. We gasped. Was it really *that* hot? Now we felt hotter than ever.

317

The guide told us the isle of Luzon was called the Isle of Gold by the Chinese traders in the third century, but the gold industry practically collapsed due to the Pacific war during World War Two.

We were shown the gold veins, black lines running along the rock wall, and were given a small rock with a vein running through it to keep as a souvenir. As we stumbled along on the rough rock floor, we were led deeper into the dark cave. We were asked to climb up onto a ledge which was hewn out along a shaft which wasn't very high. It was open on one side, so we found ourselves bent over and trying to balance along the very narrow walkway. The footing was difficult as we were hobbling along on loose rocks and stones.

However did the miners work in conditions like this? The Filipino men were smaller and a lot shorter than us so they could at least stand upright but how did they endure the heat? I had never felt so uncomfortably hot and never had I perspired so much in my life! In that claustrophobic, steamy hot space I was dripping and at the point of losing my composure.

Soaked through and beginning to feel disturbingly light-headed in these cramped conditions, I had to keep talking to myself: don't stop, put one foot in front of the other, it can't be much longer.. Keep going, no matter what. I risked a look ahead and saw the captain and pilots plodding along, bent over under the same confined surroundings, and I thought if they can withstand these conditions, then I can too. After all, I was one of the youngest in the group.

At long last we reached the end of that torturous trek and could jump down off the rocky ledge onto surer footing. My legs felt wobbly and detached from my body. My hair was soaked under the metal helmet as I joined the others to eagerly climb back in the mine tram to be shunted up to the surface and to cooler, fresher air.

The girls were led to a changing room with showers and toilets. We looked inside and were horrified to see a line of toilets on one side of the long narrow space with NO doors at all – nothing – merely open to the large room. They looked like a long line of urinals and were looking rather worse for wear, gaping wide open showing ugly patches of rust and murky brown water. Ugh! A long mirror, cracked and pot-marked hung opposite behind the wash basins. We quickly forgot about modesty and succumbed to desperation.

Then we had to face the showers and there were no curtains or doors. A row of rusty-looking shower heads poked out of the crumbling ceiling. We had no choice so, frantic to get clean, we turned on the taps and felt the water shooting out – frigidly cold. As uncomfortably hot as we were, the icy jets felt deliciously refreshing as we let the water wash over our steaming bodies. We tried to get as clean as we possibly could – with no soap. It was a good thing the air was hot as the towels were practically threadbare.

Our dry clothes were waiting for us where they were left and we dressed quickly, feeling the bliss of being momentarily cool and clean before venturing back into the heat outside.

We thanked Captain Gilbert for the unique experience and boarded the van for the drive back to the hotel.

My souvenir rock with the gold vein was regrettably tossed into the wastebasket one day while cleaning out for one of our moves.

50

RAYMOND BURR

On a flight from Manila to Saigon we had many Australian military personnel on board. The galley had been stocked with lots of calamansi juice – a fruit native to the Philippines resembling a small round lime. When ripe the skin, pulp and juice turn tangerine orange in color and the juice tastes similar to lemonade. The Australians had never heard of the fruit but tasted the juice, loved it and drank up *all* of our supply. When that was gone, they were happily drinking *all* the beer and buying *all* the English cigarettes we carried on board. But, on arrival at Tan Son Nhut their happy-go-lucky attitudes became shrouded with a solemn mask and they disembarked in a subdued and quiet demeanor. We were becoming used to this reaction. Thoughts of the war that awaited them had a sobering effect on everyone.

Back in Burlingame Bonnie told us she had experienced Australian soldiers on board a flight returning to Da Nang after an R&R (rest and recuperation) in Taipei.

"One of the young soldiers went beserk and in a rage smashed the mirror in the bathroom. The Pan Am captain was informed and he must have called ahead as the MPs were waiting for the soldier when we landed. We rushed to tell them he was not dangerous just drunk and upset about having to return to the war." Bonnie got this information from the other soldiers sitting in his row and she said it was very sad, under the circumstances, to see this young fellow handcuffed and escorted off the plane.

We were the fortunate ones continuing on to in Singapore. After leaving the soldiers behind in Vietnam, this layover had a pall hanging over our spirits.

We spent two days shopping and sightseeing before we had an early pick-up the following morning. I ordered room service breakfast for five-thirty a.m. and the scrambled eggs, toast standing in a rack, marmalade and a pot of tea arrived right on time. I loved Singapore because of the British traditions that had remained.

At the airport I was asked to work the First Class cabin as purser but we only had three business passengers to Saigon – that was an ideal number to attend to without being rushed for such a short flight. We served our chilled Charles Heidsieck champagne and fresh orange juice followed with hot gooey-cheese omelets and bacon.

At Tan Son Nhut a Pan Am representative came aboard and advised me that we were picking up a special passenger in First Class, Mr. Raymond Burr.

This was 'the' Raymond Burr who was the actor portraying the Los Angeles defense attorney in the successful and popular television series "Perry Mason." I was so surprised to see him climbing up the ramp and appearing so tall and large in build. He seemed to fill up the entire doorway as he entered the plane.

I welcomed him aboard, introduced myself, and showed him to his first row seat making sure he was comfortable. The announcements were made and after take-off I approached Mr. Burr and asked him what he would like to drink. He didn't hesitate to say he'd love a 'Gin and It.'

Oh dear, I had never heard of that one. Whatever was the 'It' part? True to training and not admitting I didn't know what 'It' was, I hurriedly went through the cabin and asked the other purser in the back for help but she hadn't heard of it either.

In desperation I felt at least one of the pilots should know, so I tentatively knocked on the cockpit door, stepped in and explained my dilemma.

"HELP! What is a Gin and It? Raymond Burr has ordered one and no-one on the crew knows what the 'It' is."

They all thought for a few moments and much to my dismay they shook their heads and declared they had no idea either. I was crushed and had no other way out but to go back to Mr. Burr and ask him, which I did.

"Mr. Burr, what is the 'It' part with the Gin? I've asked the pilots in the cockpit and the crew members in the cabin and not one of them knows." He looked up, grinned widely and explained, "The 'It' stands for Italian Vermouth."

So simple, but now I knew!

Mr. Raymond Burr got his Gin and It. In fact he enjoyed it so much he ordered another. He told me he was happy to sit back and relax as he had been busy entertaining the American troops in South Vietnam on behalf of the USO (United Service Organization). He enjoyed his Malayan Chicken Curry with a glass of cooled white Chardonnay wine for lunch. When he disembarked in Manila he gave me a heartfelt handshake and a "Thank You for excellent service."

Yet another interesting celebrity experience.

After that highlight, things went downhill. Leaving Manila for Guam we were delayed due to a shortage of meals. We were to serve a full lunch course with bar service and we had been supplied with half the amount of food we needed. Now we had to wait for the local commissary crew to deliver the extra food, which in good time they did. But our passengers were becoming agitated as they were now going to be late for their arrival in Guam.

When the meals were delivered, we closed the doors and took off. The passengers relaxed and the cockpit was able to make up some of the lost time so we were only forty-five minutes later than scheduled.

From Guam to Honolulu we had a maximum load passengers in the back and sixteen in front. Just as everyone was settling down, the Stewardess Alert button rang persistently and I walked down the aisle looking for the flashing red light to see what was needed.

As I approached the seat row, I was confronted with a rather obese male passenger flailing his arms and demanding to see the captain. When I politely asked him what was bothering him, he became irate and started complaining at being seated next to a mother with a baby on her lap!

I was concerned this large irate man could become a danger to the child so I asked him to follow me to a rear empty First Class seat (there were no empty seats aft). He then became more belligerent, raising his voice so all could hear and demanded to get off the plane. I knew it was time to call the cockpit and ask for help. The captain was busy preparing the plane for take-off, so the navigator, Jack, came out and strode up to the offending passenger. He calmly talked with him while trying to avoid the flailing arms or a punch in the jaw.

Fortunately the navigator was able to subdue him and with a firm hand escorted him to his original seat in the back of the plane. I had to keep a wary eye on this unpredictable passenger throughout the entire flight but he did eventually settle down.

We started with the liquor service and quickly found out we had some heavy drinkers on board so we hurriedly handed out the nighttime snack of assorted sandwiches. The food helped and soon most of the passengers were sleeping.

I asked the stewardesses, Anne and Francis, if they would mind working in the galley together to scramble the eggs for the breakfast service – that's a lot of scrambling for a full load of passengers.

The girls were happy to work side-by-side despite the limited space in the galley and I relaxed thinking all was going well. My contentment was short-lived. Anne and Francis soon became distraught when they discovered half the eggs were missing. They only had enough for thirty passengers!

First we'd been delayed in Manila without enough food, and again we were facing the same discrepancy from Guam Commissary. Was there a conspiracy afoot?

Unlike First Class where the eggs were whole, in the back they came already broken and semi-beaten in pans. I dashed up front to the First Class galley and begged for some eggs from their supply. They could only spare a few but nowhere near enough for all our passengers in the back. The girls scrambled all we had and I regretted having to severely cut down on individual portions when serving onto the plates. We handed out the trays of food as fast as we could as time was not in our favor.

As we pushed to continue our breakfast service, we were shocked to hear the intercom message from the captain announcing our descent – much sooner than expected. This announcement meant my timed meal service should have been started much sooner. What a dilemma! We still had breakfast trays out. With so little time left, we stopped scrambling and rushed to pick up what we could and stacked everything on the galley floor. Much to my embarrassment, a few passengers forward had to be left unfed. Time was fast running out for us to reach our crew seats and buckle up for landing.

I had to write a detailed report of this nightmarish 'eggceptional' service. I was responsible for the mess but I explained, with one-hundred-and-twenty-plus passengers, scrambling eggs was NOT a good meal plan. There simply was no time to prepare everything – especially when supplied with half the number of eggs needed. I was hopeful that scrambled eggs for that number of people would be discontinued from the breakfast menu from that time on.

We arrived at our hotel in the early morning hours and I was so exhausted I changed out of my uniform and slept till two in the afternoon.

I did have a fun surprise when I bumped into Tina walking toward the beach, so I joined her as I was headed in the same direction. We camped out on the sand and I told her the harrowing egg saga and she replied, "That's nothing compared with what happened to me."

She had been working the galley in the Economy section on her flight from Tokyo and she told me, "I had changed into my clean, freshly ironed smock and was all ready to start work. I placed the big pans of eggs on the narrow work counter and, working by myself, was happily busy with the scrambling fork. In the middle of my routine, with absolutely no warning, the plane hit an air pocket and the next thing I remember was sinking down toward the floor. But, as I was dragged down, the raw eggs flew up out of the pans in a liquid sheet of yellow.

"The eggs did fall down – rapidly – but all over me," she said. "What a mess that was to clean up, not only the galley but me too."

Yet again, being a stewardess was certainly not 'glamorous' all of the time.

51.

NEW YEAR'S EVE IN GUAM

New Year's Eve 1965 and we were flying a plane from Singapore to Guam. On arrival at Agana the crew disembarked and boarded the bus to the hotel. The captain and crew were merrily planning a party to celebrate the New Year. However, on arrival at the hotel the receptionist told us a formal invitation had been delivered and she handed it to our captain.

The captain opened the envelope and pulled out an enclosed card. He took his time scanning the message and then announced to the waiting expectant crew that we had been invited to attend a New Year's Eve Party given by the Commanding Officer of the Navy Destroyer docked at the Naval Air Station.

We were excited at the prospect of a *real* party and all thought it would be a lot more fun and agreed to attend. The girls on this crew were a mix of nationalities as I was English, Brit was Swedish, Ula was German, Sin Kit was Chinese and Kari was from Holland.

That evening we took our time dressing and primping for this special occasion. We boarded the crew bus and one of the pilots drove us to the Commanding Officer's base home. We were looking forward to meeting some young officers and having a good time.

The Commanding Officer's wife graciously welcomed us into their home and introduced us to the married officers and their wives. The room felt tropical with rattan furniture, bamboo patterns on the window drapes and fans buzzing overhead. With the introductions over, we were soon surrounded by the eager young bachelors. They were fascinated we were from so many different countries and we chatted for awhile munching on chips and dips while sipping refreshing gin and tonics.

One young man stood out to me and he came over and introduced himself as Freddi. He was a young Ensign who appeared quiet and charming, and told me he was the chaplain on the ship. I thought he appeared much too young for such a position.

There was plenty to drink and lots of good barbecued ribs and hamburgers to eat. We talked and danced until the midnight hour approached when Freddi *suddenly* suggested taking me for a drive around the island. What fun! I told him that was a super idea and he took my hand and escorted me outside to his car. The roof was down and we jumped in and off we drove.

Here I was with this dashing young officer at the midnight hour on New Year's Eve. We explored this beautiful island until six in the morning – it really was a paradise by moonlight. The air was refreshingly cool as we drove along beautiful palm-tree-lined beaches, the water looking ebony black against the moonlit white sand. Everywhere everything seemed still and asleep and we felt like intruders disturbing the quiet hush of the island's night. What a special romantic way to usher in the brand new year of 1966.

The spell was broken when Freddi rounded a curve in the road and there we were back to the stark outline of the hotel. He slowed to a stop, jumped out and led me to my door. Standing on the doorstep he told me he would be honored to have me join him and his fellow officers for their New Year's Day celebration dinner aboard the ship that same evening. This was a very special invitation and I was extremely flattered.

I fell into a happy sleep for most of the day having been up and awake all through the night. I was thrilled and excited to be going aboard a US Navy Destroyer but especially to be seeing Freddi again.

Fortunately, I had packed another favorite dress, handmade in Bangkok of deep green Thai silk, and I wore my wine-red sandals. Right on time a Navy truck drove up to the hotel and parked outside my room. I was somewhat surprised because it wasn't Freddi who jumped out.

What is going on? I thought.

The stranger in uniform knocked on my door. I was wondering who it was but opened the door and he introduced himself as Gerry. He saw the perplexed expression on my face and explained that Freddi had sent him to pick me up. Again, I was taking off with a total stranger as I climbed into the truck and was driven to the Navy base. Gerry led me to the ship where I was relieved and happy to see Freddi waiting for me, dressed in his very smart white uniform.

Being the only girl on the ship was daunting especially when I was escorted into the formal Ward Room. There, standing at attention, were all the officers in their full white uniforms waiting for me to be seated first at the long table. The captain was at the head and I was in the middle of the table feeling both very special and very nervous. Freddi was seated next to me.

Everything was extremely formal. The food was presented on silver platters and served at each place. I picked up the silver knife and fork and was amazed at how heavy they were. The food was delicious and I enjoyed the entire evening. I was thankful for all the manners and table etiquette that had been drummed into me throughout childhood.

When the evening was over, Freddi drove me back to the hotel. He explained that his ship was about to go out to sea for two weeks and he would like to write to me and asked for my address. I was only too happy to give it to him.

What a memorable New Year's Day!

Back in San Francisco I tried hard to schedule another Guam flight and was lucky to have one show up on my line the following month. I wrote to Freddi and told him I would be back again in three weeks.

Freddi confirmed that his ship should be at the base around the time my flight was due in. I was excited to be seeing him again and when our crew arrived at the hotel and I had settled into my room, he called and invited me out for a casual dinner. We enjoyed the evening telling stories about our adventures.

Again, he surprised me by saying he loved flying and would I like to go for a flight in a small plane to see the sun rise over the island. This young man was full of wonderful ideas. What a thrill that would be so I didn't hesitate to say, "YES – when?"

Freddi said he'd drive over to the hotel to pick me up at three the following morning. This was in the middle of the night, so I called the hotel desk and asked for a wake-up call and also set the room alarm clock. I didn't get much sleep as I was so afraid I wouldn't hear either the alarm or the call. However, I heard both at two-thirty and sprang out of bed, cleaned up and hastily pulled on a pair of long white Bermuda shorts and a cool navy blue shirt for this next adventure – at the same time hoping Freddi wouldn't forget.

But, at three on the dot, there was a gentle knock at the door and there he was.

In the early morning quiet we stole away and drove to the airfield where he showed me the plane. This was going to be fun as it was the very first time I'd be flying in a small airplane.

I was reassured to see Freddi methodically checked everything before we climbed in. The plane taxied and rumbled down the runway and off we soared into the inky blue sky. What a difference from the huge 707 jets. The island was so much more beautiful seen from the air and even more enchanting in the dawning light as the sun began peeking from behind the hills.

We were touched by the sudden blaze of light. The watercolor glow of pale pinks, mauves and yellows hung over the tropical coastline with its arching, swaying palm trees, the silver sandy beaches, the sheer limestone coastal cliffs, and all the lower hills inland. Freddi was flying us around the entire island and we were awed by the reverent stillness. The scene below us was one of early morning peace and calm – no traffic and no people disturbing the tranquility.

All of a sudden, Freddi turned to me and asked me if I'd like to take the controls and fly the plane on my own.

"What, *me*, steer the plane?" I balked.

Then I thought, "Why not! I'll try anything." And there I was up in the skies pulling on the rudder and veering over left and then leaning right, and probably making Freddi a bit tense though he never showed it.

I was thrilled for the piloting experience but was happy to pass the controls back to Freddi. We continued swooping around the lush green hills and over beautiful little coves and sandy beaches with ever more palm trees bending gracefully toward the water – this unspoiled island did truly look like paradise. We were one with the rising sun and flying free in its magical light.

Freddi landed the plane smoothly. Morning light had dawned and he drove me back to the hotel as he had to get to work on the ship and I had to prepare for a flight to Hawaii and on home. It was a long farewell but we promised to write and keep in touch.

This is what I loved about being an international stewardess – all these unique experiences that came our way.

Nowadays, this once picturesque island is overdeveloped with huge blocks of highrise hotels lining the beautiful beaches. How fortunate we were to have seen it in its unspoiled natural beauty.

52

THE ERRANT PILOT

Scheduled for a flight to Japan with a stop in Hawaii, I drove to the airport and checked in at the Briefing Room. Captain Richards introduced the pilots joining him in the cockpit and the Senior Purser asked me to work the First Class cabin on the leg to Hawaii.

As purser, I boarded the plane early. I was busy setting up the front lounge area, laying out the new monthly and weekly magazines, the newspapers, and the Pan Am packets of cigarettes. Then I heard the pilots on the boarding ramp.

As I happened to glance up, the good-looking younger pilot stepped into the plane and caught my attention. He was strikingly handsome, especially in his uniform, with short dark hair and deep blue eyes. He was quite oblivious of my presence and was standing in the doorway before entering the cockpit. I was curious to see him tugging at a ring he was wearing on the third finger of his left hand which I assumed to be a wedding band. He succeeded in taking it off and nonchalantly dropped it into his jacket pocket. I didn't think much more of it at the time, as many pilots didn't wear rings as a safety precaution, and continued with my duties.

I had two newly-graduated Swedish girls, Lotta and Sidsel, working with me up front. As the flight to Hawaii progressed, I noticed the 'ringless' pilot making an obvious attempt to get to know the very attractive tall, blonde stewardess, Lotta. He kept coming out of the cockpit on a number of excuses and I couldn't help but notice that Lotta seemed quite flattered with his attention.

The same crew continued on to Japan after a three-day layover in Hawaii. Lotta and Sidsel were working the aft cabin with me and Lotta confided that the handsome pilot, Tommy, had wined and dined her during the Honolulu layover. On hearing this and seeing how smitten she was, I was in a dilemma.

Did I interfere and forewarn her of what I had seen or did I just stay out of it?

I agonized over this during the entire flight – eight long hours. On arrival at the hotel in Tokyo, I determined if I were the one in the same situation, I would want to know.

At an opportune moment, when we were signing in at the hotel front desk, I approached Lotta and asked her to come to my room as I had something I needed to tell her. An hour later she knocked on my door and her roommate Sidsel was with her.

We sat down and I got straight to the point. I told Lotta, "I've noticed how the young pilot, Tommy, has been spending a lot of time with you. BUT I feel you should know that when he boarded the plane in San Francisco, I did see him remove what appeared to be a wedding band from his left hand and he hasn't worn it since. I just want you to be warned so you don't make a fool of yourself."

Lotta was shaken and saddened, but also thankful I had bothered to let her know. I was relieved I had done something about it too. Now it was her decision to confront him or not!

The next morning the cabin crew met in the hotel dining room for breakfast. Another Swedish girl on our crew, Christina, asked me if I would join her for a train ride to Nikko – a big tourist destination. Nikko, which means the light of the sun, is the center of Shinto and Buddhist mountain worship with many shrines and temples.

We had a three-day layover so I said, "That's a great idea, let's go!" Captain Richards granted his permission and advised us to be very careful. The hotel gave us the information we needed for transportation and told us a tour bus would pick us up at the front entrance.

This was a big adventure for the two of us as Nikko was about eighty-eight miles north of Tokyo. The bus dropped us off at the railway station and we were thrilled to board the sleek, long bullet train.

We were immensely impressed. The interior's spotlessly clean, pale yellow upholstery and décor made quite an impact. We sat in comfortable seats that reclined and swiveled. With all the train rides I had taken in England with British Rail, I had never seen anything this modern. On the down side, the train was traveling at such high speed we didn't see much of the countryside which became a never-ending blur as we sped by.

Disembarking we boarded a small bus to continue our journey. The hills appeared unusually pointed in shape as we began an incredible climb up a steep mountainside to Kegon Falls.

We were on the Irohazaka Driveway and as the bus wound its way upward through forested mountain slopes, we could see the sharp hairpin bends zig-zagging below us. There were forty-eight of them and the driver told us this was because of the forty-eight letters in the Japanese alphabet. The bus slowed down noticeably to maneuver around these tight turns and we were glad it did when we looked down and saw the steep drop off the edge of the road.

When we arrived at Nikko we were escorted to the Lakeside Hotel for lunch. Two young Mexican businessmen asked to join us at our table and sat down before we had a chance to say NO. However, they were very friendly and treated us to beer and cognac with our lunch. The lake outside our window appeared unusually serene and dainty swirls of mist drifted across the water.

We climbed aboard the bus and continued our journey to the Futura-san shrine. There we ascended a steep stairway of narrow stone steps to see a demonstration of the Kagura dance of Shintoism – the Mikokagura was danced by two girls who were the Shrine maidens. Their extremely long black hair was tied in white paper strips. Their ritualistic dance steps depicted the trampling down of evil spirits and are tied to the rhythms of their agricultural calendar.

The same two Mexican men were following behind us and trying hard to engage us in conversation, but we declined their advances as they were becoming annoying.

We ambled down a long narrow path to the Toshuga shrine and had to cleanse ourselves with the pure spring water before entering. This magnificent shrine is the mausoleum of the first Tokugawa Shogun and is covered with the intricate carvings and decoration of the seventeenth century artisans.

Walking on, we passed by the horse stables where the three famous monkeys were carved over the door – See no evil, Hear no evil and Speak no evil – they were there supposedly to cure all the horse ailments of the past.

A large colorful sleeping cat was guarding the doorway leading to the mausoleum entrance of the Okusha inner shrine. The beautiful image was carved by the left-handed sculptor, Jingorou Hidari. We were told the incredible story that he cut off his right hand in appreciation of his master!

Further along the winding walkway we came to the Togoshu Treasury Shrine. We were asked to please remove our shoes before entering. There was an endless line of footwear of all sizes and shapes lined up neatly along the low stone wall and we hoped ours would still be there when we came out.

Stepping inside, the atmosphere was dark and the smell of incense hung heavy in the air. We faced an enormous circular mirror which determined whether the mind was pure or evil; alongside hung many tricolor tassels representing black for the future, red for the present and yellow for the past. The small space was crowded and oppressive and we were anxious to get outside into the fresh air.

The ever-growing line of shoes under the wall looked like forsaken brown weeds. We were happy to find ours patiently waiting for us where we had left them.

Far off in the distance we saw the Sinkyo Bridge, then a national treasure, crossing the Ariyo River. It was a sacred bridge built one-thousand-three-hundred years ago for the Emperor and his messenger who were the only ones allowed to cross.

Christina and I were tiring with so much walking and so much to comprehend and remember. We were only too happy to board the bus and rest our legs for our return journey to Tokyo.

It had been a long day but what an interesting, enriching adventure. I thought back to my routine life in London and had to thank Pan Am for the opportunity to experience these exotic foreign cultures and customs – all so fascinating and mysterious.

The following morning I met the other girls on our crew and they were excited about an Ikebana Flower Arranging Class they had heard about and asked me to join them that afternoon.

We took taxis to the Sogetsu Art School and there we were led to the Ikebana classroom. Four of us joined six local Japanese ladies which made the whole experience so much more culturally interesting.

The instructor entered the room. She was a short, very attractive Japanese lady who spoke English, "A little," she said with a smile. Her black hair was pulled straight back into a tight bun.

She explained that Ikebana means 'living flowers' and is the Japanese art of flower arrangement. We learned it is a disciplined artform of graceful lines and minimalism and were told to follow her lead in silence to appreciate and feel close to nature. She said, "The living arrangement brings nature and humanity together."

Before each of us were the kenzan metal flower holder, a low black ceramic container, and shears to cut the branches and blue iris flowers to the desired lengths. We struggled to create a presentable arrangement. For something so simple, it was not easy to create, however, we did very well. Unfortunately our floral creations had to be left behind.

We felt enriched by the harmony and beauty of the Ikebana experience especially having learned something new.

53

UNUSUAL ENCOUNTER

I met Captain Robb and the crew at the airport briefing office when checking in for a flight to Hawaii. This captain was in his early fifties and very sure of himself.

We arrived at our hotel in Honolulu late in the evening and across the lobby I saw Roberta. I called her name and she turned around in surprise. She told me she was rooming with Karin our classmate and suggested the three of us meet for an early sunrise breakfast in the Royal Hawaiian beachfront restaurant at six o'clock.

I felt rejuvenated after a good night's sleep and woke early to meet the others. We sat outside on the deck looking out over the deserted sandy beach and crystal clear Pacific Ocean. We were mesmerized by the emerging glow of the brilliant sunrise spreading across the horizon. We relaxed in the early morning balmy sea air and enjoyed our fresh papaya and flaky sweet rolls with steaming hot coffee. The beach was pleasantly and unusually quiet so early in the morning which added to the beauty and tranquility of the scene before us.

Later, Roberta and I spent a couple of hours sunbathing and swimming before I had to return to my room to prepare for my next flight out to Los Angeles. The phone rang shrilly and I tentatively picked it up, always wondering if it was a flight change. I was taken aback to hear a familiar voice on the other end – Captain Robb. I was even more surprised when he asked me out for dinner that evening. This was quite an honor and quite flattering coming from a *captain*. I explained I had a pick-up that afternoon and regretfully couldn't join him. He told me he was sorry but was also leaving the next day for Los Angeles. And I didn't think any more about it.

In the Los Angeles hotel we were informed our trip to Honolulu had been cancelled and we were to stay in Los Angeles for two more days to take a London flight up to San Francisco. I was now used to our flight plans changing unexpectedly and retired to my room.

Later in the day I noticed a red flashing light on the room phone so I picked up for the message and was astounded to hear Captain Robb's voice – again. He'd flown in on a later flight and said he would like to take me on a tour of Beverly Hills the next day. Amazed at the offer and regaining my senses, I agreed to meet him in the lobby the following morning. It seemed a fun and safe way to spend the day.

He rented a car and off we went driving all over town. He took me to the Will Rogers Memorial Park on Sunset Boulevard where we parked the car and wandered around the beautiful gardens, along meandering waterways and brightly colored well-manicured flower beds. It seemed such a tranquil and peaceful haven away from the noisy bustle of Los Angeles traffic.

Toward the end of the afternoon Captain Robb asked me to join him for dinner at the Beverly Hilton. I was quite in awe really as I was a young purser and he was an experienced older captain. He was the perfect gentleman and we did have a great time. I looked on him as a father figure but I have the feeling he wasn't looking at me as a daughter. I did wonder if he was married.

A week later I was back in Honolulu enjoying a relaxing layover before heading on to Sydney. I was on my own and decided to soak up the sun. Armed with a beach towel and a good book to read, I headed to the Waikiki beach. No sooner had I laid out my towel and covered myself in baby oil than I heard a male voice calling my name. I looked around and was startled to see Captain Robb advancing toward my spot. He explained that he'd arrived on a flight the day before and settled himself down on the sand alongside me.

The coincidences of his sudden appearances were making me wonder if they were pre-planned. Anyway, he chatted for awhile and then insisted on taking me out to dinner that evening. I could have said 'No' but, of course, I said 'Yes' as I had no other plans.

Captain Robb took me to a very special restaurant for dinner and we enjoyed the evening immensely. All very proper yet fun!
I wasn't interested in encouraging a romantic liaison and was quite relieved when there weren't any further unusual encounters.

On the flight to Sydney I was working in the Economy section. It was nighttime when we landed at Nadi, Fiji, for refueling. I walked the aisle checking on the needs of the passengers. The lighting was dimmed and a rather obese male passenger was hanging over his seat into the aisle – fast asleep. I was trying hard not to wake him as I climbed around him to squeeze by.

Much to my annoyance I wasn't careful enough, tripped and fell waking up the sleeping passenger in the process. On pulling myself up off the floor I felt an intense pain in my hand and realized that while falling I had bashed my thumb backwards – hard. I tried to ignore it and continued walking down the aisle as if nothing had happened. The pain was intense and I didn't like the feeling of light-headedness that was creeping over me. I almost fainted right there in the middle of the cabin but managed to stumble back to the rear crew seat and sit down.

One of the stewardesses ran forward and asked the senior purser to come back to check me over and he didn't hesitate to grab the intercom to ask if there was a doctor on board. By now the whole cabin was awake and an elderly gentleman approached. He said he was a doctor and he very carefully examined my hand.

I hated all the fuss and felt so silly and embarrassed because to me the injury was minor but the doctor advised me to stay seated and rest. This meant the crew had to do the breakfast service to Sydney without me and that made me feel even worse.

Thank goodness I was feeling much better by the time we reached Australia. These incidents, no matter how trivial, had to be written up in the flight log and I was told to call the Pan Am doctor when in Sydney.

The Pan Am office gave me the name and phone number to call which I did from my hotel room. I had to get a taxi to see a Dr. Mallett having no idea where in Sydney the office was. The doctor was very pleasant, middle-aged, and made me feel comfortable. After hearing the story, he insisted on X-rays being taken, thankfully, right there in his building.

The next day Dr. Mallett left a message on my room phone with the good news that no bones were broken and I was granted an okay to continue flying on my scheduled flight.

I was so happy not to be stranded in Sydney, losing my line, and not knowing when and how I would be getting back home, which would have been the case with a more serious injury.

Arriving in Hawaii and entering our hotel, I saw Mona quietly sitting in the cool of the lobby. I waved and she beckoned me over. She had returned from a Sydney trip the day before mine. I thought she looked pale and not as peppy as usual so I sat down next to her and asked if she was all right. She quietly explained to me why she wasn't feeling so good.

"Our crew checked in early at the hotel in Sydney, so we all decided to enjoy some cool beer and local mussels down by the wharf. We entered a fun restaurant hanging out over the water and were escorted to a table on the deck where we soaked up the sunshine and enjoyed the views.

"The waiter brought us huge bowls of local mussels and lots of ice cold Australian beer. We ate heartily and drank thirstily. Pretty soon we were feeling drowsy from the effects of our overindulgence and the staggering time difference. We decided it was time to leave so we hailed taxis to drive us back to the hotel.

"Well, as soon as we reached our rooms we ALL became sick, but my roommate and I became very, *very* sick. We were feeling so ill we stayed in our room for the entire three-day layover. The

Pan Am doctor had to visit several times each day to give us shots and pills. Oh God, I was so sick. I'll never ever eat mussels again," she wailed.

Reliving the experience was making Mona look paler than ever but she continued her story. "By the end of the layover we didn't feel much better. The ordeal had left us very weak as we hadn't been able to eat a thing for the entire three days. The bad news was there was no spare crew on hand to take our places on the plane leaving for Hawaii. We had no choice but to get dressed in our uniforms and report to the Briefing Office."

Mona said they looked like ghosts and had sagging energy but had to work all the way back to Honolulu – a long ten hours with a refueling stop in Fiji.

"The whole crew was feeling wonky and woozy. In desperation we opted to block off one of the lavatories in the front and one in the back and put up signs on the doors that read 'Out of Order.' That way the crew could just run in when an emergency struck without having to wait in agony at the end of long lines of passengers. What a miserable flight. But we put on our smiles and somehow got through it and gave the passengers the best service we could muster under the appalling circumstances.

"Thank goodness I'm here in Hawaii for three days to recuperate. I don't have any desire to go outside. I'm just staying here in the cool air," Mona added weakly.

Mona surprised me by adding she was thinking of relocating to the Seattle base because her boyfriend was going to school there. Another member of our class about to leave for the next chapter of their lives!

Gunnel and Don had married in Hawaii and Tina and Greig married not long after but were living in San Mateo and Tina was still flying.

I left Mona in the lounge and wished her a quick recovery so she could work her flight back to San Francisco and not get stuck in Honolulu for days on end.

I'd eaten a lot of seafood in Sydney and was thankful I hadn't become ill with what appeared to be a severe case of food poisoning. My injured thumb incident paled by comparison.

54.

THE AIR FORCE DOCTOR

On a routine flight landing in Hawaii we were told of a change in plan. The cabin crew was being sent to the Ilikai Hotel on Ala Moana Boulevard because the crew hotel and the Royal Hawaiian were both full. This was a surprise as I'd never stayed in this high-rise hotel but it looked very impressive and elegant right on the beach near Waikiki. We signed in and were given our room keys. I settled into my comfortable room and was astounded to have a view right out over the ocean.

It was early afternoon and too soon to retire. I thought I'd relax by the pool, soak up some sun, and read a book. I found my favorite two-piece navy blue and white striped swimsuit buried in the bottom of my case and put it on, covered up with a short muu muu, grabbed a towel, my book, and sun screen. Walking the length of the hallway, I found the elevator, pushed the 'Down' button and followed the signs to the pool.

I did a quick glance around the crowded pool area and was annoyed to see every lounger taken, bronze bodies sprawled everywhere. I was standing there in a quandary as I just didn't feel like venturing on to the beach. Then one of the sun-soaked bodies slowly rose up and prepared to leave. I wound my way around the pool and claimed the newly vacated chaise and was happy to see it was partly in the shade of a huge white umbrella.

I laid out my towel and slipped out of my cover-up dress and got comfortable on the lounger. I escaped into my fascinating book, an autobiography and history by Han Suyin, a China-born Eurasion, titled "A Mortal Flower."

Time passed and I was engrossed in my story relaxing in the warmth of the afternoon sun. Lost in my quiet reverie, I had the shock of my life when I was rudely jolted, almost levitated in the air as the foot end of my chaise suddenly sank down hard. I gasped and dropped my book which landed with a thud on the ground.

The cause of this commotion was sitting at my feet – a good-looking, sun-bronzed hunk of man.

He was a total stranger to me yet nonchalantly introduced himself as Jake and tried to engage me in conversation. I wanted to be left alone.

I looked around embarrassed, certain all eyes around the pool were watching this little scenario with great anticipation.

"Please go away," I begged in a low tone. To no avail.

"Please leave me alone," I pleaded again and again.

But he just sat there and refused to move. I was a little leery as I didn't know this fellow at all, but he really was handsome, tall, and appealing. I kept asking him as politely as I could to leave. He ignored my requests and with a broad grin told me he was staying at the hotel.

He was telling me he was a pilot and doctor with the U.S. Air Force. I told him I was with Pan Am and hearing that he asked me, "Do you know a Pan Am stewardess called Gunnel from Sweden?"

Hearing Gunnel's name hit me like a lightning bolt as Gunnel was my good friend from our Pan Am class and with that revelation, I relaxed and opened up. He knew someone I trusted and I asked, "How do you know Gunnel?" Thinking if he knew her he must be all right. He told me he was a good friend of Gunnel's Air Force officer husband Don.

On hearing that my resolve was gone!

Time passed and Jake invited me to his hotel suite to have a cool drink as the temperature was becoming uncomfortably hot by the pool.

All eyes were definitely on us as I picked up my things and casually followed him out of the pool area. I kept telling myself if he's a friend of Gunnel and Don's he must be okay.

We had a great time looking at photos and enjoying a drink or two and I could feel myself being drawn in. He told me he was a dermatologist. In those days coming from the National Health System of England, I'd never been to a specialist doctor in my life and in all honesty didn't know what a dermatologist was.

We had a lot to talk about as we were flying to the same exotic places across the Pacific. I stayed a long while till I had to get back to my own room. After all, I was expecting an early morning pick-up for a flight to San Francisco.

Most of us lived in fear of sleeping in, dreading the hotel would forget the 'wake up' call, and missing the crew bus. I wasn't about to face that fate.

Jake reluctantly walked me to my door and did ask me to call him when next in Hawaii.

And, of course, the next time we landed in Hawaii, I did call him. The crew wasn't staying in the Ilikai Hotel as that was a rare occurrence. Jake fortunately had the time off and suggested we spend the day on the beach.

He stopped by the Royal Hawaiian and together we enjoyed a lazy day of swimming and sunning, talking and getting to know more about one another. But, at the end of this wonderful day, he gave me a big hug, and with a sad expression in his eyes, told me he had just been assigned to a new base in Thailand. As we parted, he whispered, "Please wait for me!"

We corresponded and I begged Dwayne in Scheduling for a Thailand flight. In time I was thrilled to get one and wrote to Jake to tell him I'd be in Bangkok in two weeks.

When the flight finally landed in Thailand, we left the plane to find our bags and boarded the crew bus. At the hotel we were given our room numbers and room keys. I took my bags and headed to my room.

I called Jake at his new base but sadly, because of his scheduling and mine, he could only meet me for dinner at the hotel dining room that evening. We agreed on an early five o'clock. I had enough time to unwind, have a shower, wash my hair (we were forever getting our hair washed because of the cigarette smoke on the planes and the residual obnoxious odor left on our bodies and all our clothes) and dressed in my favorite green dress and red sandals. I took the elevator down to the restaurant.

I peeked into the empty dining room and Jake was nowhere to be seen and I wasn't happy to be there first. I told the maitre d' that I was expecting a friend any minute so I was shown to a table and sat there waiting, hoping beyond hope that he would show up.

Then I saw him enter the far end of the room and he smiled.

I instantly relaxed and was thrilled to see him again. We enjoyed yet another fun, romantic evening but because of schedules he had to leave early. With sad goodbyes, I told him I could hopefully bid another trip to Bangkok the following month.

This was not the easiest way to develop a relationship.

55

HONG KONG

At the San Francisco Briefing for a Singapore trip, the senior purser asked me to work the aft cabin to Honolulu. We were happy to see very few passengers.

The two stewardesses were setting up the drinks cart before starting the meal service. I was walking up and down the aisle making sure everyone was comfortable, handing out magazines and pillows and answering questions.

I noticed one lone middle-aged gentleman sitting by the window with two empty seats next to him. He never looked up and was totally absorbed in something he was holding in his hands. He seemed very quiet and lost in thought. He didn't move, he didn't ask for any refreshment, he just sat there and looked very sad. I felt the need to give him some reassurance so I asked him, "Excuse me sir, are you all right? Can I bring you anything?" He gave me a doleful smile and said he didn't need a thing, but I continued, "May I ask what you are holding that has your total attention?"

He handed me a small black and white photograph and told me, "This is a picture of my wife."

He slowly opened up and quietly explained to me that all their married life his wife had dreamed of going to Hawaii. For years they had saved their money and planned the trip of a lifetime. Then a week before they were to leave, she became ill and died suddenly. He was devastated but felt compelled to go on the trip, alone, as that is what she would have wanted and he was taking along her photo to share everything with her.

By this time I was getting teary-eyed. It seemed such a romantic yet heart-breaking story. I had to leave him sitting there all alone with his memories. I wished him well and hoped he would have a happy vacation.

I felt very sad saying goodbye to this lonely passenger as he exited the airplane.

After a three-day layover in Honolulu we boarded our next plane to the Philippines and this time had a full load of passengers. On arrival in Manila, an official came aboard with a solemn expression and told the crew we had to forfeit our three-day layover and continue flying to Guam. After the busy non-stop working flight, we were expecting three days to unwind and now, with no forewarning, we had to stay on the plane and carry on.

We worked through intermittent turbulence trying to prepare baby milk from powder for an unusual number of babies on board while at the same time serving a regular hot lunch. We had to rush due to the short flight, and were looking forward to the much-needed layover in Guam.

At Agana we were told by another Pan Am representative that we had to turn around and take a flight back to the Philippines the very next morning. Our normal schedule was completely torn apart. We had no idea now where we would be sent next or when we could expect to get back home.

Barely rested the next morning, the crew was driven to the Anderson Air Force Base where we climbed aboard another plane and with a full load of passengers headed back to the Philippines. The Senior Purser Harry was sensing our fatigue and being a fun-loving fellow he gave his take-off announcement introducing his crew to the passengers as "Harry and his girls – Dimples Peters (I had the dimples), Saigon Sadie (a Niseii girl), Bubbles Booth (Judy had lots of curls) and Svenstam Swede." We loved him for lifting our spirits and, of course, the passengers enjoyed the fun as well.

On all flights we served the meals two at a time, one tray in each hand, walking up and down the aisle constantly until every passenger was served. Only the drinks in Economy were served from a cart.

At the Manila Hotel we retreated to our rooms and didn't come out until the following morning.

Our next flight was a military charter to Saigon and at Tan Son Nhut the military passengers, as always, were reluctant to leave the security of the aircraft.

We had a two-hour stopover at the airport so the crew was given permission to get off the plane and spend some time in the terminal. We bought postcards, wrote some notes home, and mailed them from there.

A boisterous load of passengers boarded the plane - all smiles to be heading home. Six Vietnamese military members joined them and one was an air cadet heading for Texas to learn radar training. He was so pleased when I showed an interest in his language and asked him to try and translate the Vietnamese phrase the airport lady had written down for me. He explained the meaning to be – *a long journey measures the strength of the horse.*

I spoke with an Army Special Intelligence Officer who had been stationed in Da Nang. He told me the horror of a young Vietnamese child who had entered their base holding a live grenade in his shirt.

We flew another flight back to Manila yet again and a fresh crew took the flight on to Hawaii.

The Pan Am representative in Manila told us our crew schedule had been changed and we were now being deadheaded to Hong Kong. That was exciting news as I'd never been to Hong Kong and made all the upheaval of schedule changes well worthwhile.

Our crew boarded a Philippine Airlines plane and enjoyed playing passenger to Hong Kong – not a long flight but a chance to relax and be waited on for a change.

We disembarked in the early evening and were taken to the prestigious Park Hotel in the heart of Kowloon which had just opened in 1961. Not wanting to waste any time, three of us, Birit from Sweden, Missy the American, and I, decided to venture out to explore Victoria Peak, the highest mountain on the island.

We changed into cool dresses and met in the lobby. As the evening light was fading and the last bus had gone, we hailed a taxi and squeezed in for a ride to the ferry terminal. We hastily bought tickets and felt ourselves jostled and pushed onto the busy ferry crossing the bay to Victoria.

We were disappointed to find out we had narrowly missed the last tram to the top of the Peak. That news didn't stop us so we called over a waiting taxi and the driver was only too happy to drive us all the way up the very steep incline.

By this time the sky had darkened to a deep indigo blue and when we reached the top of the Peak a magnificent sight loomed before us. We paid the taxi driver and he sped off down the hill. It was a crystal clear evening and we stood in silent awe at the magical views – more spectacular with all the twinkling lights sparkling on the Victoria Harbor waters and many surrounding islands below.

Standing alone the thought struck me – here I am surrounded by this world-renowned panorama and there isn't anyone meaningful to share it with.

The three of us wandered along the ridgetop pathway as there was so much to see. We were forgetful of the time and as lights were shutting off, darkness enveloped us.

I looked at my watch and was surprised to see it was past eleven o'clock. With all the time differences we had passed through it was easy to mistake the actual time of the country we were in. We looked around and realized we were three young, lone girls stranded on the top of this mountain.

No people, no taxis, no busses in sight.

The night air grew chilly. We felt isolated and were concerned about how we were going to get down the very steep, long road and across the water to our hotel. We didn't fancy having to walk all the way down as we weren't wearing sturdy walking shoes, only flimsy sandals.

Being the purser, and the other two were fairly new stewardesses, I was felt the weight of responsibility. I tried to remain 'calm' as we stayed together searching for a sign of life.

Straining our eyes through the bushes and trees, we spied a lone distant light peeking through the dense undergrowth. We slowly tiptoed along a narrow path drawn toward this flicker of civilization. My feeling of unease lifted as a small hut-like building appeared and through an open window we could make out two or three Chinese men inside wearing some kind of uniform. We had stumbled upon a radio communications facility!

Desperate for any kind of help, I tapped on the door and one of the men opened it and stepped outside. He looked aghast. His eyes opened wide in surprise to see three young Caucasian girls standing there at such a late hour. We tried speaking to him but he responded in clipped Chinese.

The other men came out curious to see what all the fuss was about. We tried gesticulating and pointing down the hill and they gradually understood what we needed. In broken English they nodded their heads and repeated, "Taxeee, taxeee – we call."

We had obviously missed the last bus, the last tram, and the last taxi.

After an interminable wait sitting on a low stone wall at the top of the mountain, an old beat-up looking vehicle appeared around the corner. This had to be our ride and mercifully it was. We thanked the Chinese men for their help, climbed in and set off down the steep, winding road.

The driver raced down at great speed and we jostled from side to side as he careened around the turns. We understood why when he slammed to a stop at the terminal just in time for us to board the very last ferry to Kowloon.

On reaching the other side we were fortunate to find another taxi to deliver us to the safety of our hotel.

We all slept soundly after that adventure.

The next morning, I met Missy and Birit in the hotel restaurant. We enjoyed a good British-style breakfast of bacon, fried eggs, grilled tomatoes, toast in racks, and pots of good loose-leaf tea. Well fortified, we decided to explore the shopping district in the heart of Hong Kong.

The hotel concierge advised us to try a couple of stores for cashmere sweaters and another for jade. We set off on foot and were enthralled with the swarms of colorful people everywhere. There was hustle and bustle all around us as we passed many open-fronted stalls selling beautiful artifacts, silks, jewelry and spices. Enticing smells of food sizzling on huge open woks and small barbecues wafted down the streets.

How different, exotic and exciting.

Following the street signs we eventually found the jade shop. We had to climb up some narrow, well-worn wooden steps to enter through the open doorway and into a very small cramped space. There were collections of jade in a myriad of colors lining many dusty shelves. We had no idea how authentic any of it was but I fell in love with a beautiful green jade elephant. The salesman showed me two which he had brought out from the back of the store and stood on the counter before me. I was trying to make up my mind when he asked if I'd be interested to see some ivory.

Before I could say a word he produced a beautiful ten-inch-high Chinese fisherman carved from a tusk. The chiseled face was full of oriental character. I was told the detail proved its authenticity, as years ago men had the time to spend carving all day long to show the great detail.

I believed the story and agreed to buy it in place of the jade elephant, although they tried very hard to get me to buy BOTH. They suggested they could ship it to my address in San Francisco, a sensible idea with which I agreed. Later I realized it would be a miracle if the fisherman ever turned up on my doorstep so far away.

We walked on to the quaint little cashmere shop and were surrounded by beautiful soft sweaters of all colors and styles hanging from floor to ceiling, and piled high on tables all round the small room. The prices were so reasonable we bought two each. I decided on a super soft black, button-down cardigan and a pretty pink short-sleeve summer sweater. (Both were worn over and over again – till they were practically threadbare).

We stumbled upon an intriguing shoe store and longingly looked at the beautiful leather shoes and exotic sandals in the window. We couldn't resist venturing inside and were soon trying on many styles. They were so reasonably priced and we decided we couldn't leave without buying a pair each.

How very dismayed we were to find out they adamantly refused to accept personal checks. We were deeply disappointed, and reluctantly put the shoes back in their boxes and walked out empty-handed.

Credit card convenience was way in the future!

Our adventurous short stay came to an end and we had to board a Pan Am plane back to Manila and from there work our way back to San Francisco.

I honestly believed I'd never see my ivory fisherman again. At least eight weeks passed and I'd almost forgotten about him.

One morning when I was home, the mailman knocked on our door and delivered a wooden box covered with brown paper and lots of colorful stamps. I rushed indoors to rip off the paper and pry open the lid, hoping I wouldn't find bits and pieces. But there, lying supinely on a bed of straw, was the ivory fisherman. I'm still amazed they packed and shipped it all that way.

I treasure my fisherman to this day along with all the memories.

56.

NEW UNIFORM

Rumors were in the air that our uniform was being re-designed. Not long after we all received a letter to inform us our current uniform was to be replaced with a different, slightly more-relaxed style.

The new hat was round with the gold Pan Am logo pin on the side and could be worn back on the head and not over the forehead as required before. This seemed to please most of the girls but did detract from the uniform look of the old hat. The jacket was much the same style, not as fitted, and the white blouse collar was to be worn under the jacket not over the lapel. The color remained the same Pan Am Tunis blue.

These subtle changes were ringing in a less formal look – and attitude.

Mona was now home and fully recovered from her bout of food poisoning. She stopped by to bid us goodbye before leaving for the Seattle base.

As always, we were telling Pan Am stories and Mona settled down with us in the living room and told us she had just flown with the first black stewardess hired by Pan Am. Coming from Norway in the mid-Sixties, Mona said she had hardly seen any black people and had never talked with one, and that applied to me, too, coming from England.

Mona said she and Roxanna had become good friends as they were flying to Sydney together. Roxanna had worked in the

Personnel Department of Pan Am in New York and had been asked to apply for the job as stewardess. The one incident that left quite an impression on Mona happened on this trip.

They were both assigned to work the First Class section with Mona working in the galley and Roxanna in the cabin assisting the purser. Mona was preoccupied with cooking and preparing the food, when, she recounts, "All of a sudden Roxanna came running back to the galley, crying so hard and trying to explain between sobs that a passenger had told her he didn't want to be served by a black person!

"Well, we sorted that out very fast as I told her to take over in the galley and I would work her place in the cabin. And that settled that!"

Sexual inhibitions were also relaxing as Mona told us how mortified she had been on a flight from Tokyo to Honolulu.

"A handsome young man and a cute girl, not travelling together, happened to be sitting in the last row with an empty seat between them. The crew noticed them talking earnestly. After a while, we were shocked to see them hugging and kissing. They had raised the armrests and were inching ever closer together when things really heated up."

Mona continued with a laugh, "I couldn't believe my eyes as they were struggling to have sex! And passengers were lining up in the aisle to use the restrooms. It was so embarrassing and I had no idea what to do, so I grabbed a blanket and threw it over them and marched up to the cockpit. I knocked on the door and just walked right in. My face must have been scarlet as I told the captain I had an emergency and asked him to put his hat on, to show authority, and come with me to the back of the plane, which he did.

"The captain raised an eyebrow when he saw what was going on. He yanked off the blanket and stood there giving them a stern lecture about airplane etiquette. After that they sat there very quiet and subdued for the rest of the trip."

Mona stayed for some tea and then we said our sad goodbyes as she was heading to Seattle and her new life there. She was looking forward to visiting Mary at the same base.

57

SURPRISE AT TAN SON NHUT

A letter to Dan in Phu Quoc gave him the flight number and arrival time for our landing in Tan Son Nhut. He had sent me his schedule of R&R (rest and relaxation) in Bangkok and his flight was returning to Vietnam shortly before we were due to land. I was hopeful, but also knew it was highly unlikely, that he would be able to meet our plane.

Our flight landed at Tan Son Nhut late in the afternoon in the midst of a heavy monsoon. Rain was lashing down in torrents and hit the ground with such force the runway appeared flooded. The dark sky hung low and the clouds were an ominous grey but our passengers had to disembark despite the unwelcoming weather.

The captain told us to stay aboard the aircraft as the rain was too heavy to venture outside. We only had an hour before curfew and take-off time. Sitting in the first class lounge area we could hear the rain pounding against the plane.

Some minutes passed and in the quiet of the cabin, we heard a knock against the airplane door. Wondering who it might be out there in such a deluge, one of the pilots opened the door slightly not wanting to get drenched. We all craned our necks to see who was there and a young officer in jungle camouflage uniform asked to come aboard. The captain looked him over, gave his OK and in he came.

What a shock when this young fellow asked the captain if there was a 'Lesley' on his crew. Hearing my name I looked up and it took me a while to recognize the young officer as the Dan I had met months ago in San Francisco. I hardly recognized him – after all, a long time had lapsed since we met for such a short interlude.

The captain allowed him to stay on the plane and the two of us retreated to the cabin seats. How uncomfortable we felt. All eyes were watching us! The crew was full of curiosity as to what this was all about and we felt awkward trying to talk privately. Dan sensed this and I was thankful when he approached the captain and asked if he could have permission to take me into the terminal.

The captain looked me in the eye and said, "Yes, but I want you back on the plane *before* the curfew hour."

The rain had subsided slightly so Dan and I made a mad dash to the cover of the terminal. We found the makeshift cafeteria which showed signs of the recent bombing with boarded up walls and a gaping hole behind the counter. A battered metal table for two was empty so we sat down on the equally rickety chairs and Dan ordered two Cokes. Seeing him again was a surreal sensation especially in this war-torn setting. He'd been at war for eight months living aboard a Vietnamese Navy junk. I was surprised he wasn't looking emaciated having been on a diet of fish and rice for most of the time.

His flight from Bangkok had arrived a few hours earlier. He had been able to get permission to delay his return to Phu Quoc to see if I would be on the next Pan Am flight due in.

All too soon we heard the boarding-time announcement blaring overhead through the tinny loudspeakers. We left the café and jumped and skipped our way around the deep puddles toward the waiting plane.

Nightfall had stealthily crept in, hence the curfew for our plane to depart by seven, and the blinding rain had become a light drizzle. Dan steered me to the underside and protection of the enormous Pan Am jet's airplane wing. We could see white flashes of flares and gunfire in the distance, intensified against the darkening sky. Thunderous loud cracks and bangs of guns blasting filled the air, followed by streaks and flashes of brilliant yellow light shooting skyward from ground explosions. Despite the reality of our proximity to these horrors of war, it seemed so romantic standing there in the arms of this dashing young officer, under the paternal protection of the airplane wing.

I was so disappointed to see one of the pilots advancing toward us and I knew it was time for me to leave. The navigator told me the captain wanted me on board *immediately*. As I stepped into the jet, I looked back and saw Dan disappearing across the wet tarmac and into the bomb-blitzed terminal.

The captain surprised me by inviting me into the cockpit for the take-off to see Vietnam at night as we were flying overhead. He told me he knew of a Naval officer who was doing a tour of duty in the River Patrol, similar to what Dan was doing.

Looking down from the safety of the cockpit it was extremely disturbing seeing the flares and explosions from the deadly battles on the ground below. The captain showed me the route on his map and I felt privileged to be receiving all this attention. He told me he was ex-military himself and sympathetic toward my friend who was fighting a different war.

The plane leveled off and I had to return to the cabin to start the drinks and meal service. Busily popping champagne corks made seeing Dan remotely surreal and a dream-like fantasy.

My emotions toward Freddi and Jake were now in turmoil.

58

RETURN TO THE U.S.A.

The metal mailbox lid creaked open. I grabbed the letters and bills stuffed inside in one mindless routine motion. The kitchen table was cleared of breakfast dishes and I dumped the mail to sort into stacks – mine and Roberta's. During this mundane sorting, I was jerked into the present when I spied the familiar military address and handwriting – from Dan.

My adrenaline soared and I eagerly ripped open the envelope. On a single page he told me he was due to fly back home. He was scheduled to land at Travis Air Force Base the following month – September 1966. His one year tour of duty in Vietnam was coming to an end.

I checked the date on my calendar and was horrified to see his return was the very same day as my ex-roommate Mary's wedding to Ralph in British Columbia. What was I to do?

The chemistry of romance won over and I decided to be at the airport to greet Dan from his ravaging year at war – remembering so many of the heart-rending stories of returning soldiers on the return flights from Vietnam.

I apologized profusely to Mary and hoped she would understand, which, thankfully, she did.

The long-awaited day arrived. I left early in the morning and drove to the Travis Air Force base in Fairfield. Gunnel and Don had married in Hawaii the year before and Gunnel was aglow in her first pregnancy. They kindly invited me to stay with them on base and welcomed me into their charming home.

Dan's flight was due later that evening and Don very graciously offered to drive me to the Arrivals Terminal and Gunnel insisted on coming too. I was brimming over with mixed emotions – anxiety, excitement, and anticipation.

We waited, and waited – and waited. The sky had become black as nightfall surrounded us. Just as we were giving up, we heard the familiar whine of an approaching plane. It touched down and taxied to a stop and the throng of family and friends surged forward. The military personnel disembarked and I was scanning them all looking for Dan. As each passenger headed toward the terminal I saw no sign of him. I was disappointed and disheartened.

Don was surprised and he left me with Gunnel to find out what had happened. He came back shortly and explained that Dan wasn't on the flight list of passengers and would very likely be on the next plane, which wasn't due in until early the next morning at five o'clock. I was with very dear friends and they offered to let me stay overnight and take me again in the morning – at four-thirty. I was feeling greatly indebted to them both.

We crept into bed knowing we had to be up before the crack of dawn. I was concerned about Gunnel but she was adamant about coming with me despite her pregnancy.

I didn't get much sleep, tossing and turning with a myriad of thoughts. The alarm jangled us awake and we got up wearily and dressed. At that hour of the morning much of the excitement had worn off but we bundled into the car and set off for the second time.

I was thinking if he wasn't on this flight, I was going to forget the whole thing and drive back to Burlingame.

We waited through yet another plane load of disembarking military personnel surrounded by raucous expectant families with lots of young sleepy children. Amidst the throng I finally spied a familiar face and there he was. He had on his khaki uniform and looked very tired but I ran up to him and gave him a big welcoming hug. He was one of the lucky ones who had survived to return home to the USA.

Dan was happy to see me with Gunnel and Don and they drove us back to their house so he could freshen up. We felt they needed some time to rest, so we soon said our goodbyes and drove south to the Peninsula.

Dan had allowed a couple of days before continuing on to his home in Michigan. When we reached the apartment, he took a refreshing shower and then spent time on the phone talking with his parents who couldn't understand why he wasn't flying straight home. He told me some of his Vietnam experiences had been quite unpleasant, and he felt he needed 'quiet time' to adjust before the whirlwind of family reunions.

The weather was gloriously hot and sunny so we spent most of our time relaxing by the pool sipping champagne. I was on cloud nine the whole time not quite realizing he was actually here in the apartment after a whole year of letter writing back and forth.

Dan had orders to report to Naval Station Treasure Island in San Francisco Bay for duty. He could have been stationed almost anywhere, and most any other posting would have put our relationship against quite long odds.

The days passed quickly and Dan had to fly home to Michigan. But I was taken by surprise when he invited me to his home a week later to meet his family. Making sure I had time off from flying, I made plane reservations to go – one way. The plan was that he would buy a car while there and then drive back to San Francisco. It would be a wonderful way for me to see more of the United States – if I was willing to drive back with him. I didn't have to think twice about that offer and agreed I would be experiencing another fantastic adventure.

And, I did!

His parents welcomed me with big hugs (coming from England I still wasn't used to such a welcome from total strangers). For three days I luxuriated in a home setting, enjoying good Mid-West home-cooked meals and a warm visit with the family.

We left in Dan's new blue Ford Mustang and drove for eight hours a day for three days through some breathtaking American scenery in Indiana, Illinois, Iowa, and Nebraska. Fall in Colorado was a spectacular sight of glorious golden aspen leaves 'quaking' in the breeze – a magical sight. We drove on through Utah, Nevada and over the Sierra Mountains down to the San Francisco Bay Area. An exhilarating three days!

I had to relinquish my line and return to On Call status due to the requested time off to be in Michigan. This meant staying close to home, ready to answer the phone at any hour, in case I was called with short notice to report for a flight to 'anywhere.' These were emergency cases when a purser called in sick at the last minute, or worse, didn't turn up or was late.

Dan was working at Treasure Island and driving over to see me many evenings while Roberta was away on a Tahiti trip. Because I was biding time on standby, I invited Dan to a home-cooked supper.

I opted to make a very English country dish called Shepherd's Pie, which was easy to prepare and could be made ahead and put in the oven later to reheat. Liver and onions were definitely not on the menu!

I took time setting up our small kitchen table for a cozy dinner for two. I even picked a small posy of red geraniums from the window box outside. This was the very first meal I had cooked for 'us,' and I waited expectantly for Dan to arrive.

He drove up on time – military punctuality! I led him to the kitchen and he opened a bottle of wine I had been keeping chilled in the refrigerator. The pie was sending a delicious aroma throughout the apartment. The chopped beef with peas, carrots, and onions in gravy was covered with a layer of creamy cheesy mashed potatoes and was sizzling in the oven. I didn't have much of a cooking repertoire in those days as we ate out most of the time.

We were sitting in the small living room listening to Beatles records and Dan announced he had been transferred to the Mare Island navy base to become a Combat Operations Instructor for

Army and Navy units leaving for riverine service in Vietnam. That meant he would have to relocate further north. This was not good news, but considering the distance was just a matter of a few miles and not out of state, we weren't too devastated.

The oven timer buzzed. The pie was ready. We sat down and helped ourselves to a green salad and generous servings of the Shepherd's Pie. Dan was regaling me with more of his war stories as we began our meal.

RRRRing, RRRRing.

The phone rang irritatingly as an unwanted interruption in the middle of this special evening. I wanted to ignore it. But I had to answer the call because we were expected to pick up the phone at any hour of the day or night in case it was an important call from the Scheduling Office. I left the table and moved to the phone on our living room table and hesitantly lifted the receiver.

"Miss Lesley Peters?"

"Yes," I replied in barely a whisper, guessing what was coming.

"This is the Pan American Briefing Office and we have a purser no-show for a flight to Sydney, Australia. The passengers are boarding as we speak and we request your reporting here within half-an-hour to join the crew on this flight!"

I gasped and could barely squeak out the words, "Yes, I'll be there."

I looked crestfallen at my beautiful table, the food still left on the plates, the wine in the glasses – and Dan. I explained I had to cancel everything to change into my uniform and pack my suitcase for a *ten-day* trip to Sydney, and be on the plane in thirty minutes or less!

Living close to the airport begged for an emergency call such as this one. With so little time for a crew member to get to a waiting airplane, they called those living closest to the airport first.

Rushing into the bedroom I grabbed my suitcase and threw in my clothes. A swimsuit first as we always stopped in Hawaii, then the sundresses, a sweater, and sandals for Sydney. There was little we could pre-pack as we never knew 'where' we would be sent – to the chilly cold of Alaska, the oppressive heat of Manila or the city life of Tokyo. The uniform was always cleaned and pressed ready to wear. The purser bag and carry-on bag with a change of shoes and cabin smock were waiting by the door.

Dan was left alone sitting at the table. He did finish his dinner while I was packing and getting ready. He cleared the table for me and cleaned up as best he could and left when I did.

What a crazy date!

In a mad rush I climbed into my little Sprite and tore off down the road to the airport with little time for fond farewells. I arrived at the Briefing Office breathless, and signed in.

I was mad at having my romantic first-time dinner so rudely interrupted. I got caught at a bad time but knew there was a chance it could happen.

I was given a fast ride out to the plane and could see the captain anxiously waiting in the cockpit. Passenger faces were staring out the small windows fretfully waiting for my arrival so they could be on their way without any further delay. They clapped thankfully when I appeared in the doorway – I felt like a reluctant hero.

The two stewardesses working with me in First Class were Britt from Sweden and Marianna from Germany. I immediately started the welcome announcement with an explanation for my late arrival.

I had been torn from the one extreme of a romantic dinner with Dan and dropped into the practical business of running the First Class cabin service in less than thirty minutes. I must have worn a flimsy mask of disaffection as one of the male passengers brought me down to reality by telling me to 'smile.'

I learned from the passenger roster we had young newlyweds in First Class and a wedding cake had been delivered on board as a surprise. We had ten passengers and served a light dinner. The charming newlyweds were a handsome young couple, and they appeared so much in love, holding hands and beaming at each other most of the flight.

I told the happy couple we had a special wedding cake just for them and they were so excited they didn't hesitate to tell me they would like to share slices with the other passengers.

Britt and I set up a beautiful serving cart with fresh white linen. We carefully placed the wedding cake in the center; a two-tier round cake, beautifully decorated in white icing and covered with pale yellow frosting roses.

Marianna passed out glasses of chilled champagne as Britt and I walked the trolley down the aisle. I carefully cut the cake and handed a large slice to the lucky couple and a serving to each passenger in lieu of other desserts. The newlyweds enjoyed a celebration party in the sky en route to their honeymoon in Honolulu. There was so much cake left over, they were happy to have me offer slices to the pilots who were thrilled with the gesture and ate it hungrily.

In Hawaii I was able to calm down in the island's relaxing, warm atmosphere and three days later was ready to board the plane to Sydney. We were on a night flight and the sky was ominously dark. I was working the First Class cabin as the other purser insisted on staying in the aft section. This leg the stewardesses helping me were Britt and Sin Kit, as Marianna had been rescheduled to another flight.

Three hours into the flight, the passengers craned their necks to stare out the windows. I wondered what was happening and they told me there were enormous streaks of lightning in the sky. They were becoming increasingly alarmed so I entered the cockpit and asked Captain Parker to please make an announcement to allay their fears. He was happy to do so and then invited me to stay so I could see the distant storm from the front cockpit view. I quietly sat in the spare seat behind him.

What a sight to behold flying high in the night sky, ebony black one minute and brilliantly lit the next. Blinding streaks and jagged shapes of scintillating lightning flashed across the heavens in enormous wide flares way ahead of us. The pilots seemed unconcerned about our flying into this heavenly firework display so I assumed they knew what they were doing. The experience was quite eerie, almost otherworldly, as if we too were a part of this spectacular power of nature.

I thanked Captain Parker for the opportunity to view such a unique show and returned to the cabin. The dazzling, yet chilling drama held us in thrall for a long time, and there was a quiet hush throughout the cabin as the passengers were mesmerized by the diversion. We could hear disappointed sighs as the plane gently veered away and left the violent storm shrinking and disappearing behind us.

We flew on to Fiji for a refueling stop and there the Fijian commissary re-stocked our galleys for the dinner service on to Sydney.

On this short hop from Fiji to Sydney we offered the Prime Rib Roast Beef. Sin Kit was working the First Class galley and was taking pains to organize everything to facilitate the service. I was at the bar area filling the drink orders brought in by Britt. Halfway through my mixing and pouring, I heard a long, high-pitched cry emanating from the galley. I stopped in mid-pour when I heard Sin Kit urgently calling me to come quick. I asked Britt to continue mixing the drinks while I approached the galley.

I found Sin Kit standing in the middle of the galley holding the huge hunk of beef. Her face was stricken with panic, and so was mine, when I saw the Fijians had delivered the prime rib roast to the plane – frozen solid!

This was a short three-hour flight and I could see there was absolutely no time to set the meat out to thaw. There were no microwaves in those days. To make matters worse, I had already taken the entrée orders while the plane was on the ground prior to take-off. This saved precious time and, of course, most of the orders were for the Pan Am specialty prime rib roast.

What an embarrassing situation, but this time being the purser I could see we were not at fault. I approached the passengers who had ordered the roast beef and apologized as I explained to each of them the absolute truth that it had been delivered in Fiji too frozen to roast and would they mind ordering another entrée. Some passengers sighed and groaned with disappointment, and I didn't blame them, but everyone was very understanding and did order an alternate meal.

After this minor setback, the service continued smoothly with no other problems and we arrived in Sydney on time.

I was ready for a three-day layover.

59.

CHANGES

Dan was now at Mare Island as an Instructor in the Riverine Warfare School. He had a military business trip to San Diego for a few days and asked if I would like to join him. Never having been to San Diego I jumped at the opportunity. I had a few days off between flights and could stay for a couple of days.

San Diego was warm and sunny and Dan drove me around exploring the city, the Old Town district, and the natural deep water harbor. In the evening we found a wonderful restaurant on the waterfront with spectacular views.

We enjoyed a special Surf and Turf (steak and lobster) dinner. Lost in romance and full of emotion, Dan took my hands across the table and shocked me by asking me to *marry* him. I wasn't expecting a proposal at all! He obviously wasn't either as he apologized for not having the ring which was at his parents' home in Michigan for safe-keeping. I was so enraptured by the moment, I instantly said YES!

I was ecstatic. I was madly in love. My life was changing rapidly and I sent a telegram to my parents in England to tell them the wonderful news. I was committing myself to a fellow they had never met!

The tough part was telling Freddi and Jake. I had a flight to Guam coming up on my schedule. As soon as the plane crew checked into the hotel, I called Freddi and told him I'd like to meet to talk. I was not looking forward to this as he was a very dear friend, I truly respected him and we had enjoyed many fun times together. He must have wondered what was going on as he turned up with a fellow officer. When I broke the news of my engagement, his first reaction was to look at my left hand and he said, "Where's the ring?" He had noticed I wasn't wearing one and seemed troubled by the fact. It was a heart-wrenching evening but we parted amicably.

One evening, shortly after my return from this flight, Dan drove over to visit and surprised me by producing the long-awaited diamond ring and placed it on my finger. It was a beautiful marquis.

Our engagement was official.

A few days later I received a surprise phone call from Freddi. He was in San Francisco on his way back home to the East coast and wanted to stop by. It was an emotional visit and I felt he was checking to make sure I did have a 'ring' on my finger. It was hard saying goodbye to such a dear friend and he felt it wasn't right to continue keeping in touch!

Roberta was unsettled as we had lost Mary to marriage and now she would be on her own. I worried about her as she didn't take well to 'aloneness.'

I was in a dilemma about marrying in England or the United States. Kate had married in England, Gunnel in Hawaii, Tina in California and Mary in Vancouver. I was very lucky to have had a flight with another English girl, Pam, and I was telling her of my indecision and she very sensibly told me, "You have to go home to get married. As the oldest daughter, your parents have waited for this day all their lives and you shouldn't take that away from them." I took her excellent advice and am so glad I did.

Eight months later on a sunny spring day in England, Dan and I were married in St. Stephens, our eight-hundred-year-old village church.

I was thrilled Barbara attended as the sole Pan Am classmate; and I was especially happy to see my good friends Linda and Susan from my London days.

We enjoyed a short honeymoon in the New Forest with a memorable romantic picnic in the bluebell woods on the mossy bank of a babbling brook – only in England!

Three days later I faced a tearful family farewell at the Heathrow airport. I'm sure my parents wondered when they would ever see me again.

The flight was full and we sat in the front row Economy seats. The senior purser on the flight made sure we had copious champagne to drink as a celebration – quite frequently a disembodied hand would appear through the bulkhead curtain and a champagne bottle would surreptitiously fill our glasses!

As soon as we returned to San Francisco, Scheduling called and asked me to take a ten-day trip. I wasn't happy at the prospect of leaving my brand new husband for that length of time and agonized over what to. The next day I walked into the Pan Am offices at the San Francisco International Airport and announced I was quitting. I handed in my uniform, which for some reason was requested at that time, along with the purser bag and all its contents.

There would be no more reduced-fare tickets to London, or anywhere else.

We received zero benefits!

Dan was leaving the Navy, and planned to relocate to the mid-west.

I had packed these wonderful three years of my Pan Am life with an incredible mix of international travels, exciting adventures, and lasting friendships with the Girls in Blue.

EPILOGUE

In reliving personal and group memories for the writing of this book, I recognize how much has changed in airline flying since those years.

Intense attention to detail dedicated to everything from soft-boiled eggs and the perfectly cooked prime rib, to proper hairdos and representation of Pan Am both on and off the job, has faded to microwaved meals in tinfoil, oversold flights, laxity in dress codes, and inability to even touch or aid passengers in certain situations over fears of legal action. While certain expectations and behaviors may these days be considered examples of sexual harassment, cultural insensitivity, or overt racism, the experiences of this bygone era also highlight a time of chivalry, kindness, and personal attention, perhaps lost in these present times.

In the 1960s most of us girls were under the old-fashioned notion that we were 'on the shelf' if we hadn't any marriage prospects by our early twenties. But despite the widespread notion we were jumping into bed with every pilot we met, most of us were not about to jeopardize our careers by an unwelcome pregnancy. Birth control pills were practically non-existent and only just making an entry onto the market.

In that short span from 1964-1967 Kate, Gunnel, Mary, Tina and I were married. Karin and Reidun returned home to Sweden, married and stayed. Mona married in Seattle and eventually returned to Norway. Barbara was still in England but returned to flying and eventually returned to San Francisco. Edith continued flying out of San Francisco as did Roberta. Bonnie now resides in Nevada.

The Girls in Blue, our Pan Am Class 12, have kept in close touch over the past fifty years and is the only class in the history of the company that we're aware of to do so. Those of us living in the Bay Area – Gunnel, Tina, Kate, Edith, Barbara and I – frequently meet for lunches in our homes and casual get-togethers elsewhere. We celebrated and participated in our children's weddings and the growth of our grandchildren. Though a diverse group, we have shared many intimate moments as only a 'family' can and thank Pan Am for bringing us together.

We enjoyed reunions every ten years and now, with our advancing years, every five years. One memorable reunion was in Sweden to accommodate our Scandinavian friends and Dan and I were fortunate to spend time with Mona in Norway.

In recent years we were saddened to learn of the deaths of Roberta (cause unknown), followed by Lilibi who continued flying for many years and sadly succumbed to bone cancer, and Sigi who died tragically in a Pan Am plane crash in Tahiti. We made many attempts throughout the years to connect with Louise and Jenny but to no avail.

Early in 1970 Pan Am was about to launch a new fleet of Jumbo Jets, the 747s, two-and-a-half times the size of the 707. A huge hiring campaign was underway as the airline needed to jump from six cabin crew members to eighteen to staff these enormous planes.

Those of us who had left Pan Am before this major change, and those who continued flying, felt we had certainly enjoyed the 'end of the good old days' of half-empty cabins, time to visit with passengers, small intimate crews and seeing the old world of the

Pacific route countries before all the changes in the name of progress.

The Girls in Blue of Pan Am Stewardess Class 12 1964 are proud to be celebrating their 50[th]ANNIVERSARY in 2014.

ACKNOWLEDGEMENTS

My sister planted the seed to write this book about my exploits with Pan Am. She was in college during those years and knew little of my experiences.

Joanna, my younger daughter, encouraged me and continued her support through the long, arduous process of writing, re-writing, and editing. We had many spirited discussions about the spelling and grammar variances between the English and American styles. Some inconsistencies may still exist in the book.

Lots of gratitude to my older daughter Lauren and granddaughter Hannah for their input – and, of course, husband Dan for his patience and invaluable advice.

My Class 12 friends willingly provided me with their stories and I thank you all for delving deep into your memories: Mona, Tina, Barbara, Gunnel, Mary, Kate, Karin, Edith, Bonnie and Reidun. Thank you for laughing at my own stories and insisting I not delete some of them.

The sayings throughout the book were gleaned from many books read during these flying years and noted in my travel diaries.

Many names have been changed to protect privacy, and any errors are all mine.

Lesley Peters Robson was born in England and moved to the United States in 1964. Following three memorable years with Pan Am she married and, after some years living on the East Coast, returned to the San Francisco Bay area. She is an avid watercolorist and loves gardening and baking. Lesley and her husband Dan live in the Napa Valley with their two daughters and two grandchildren nearby.